A must-read for anyone who leads an Agile team.
~Steve Kotsopoulos, ScrumMaster

Gil puts the importance of the Agile team leader's role into perspective. He clearly identifies the shift in thinking and attitude from traditional project leadership and management to the Agile servant leader: understanding that it's about the people is at the core of your success.
~Steven "Doc" List, National Agile Evangelist, Neudesic

Gil's understanding of Agile and people is remarkable, and he brings comprehensive guidance in order to inspire, guide, and grow your Agile team.
~Dan Douglas, Senior Software Consultant, Douglas Information Systems Corporation

Finally, a book about team, self, and organizational reform.
~Scotty Bevill, Founder & CEO, Bevill Edge

If you've just become a Certified ScrumMaster, or you're a project manager transitioning to Agile, this is the missing guidebook to effectively working with your team. Even if you've been doing this work for years, there are suggestions and reminders to help you become better. I'll be keeping this book handy, and I suggest that you do so, too.
~George Dinwiddie, software development coach

Have you wasted years applying Agile-like processes in your teams, but are still waiting to see great results? Gil explains how to grow highly effective, truly Agile teams. Take his pragmatic advice on providing strong leadership, forming the best team, and cultivating the right culture. There will be no looking back!
~Naresh Jain, Founder, Agile Software Community of India, and recipient, Gordon Pask Award

Pragmatic advice and principles for successfully facilitating team communication, collaboration, and conduct, and ultimately helping team members embrace small, incremental, continuous change.
~Chris Sterling, author, *Managing Software Debt: Building for Inevitable Change*

Readable, pragmatic, and complete! I am pleased to add The Human Side of Agile *to my list of recommended readings.*
~Peter Stevens, Agile Coach & Trainer and Co-initiator of the Stoos Network

What People Are Saying About The HUMAN SIDE of AGILE

I just found the next must-read book for our entire leadership team.
~**Tricia Broderick**, Director of Development, TechSmith

Gil Broza has done a superb job of cataloging the myriad issues facing the Agile team leader. He proposes a solution (and many times, more than one possible solution) to each issue, specifically noting the impact on team and personal dynamics. A masterful achievement.
~**Jeff McKenna**, Agile mentor, coach of the first Scrum team in 1993!

Gil's book covers the human side of Agile teams not discussed anywhere else. He handles the in-depth people aspects in lighthearted prose that is also easy to understand and put into practice.
~**Joy Kelsey**, senior Agile lecturer and Scrum professional

There is only one side of Agile—the human side! Rediscover the simple but profound practices and behaviors that transform the human discourse into creative solutions. It's a must read for anyone who wants things faster, better, and cheaper.
~**David Spann**, President, Agile Adaptive Management

Software delivery is a field dominated by logic and science, but it is ultimately accomplished by people and people are inherently complex. I was concerned when I picked up a book about the human aspects of Agile that it might be too fuzzy, impractical, and unhelpful. However, Gil gives sound advice and relevant examples, in a format that I can see myself returning to again and again as I navigate my way through an Agile world.
~**Dan Snyder**, ScrumMaster

Is your Agile project missing stewardship, the facilitation that would help it succeed? If so, run to buy Gil's book, The Human Side of Agile. Chock full of stories, tips, and advice, this book will 'unwedge' your project, and position you for effective team leadership throughout your project.
~**Johanna Rothman**, author, *Manage Your Project Portfolio: Increase Your Capacity and Finish More Projects*

With its focus on people, relationships, and interactions, this book will help you make the leap to being great at Agile, and is one of the best on the topic of leading and managing Agile teams.
~Mark Veksler, Senior Director Software Development, VFA

Practical answers to the most relevant and pressing questions that team leaders ask.
~Chris Young, VP Engineering, Entertainment Group, Autodesk

Agile teams need effective leaders who 'get' the people stuff, and without that you're merely going through the Agile motions. This book gets to the heart of the matter.
~Scott W. Ambler, co-creator of Disciplined Agile Delivery

Gil's book transcends any particular approach to delivering systems. It's up there with Peopleware with respect to its focus on concrete, actionable examples that you can take away and use immediately regardless of your organization's development approach. The only difference is that Gil leverages the ensuing 25 years of software industry experience and his own decade-plus experience in the Agile world to provide recommendations that work in today's environments. Having had the great pleasure of working side-by-side with Gil, I have seen his advice being used to help individuals and teams improve. This book is a must read!
~Dave Rooney, Sherpa, Shopify

I've rarely seen so much useful, concrete advice packaged in such a simple and accessible way. If you are an Agile coach, put this on the top of your reading list!
~Henrik Kniberg, Agile coach, author, *Scrum and XP from the Trenches* and *Lean from the Trenches*

There are many good books on the technical details of Agile software development. Equally important is the human side: the Agile Manifesto says 'we value individuals and interactions over processes and tools.' The Human Side of Agile redresses the balance with intelligent insights and practical techniques to help you inspire your team to deliver more, faster, and more repeatable results.
~Ian Brockbank, badgertaming.net

At Menlo, our cultural focus is 'the business value of joy.' Joy is only possible when we sustain the humans involved throughout the life cycle of a project. Gil Broza gives us a very practical guide to the human factors in sustainable process and agility.
~Rich Sheridan, CEO and co-founder, Menlo Innovations

The
HUMAN SIDE
of AGILE

How to Help Your Team Deliver

GIL BROZA

Gil Broza
(416) 302-8120
support@3PVantage.com

Published by 3P Vantage Media

ISBN: 978-0-9880016-2-6

Book design: Heather Kirk, Graphics for Success

Book cover text: Graham Van Dixhorn, Write to Your Market, Inc.

Editing: Karen Pasley and Mark Woodworth

Indexing: Elizabeth Walker

Printed in the United States of America. Published simultaneously in Canada.

CONTENTS

FOREWORD

by Jim Highsmith

When the authors of the Agile Manifesto began talking about what was important to each of us, way back in 2001, we clearly agreed on two broad goals: improving software development performance (striving for software excellence) and creating exciting, collaborative, fun working environments. The latter — better working environments — was just as important as the former, but in the intervening years it often became sidetracked as organizations focused on stories, iteration planning, and velocity. Organizations struggled with self-organizing teams and collaboration — some struggling more successfully than others.

Agilists don't usually try to predict the future, but as we enter the second decade of the 21st century, it's clear that two things will dominate: winning customers and engaging talent. Creating healthy, engaging workplaces in which people are inspired to deliver customer solutions will be a critical management focus.

Really? Is this last statement actually true, or is it just wishful thinking? Is the human side of organizations as important as the high-performance, execution side? In *Beyond Performance: How Great Organizations Build Ultimate Competitive Advantage*, Scott Keller and Colin Price, both from McKinsey & Co., present research data from surveys of 600,000 respondents from 500 companies (including 6,800 CEOs and senior executives) and personal interviews with over 30 CEOs. Keller and Price make what many might interpret as a startling conclusion: "Organizations that focused on performance and health simultaneously were nearly twice as successful as those that focused on health alone, and nearly three times as successful as those that focused on performance alone." They defined organizational health as the ability both to execute and to adapt faster than the competition.

So organizational health, particularly the abilities to adapt to change and engage one's talented workforce, is critical to continuing success. This brings me back to why Gil Broza's book is such an important one. There are a myriad of important Agile books about practices — technical practices and project management practices — and a few books about "softer" skills such as collaboration or coaching, but until Gil's book we lacked a comprehensive treatment of how to build Agile team leadership skills. While other authors write about Agile principles and values, Gil shows us practices that help leaders actualize those principles and values.

The Human Side of Agile defines the team leader's role, describes practices for growing Agile teams that are effective and self-organizing, explains how to foster communications and collaboration, offers critical advice on forming Agile teams, and shows how individuals with different roles (leader, developer, product manager) mesh together. Gil's book covers diverse topics, from active listening and running good meetings to dealing with a team member's bad behavior, but in the end all these topics come back to a central theme: how we create exciting, collaborative, fun working environments that engage teams in the task of delivering outstanding results.

Gil's Agile coaching and consulting experience shows through in this book's down-to-earth perspectives and advice for the reader's real-world challenges and needs. He equips the reader for the entire team life cycle — assembling, creating, growing, and maintaining a solid Agile team.

The human side of the enterprise, the side that involves organizational health, was a critical element in the thinking of early Agilists, and its importance continues to be advanced by research such as that reported on by Keller and Price. *The Human Side of Agile* provides team leaders with a "how to" for developing and strengthening this all-important aspect of successful teams and organizations.

Jim Highsmith
Executive Consultant, ThoughtWorks, Inc.
Venice, Florida

FOREWORD

by Christopher Avery

Thank goodness for Gil Broza's *The Human Side of Agile*. Why? Because you are not a role, a skill set, or a process automaton, and neither are your colleagues. You are human. And your performance relies more on embracing your humanity than on anything else.

If you want to be more valuable to your team regardless of your position, this book can help. Benefitting from and providing personal leadership to the human side of Agile has little to do with your role, title, or accountabilities. As Gil explains, in Agile teams responsibility is shared and that means anyone and everyone can provide Agile leadership. Yes, Agile requires leadership, lots of it. That means applying uncommon good sense by being value-focused, courageously facing the truth, and taking ownership to move the team forward. That's what this book is about. *The Human Side of Agile* is the first book I know that succeeds at putting people before product and process.

Let me share a personal story 30 years in the making.

Technical professionals were said to not care much about relating to other humans, only machines. The year was 1983 and I was stepping into my journey as an applied organization and leadership scientist. The common excuse was that engineers and other "techies" were not required to study interpersonal communication in college. I never bought that story.

My focus then as now was on the personal — as opposed to the impersonal — side of organizing. My strong hunch was and is that high performance is never due primarily to structure and process (those great attractors of management time and attention) but to shared clarity, ownership mind-set, trust, and an integrative culture. Yes, the so-called "soft" stuff is far more profound, challenging, and high-leverage than is the "hard" stuff.

The most vexing problem I saw in organization and leadership science — and wanted desperately to address — was the persistent negative correlation between business performance and humanity. The prevailing perception has been that these two elements each occupy one tray of a balance scale: an increase in business performance takes a toll on the humanity of people at work. And an investment in greater humanity — i.e., satisfaction, health, sustainability — reduces the bottom line. Additionally, the occasional counterexample of a high-performing business that is also a great place to work is an irreproducible oddity.

This widely shared assumption of scarcity — that one of these elements must suffer so the other can gain — did not have to be true. I was sure of it.

As my friend and fellow Agile Leadership Network founding board member Jim Highsmith makes clear in his companion Foreword, that negative relationship between business performance and human health is today being replaced with a positive correlation.

This to me is pure beauty, considering how much of our lives we all will spend at work. Though we have a long way to go for everyone at work to experience this shift, this turnaround is what I most relish about the Agile movement.

To be truly Agile invites confronting that scarcity (the negative correlation) and turning it to abundance (a positive correlation). That means in order to realize greater performance we must invite more of each individual to show up at work, take ownership, and collaborate with others to produce a net gain in value. And it means that offering a more satisfying, engaging, and sane experience at work produces a greater return for the business.

Thus, compared with 1983, a far greater percentage of today's technical professionals are teaching each other facilitation skills, team skills, and self-organization through personal responsibility. They are focusing on value, priority, and sustainability. This is wonderful to see. And the assumption that engineers don't have communication skills and don't like to interact with other human beings? It could not be less true.

What a story!

As Gil shows in *The Human Side of Agile*, when you put the human (i.e., personal) side of Agile ahead of the nonhuman side, there is no end to the questions you can ask yourself about how to be both more you and more effective at the same time.

Allow me three recommendations. First, read the Preface, Introduction, and Part I with an interest in completely understanding Gil's offer and his point of view in this book. What he is saying is that no processes or tools will take precedence over your ability to understand and respond to your own and others' humanity. That's the frame from which you should then read the remainder of the book.

My second recommendation is to review all the section headings in the Table of Contents. Notice that each is in the form of a question. These are the questions that Gil has encountered and addressed over and over during his career as a developer and engineer, as an XP (eXtreme Programming) practitioner and coach, and as an Agile enterprise consultant. Mark the questions that appeal to you most.

Then third, read the book. You'll want to return to it often. And I'll tell you when to return to it: every time you are frustrated by a problem or challenge at work. That can happen every hour or two in many jobs, so keep the book handy. When you open it, rescan the questions that title each subsection until you find the one calling to you about this challenge, this time. Then settle in to expand your thinking.

Christopher Avery, Ph.D.
Comfort, Texas

PREFACE

In proper conditions, Agile teams outperform the sum of their parts. Well-functioning Agile teams are a joy to behold, a pleasure to be part of, and a privilege to lead. They use reliable methods, which they continually adapt — ones that make their lives easier, not harder. Responsiveness to changes in understanding and circumstance is second nature to them. A high-performing, engaged Agile team can handle almost anything.

Would you like to lead a successful team like that? Agile frameworks do not assume that the team has a project manager or reports to a manager, although some frameworks (like Scrum) do assume that the team has a servant leader who helps them deliver value. If you are, or would like to be, that person, this book is for you.

Over the past several years, many ScrumMasters, managers, and team leads have expressed their challenges to me. Many of them were spearheading an implementation of Scrum or some other form of Agile. I would hear them voice sentiments like the following:

"We've put in place roles, sprints, meetings, and a backlog. But I'm not seeing any of the promised self-organization, teamwork, or commitment. Everybody still works on their own piece. They'll stay stuck on a story for three days before telling anyone. In some sprints, they don't finish a single story — and there's no consequence! Where are the 'shared responsibility' and 'hyper-productivity' that we were promised?"

"We try to implement Agile, but we have some real limitations. The team is spread across several time zones. Most folks say they

are so specialized they can't share tasks with anybody; some just won't work with anyone else. They sit quietly in retrospectives, waiting for me to tell them what to change. Sometimes I wonder whether the Scrum theory works in practice."

"I used to have a solid track record as a project manager. Now, I get to feel anxious every two weeks. Will the team deliver on their iteration commitments? How will the demo go this time? Senior management keeps interfering in tactical work, asking me to increase productivity and holding me accountable for delivering this project — but I feel powerless to affect its outcome."

Even people who were running apparently successful Agile implementations expressed concerns:

"I lead the team's meetings, keep on top of their plans, and help remove the occasional impediment. But I want my role to be more significant than that! I know Agile is so much more about the people than the process or tools, but what can I do to help? Anytime they run into a serious team challenge, I'm told not to intervene — they should work it out on their own. I don't feel that I add any significant value to the team."

"We've been using Agile methods successfully for quite a while. The team has jelled, and they seem to flow smoothly with their process. But retrospectives yield only minor improvements, and I feel we've reached a plateau. How can I help our good team become a great team?"

If you see yourself in some of these people or their statements resonate with you, what would you say is the difficulty in realizing greater value from Agile?

Consider the following three P's:

+ Product: *What* product do we make?

+ People: *Who* participates in making the product?

✦ Process: *How* do we make our product and get it into customers' hands?

In the early 20th century, the world was busy manufacturing goods. Frederick Taylor was the reigning thought leader, studying how workers could use technology in the most efficient manner. With his Scientific Management approach, the most important P was process. Manufacturing ability and scale were greater differentiators than product design and quality, so the second P was product. People were the third P, as their working conditions made painfully obvious.

Since then, process and product have remained the two key factors. Most businesses still live or die by their product. The process element has been refined, standardized, reengineered, and regulated to be independent of the flesh-and-blood folks who use it. Thus people still constitute the third P.

Yet, when it came to the software industry, process turned out to be a stumbling block. Many workers in that industry realized that streamlined processes that optimize manufacturing and minimize variability really don't cut it in this type of knowledge work, where development, innovation, and customization are dominant. Agile development emerged as a natural reaction to the fallibility of the Process-Product-People value system.

The revolutionary ordering of the three P's according to Agile is People-Product-Process.

An Agile axiom is that success and failure are first and foremost about people. If you build an enabling framework for your team, tend to the members on a personal level, tap into their potential, and help them interact effectively, they will take care of the next important P, product. And to do that, they will customize the third P, process.

However, putting people first means dealing with such matters as emotions, drive, conduct, resistance, habits, and blind spots. This does not come naturally to most product development professionals.[1]

They are used to thinking of tasks, resources, job descriptions, and technical skills. And their workplaces—cubicles, standardized offices, dreary meeting rooms — conceal the fact that their inhabitants are human beings.

These professionals have few reference experiences that would enable them to recognize, welcome, and foster a core Agile principle: collaboration. Traditional environments have suppressed both interdependence and shared responsibility; people were viewed as "resources," and management tried to maximize the time they spent on their specialties. Agile moves away from keeping people busy, focusing them instead on *delivering value* in a *team* setting.

No matter how technical the system you deliver, you must deal with the people who define and build it. You can't always choose them, and you won't always like working with them. However, the Agile framework, fiercely people-first and transparent, will make any difficulties explicit and encourage collaborative solutions. You are not alone.

This book will help you master the human side of Agile so you can lead your team to greatness. You'll find useful advice, whether you first learned about Agile yesterday or have been leading a successful team for years. Whether your leadership role is formal or not, this book will help you design it for outstanding value and then grow a solid team. It will assist you in engaging people in powerful conversations and being an Agile leader. And when your team is humming along and you're ready for more, it will show you how to sustain their performance for the long haul.

If you are an Agile team member, use this book to learn what to expect from your team leader and how to apply your innate leadership to help your team prosper. If you are a senior manager, use it to better understand your organization's greatest asset — its people — and the influences on their performance in an Agile setting. And if you are a coach or a change agent, use this book when you help people integrate that brief but powerful statement from the Agile Manifesto: "Individuals and interactions over processes and tools."

Gil Broza
Toronto, Canada
May 2012

INTRODUCTION

Do you enjoy supporting your team daily — for instance as their ScrumMaster, Agile project manager, or project leader? Would you like to amplify your contribution as part of the team? Then set your sights on being the Agile team leader (ATL). This comprehensive, rewarding role has a single purpose: to help your team meet their objectives.

Being an Agile team leader has two sides to it. One is tangible, sensible, and definable — the side of *getting stuff done*. That's where you apply tools, process mechanics, standards, artifacts, and, generally, *things*. On this side, plenty of useful resources (notice that's another *thing*) are available to you.

And then there's the *human side*. That's the squishy, irrational, "But-yesterday-everything-was-just-fine" side. That's where you encounter silent or pointless meetings, resistance to change, mistrust, people who are stuck but won't admit it, and blunders. But it's also the side with delight, flexibility, passion, creativity, and "Woohoo!"

I've written this book to help you both manage the human side's challenges and enjoy more of its benefits. For years, I have been focusing my coaching and consulting practice, my studies, and collaborations with other caring experts on the human side. Here are my time-tested tips, techniques, and ideas.

You do *not* have to become an expert communicator, facilitator, sociologist, psychologist, or change management guru. Rather, this book will augment your toolkit from each domain just enough for you to handle effectively those situations in software development where people, Agile methods, and delivery leadership intersect.

The book is designed to address your needs as they arise. The table of contents lists about 80 questions that team leaders ask about the human side of Agile. Since the book's organization roughly follows a team's life cycle, you may find some chapters to be more applicable than others right now. You can also gain a broad perspective from reading cover to cover.

Part I starts by making the case for the Agile team leader role (chapter 1). It defines the role's responsibilities and relationships and explains how teams can benefit from having dedicated ATLs (chapter 2). You will learn how to adapt the ATL role for your personality, team, and context (chapter 3). Part I will be useful to you whether you're new to Agile or are ready to take on expanded responsibilities.

Part II helps you grow a solid Agile team. If you have a say in choosing the members, you will learn how to select them (chapter 4), help the chosen group become a team (chapter 5), and, more specifically, help them become an Agile team (chapter 6). Throughout the team's life cycle, you may have to manage certain behaviors that threaten teamwork (chapter 7).

In Part III you'll learn a wealth of pragmatic techniques that will be beneficial every day, and many times each day, for improving dialogues with colleagues at all levels — both one on one (chapter 8) and in meetings (chapter 9).

Communication and facilitation are vital for overcoming the tough leadership challenges described in Part IV. Even in thriving Agile environments, you will sometimes need to champion your team (chapter 10), support people through change (chapter 11), and reduce resistance to ideas (chapter 12).

Before the team reaches cruising altitude, you need to start supporting them for the long haul. Part V will show you how to help them cultivate a mentality that truly embraces change and adaptability (chapter 13), as well as how to keep the team together through thick and thin (chapter 14).

The dozens of stories you'll read are all true (I've changed the names to protect identities). Most are from teams I've coached or observed, while a few have been contributed by clients, reviewers, and colleagues.

Most chapters come with free resources, such as checklists, worksheets, and mind maps. Download these resources, as well as content updates, from the book's companion website at **www.TheHumanSideOfAgile.com**.

PART I
Design Your Role for Outstanding Value

What are Agile team leaders responsible for? Are they anything like "traditional" team leaders or project managers, and how do they differ? If the team is supposed to negotiate deliverables with the product owner and self-organize around execution, what would a leader *do*? Part I answers these and related questions. It lays out the nature and specifics of the Agile team leader *role*, and guides you — the *person* in that role — to be the best leader for your team.

CHAPTER 1

Step Into Agile Team Leadership

In every Agile implementation, teams include at least two roles. The delivery team (also called the "development team" or "technical team") constructs the product, while the product owner (also the "customer" or "lead customer") specifies its features and behavior. Many Agile teams include a *third role*, whose purpose is to support the first two in meeting their objectives and whose responsibilities include facilitating the process and removing obstacles. In Scrum teams, that is the ScrumMaster. In other teams, the role is called "Agile project manager" (APM) and, where properly implemented, the APM is a facilitative leader rather than a controller or administrator. Other variations on this third role are "delivery lead" and "development lead." It is distinct from the technical lead and the coach roles.

The Agile community has offered contradictory opinions about the leadership of Agile teams. The self-organizing nature of delivery teams and their direct negotiations with the product owner (PO) seem to imply that a specific leader is unnecessary overhead. Some teams do, in fact, enjoy shared leadership and effective self-management. Yet thousands of Agile teams exist that attribute some of their success to the person in that third role, whether called ScrumMaster, Agile project manager, or something else.

Even an experienced Agile team may experience the following challenges:

Team members cannot, should not, and will not do everything. They *cannot* perform activities for which they are not informed or authorized, for instance obtaining access to protected servers and data. The team *should not* perform some other activities, mostly because they would lose focus or switch contexts a good deal. Examples include removing certain impediments and finding support for a product they are using. Even conscientious team members *will not* care to handle certain necessary, but nonstimulating, recurrent tasks. (Personal and shared responsibility is no match for the reaction "This isn't what I signed up for!")

Self-direction does not imply smooth flow. Team members have the autonomy to make decisions and take actions, both individually and collectively, yet they are still human. As a group, they have a lot to do and a lot to pay attention to. No matter how bright, evolved, sharing, open, and self-organizing, they will occasionally drop some balls. They may forget to take a certain action, coordinate ineffectually, delay a decision too long, or fail to follow up on an expectation.

The wealth of information is staggering — even in small projects.* Some information is documented and maintained; the rest is stored in people's heads. The team and the organization must identify and manage relevant information in support of analysis, dissemination, and informed action.

Since most Agile teams work within a larger business, additional people are involved: managers, stakeholders, and sponsors. (The entire cast of participants is called the *project community*,[1] *development community*, or *product community*.) An Agile team must keep open lines

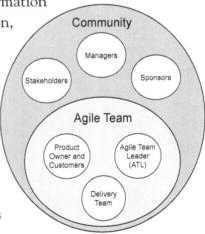

---

* A number of Agile practitioners prefer to move away from the project concept, which connotes a temporary endeavor. I agree that teams ought to persist past any single project and deliver value on a regular basis; nevertheless, I find the project concept useful when thinking about a team's effort over a specific period, such as a point release or a new product direction.

of communication with its community, which can become taxing. There can be many stakeholders; some of my coaching client teams have counted more than 15. Having a central conduit for most of that communication can reduce the team's load — albeit at the risk of delays and incorrect representation.

A team that experiences these four interrelated challenges cannot solve them with more process or more tools. They need someone to play the third role and help them overcome these challenges. To be extremely valuable to the team, however, the third role cannot focus solely on process mechanics or project administration. This facilitative servant leader supports *the people*, having the sole purpose of helping the team deliver. Hence, I call this role the *Agile team leader* (ATL). The ATL is sometimes affectionately referred to as the "glue," the "connective tissue," or "the oil in the engine."

The Agile team leader helps the entire community identify and deliver a valuable product within set parameters. Unlike a classically trained (e.g., PMI-certified) project manager, the ATL does not manage and control the work. Instead, he facilitates the interactions and activities so that the project community can do its work effectively. The ATL is a servant leader, supporting responsibility taking and team growth without need for a reporting relationship.

The Agile team leader connects the team and their work to the rest of the organization. The leader helps the self-organizing delivery team maximize their results within the constraints of scope, budget, quality, and time. By constantly observing the team's progress and learning about their hurdles, the leader can distinguish patterns, identify root causes, and stop small problems from growing into big ones.

Just as a programmer does not become an "Agile developer" overnight by joining an Agile team, you don't become an ATL merely by taking on this title. While your experience and training in managing people and projects remain valuable, you need certain additional skills, behaviors, and attitudes to qualify as an ATL. These include:

+ Comprehending and embracing the Agile principles,[2] values, and practices

+ Recognizing that you don't command or control anyone in your team

+ Believing that your team will deliver the goods and that your role is to help them

+ Being inclined and able to lead, nurture, and coach people rather than manage their work

+ Permitting yourself and others to proceed despite incomplete or changing information

Note that the Agile team leader is a *role*, not a person. In many situations, a single person plays that role full-time. However, in a tight team of a half-dozen or fewer, one that is fairly isolated from the rest of the organization and thus subject to few organizational constraints, the role may be staffed part-time.

Great Agile teams are characterized by a passion to deliver value regularly and delight their customers. ATLs, leading from within their teams, manifest that passion not by defining or developing deliverables, but by supporting those who do. Rather than apply prescribed "best practices" or process mechanics, effective ATLs work situationally, fostering a healthy alignment between the people, product, process, and project. In the next two chapters, we'll see exactly how.

CHAPTER 2

Add Value as an Agile Team Leader

To help your team deliver, your ATL role borrows heavily from the ScrumMaster role, traditional project management,[1] and pragmatic management and leadership. You undertake a wide variety of activities and responsibilities, which seems to be asking a great deal from a single person. In true Agile spirit, though, context is everything. Customizing your role to fit the actual needs of the real live team in your very real organization is far more important than sticking to a formal role description.

2.1 Who Is Responsible for Value Delivery?

I sometimes give an introductory talk to project managers, called "The Truth about Agile Teams, Leaders, and Managers." After describing the principles of Agile teamwork, I ask, "Who is responsible for value delivery in Agile?"

Many people in the audience are used to the traditional organizational model of a hierarchy ("command and control"), which gives rise to a certain power structure. At the bottom are line workers, or "individual contributors," who are supposed to spend their time performing their duties and specialties. They have limited access to information and no formal authority.

Line workers report to managers, who in turn report to their own managers. Managers have the authority and responsibility to decide who will do what when. They design the work and its environment. They are privy to more information than individual contributors. To varying extents, the same is true for project managers. In matrix organizations, individual contributors answer to people managers as well as to project managers.

In the command-and-control structure, *managers are under the gun* to deliver results. If something goes wrong with a project, managers can take "corrective action": add or shift people, mandate overtime, and the like. Delivery responsibility lies with managers.

Others in my typical audience are actively using Agile frameworks, wherein teams are empowered to make most of the decisions that affect them and their work product. By self-organizing, communicating openly, and taking a value perspective (as opposed to a task perspective), they are supposed to produce more meaningful results. Therefore, managers and project managers are actively discouraged from telling an Agile team what to do and how to do it. The Agile team's experience sometimes resembles that of the cars in this picture:

Team members are like the car drivers. They know the rules of the road, they can operate their cars, and they communicate their intentions to other drivers. The drivers self-organize to share the road and reach their separate destinations without colliding. Notice the two police officers at the top? They could be the managers. From where they stand, they can mostly influence drivers into compliance and maybe call an ambulance if an accident happens. (In newly Agile environments, managers are in an even tougher spot, because sometimes their teams know the rules better than they do!)

When I ask my audience, "Who is responsible for value delivery in Agile?" one common answer is "the project manager." Sorry, no.

Another common answer is "the product owner" (PO). Not quite; the PO is responsible for *choosing* and *defining* the value to build, but she can't cause any of it to be developed or delivered.

Other answers include "the ScrumMaster" and "the development manager." At this point I say, "Whether you are the project manager, the ScrumMaster, or the team leader, you *personally* are not on the hook to deliver. After all, you don't tell the team what to do."

After a pause for dramatic effect, I continue: "The *team* is responsible for delivering value, and your responsibility is to facilitate their commitments."

Invariably, a few seconds later, someone bursts out laughing. The reality of many of those new to Agile continues to be the opposite of my description. They may have a few Agile teams, but the managerial hierarchy still hands down responsibility, and the chain of delegation stops at the project or functional manager.

If your organization thinks *you* are solely responsible for value delivery, it is not implementing Agile properly.

But what if the team is *unable* to deliver? What if they are understaffed, or their technical skills are unsuitable for the job? In a proper Agile environment, the team members would clearly communicate their abilities, apply themselves as best they can, and consistently improve over time. If they can't possibly accomplish what's expected of them, you help them renegotiate commitments or introduce necessary changes.

In the old structure, you communicated to the team what the organization wanted them to do. Communication went mostly downward and through you. By contrast, in the Agile framework, you also communicate to the organization what the team needs from *it*. Communication is now mostly upward. You no longer serve merely the organization; you mostly serve the team.

2.2 What Is My Relationship With Each Role Player?

2.2.1 With the Delivery Team

In a well-functioning Agile community, you would be most effective as their *servant leader*. This has several aspects, a number of which may feel uncomfortable or confusing.

Since the team is cross-functional, some (if not all) members do not report to you. And even if you have formal authority over the others, exercising it ("pulling rank") can be detrimental to the team's Agility (see chapter 6).

Most team members probably report into a functional hierarchy, such as development, quality assurance (QA), or architecture. You lead, inspire, and support members' allegiance to their Agile team rather than to their functional group.

As a leader, you guide, support, encourage, and mentor the *people*, rather than oversee their *work*. You assist their self-organization in service of the common goal. In one team, that will be easy and pleasant; in another team, it will feel like herding cats. You help them be as effective and efficient as they can be according to *their* best understanding. Rather than maximize their utilization, you support them in working smart and adapting to changing needs.

2.2.2 With the Product Owner

Just as you support the delivery team, you support the product owner. Even on a small product, she will have a lot of information to capture and process, interactions to manage, and decisions to make. She is also likely to be pulled in several directions and beholden to additional objectives. You are in an excellent position to help her own the product effectively.

Many POs write backlog items, prioritize them — and then run out of time. You can tidy it all up in preparation for the next planning cycle. Another area for support is in building and maintaining relationships with the community at large. Reaching out to stakeholders, managers, and advisory boards; maintaining beneficial relationships; and holding conversations that result in useful artifacts — these and other support activities are usually quite time-consuming. As the product owner maintains the feature roadmap, she needs to talk with people who are even busier than she is, so help her establish and maintain those connections. What actually transpires during the conversation — anything to do with the domain, the product requirements, the roadmap, and so on — is usually left up to the PO.

What should you do if the product owner isn't fulfilling her duties? Lack of PO accountability is a serious risk, quite probably the team's greatest impediment to success. You may step in and help an underperforming PO *only* if she is having good-faith difficulties. Maybe she is swamped right now, needs additional training, or is temporarily away. However, if the product owner is not accountable, is delinquent in her role, or just doesn't want to play the role — *do not* step in. Make the root cause transparent so the PO is held accountable, since that is a bigger organizational problem and the solution is not in your hands.

2.2.3 With the Stakeholders

If your community is like most, it has many stakeholders: people who affect the product or the team or are affected by them.

Some stakeholders contribute product requirements or information. They may be in other teams downstream or upstream from yours. They may be key people in other business units. Many software development endeavors have stakeholders in marketing, sales, legal, training, and operations. There could be stakeholders outside your organization, such as regulatory agencies, government representatives, and vendors.

Other players, perhaps less obviously, have a stake in the team's Agility irrespective of the system they develop. Human resources plays a role in staffing, compensation, and rewards; finance provides funding; procurement (purchasing) supplies tools and specialists; and facilities looks after the team's physical setup.

One Agile team developing a Master Data Management platform had 24 stakeholders. The project community poster listed all their *names* in addition to titles and departments. Thus, the product owner and ATL knew exactly whom to keep in the loop, and whom to call when they needed something from their department. Most stakeholders were managers and, when necessary, they delegated requests.

For the product to be a true success and not just a narrow solution, stakeholders need to be continually advised and consulted. Bringing them into the project's kickoff meeting is one of your earliest collaborative, relationship-building steps. Later, invite them to visit the team and attend iteration demos. That said, stakeholders are unlikely to have daily interaction with the team, and they often communicate directly with only two people: the product owner, with whom they discuss requirements, system details, and priorities; and you, their point person for everything else. They expect you to listen to their concerns, invite them to relevant meetings, and keep them updated. If the PO is very busy and there are many stakeholders, the balance of the communication with them will shift even more heavily to your side.

Take good care of your stakeholders. Many of them are in influential positions, and if they feel ignored, there may be consequences for you and the team. Help them manage their interactions with the team in a way that maximizes the value of the team's deliverables. Be inclusive, open, and empathetic with them — they will reciprocate.

2.2.4 With the Sponsors

The sponsors, often business or engineering directors or unit heads, are key stakeholders: they represent both senior management and the company's interests in the project. They bet corporate money and other resources to run the project and reap some organizational reward. Bluntly, their necks are on the line to make the effort succeed. Many projects have one or two sponsors.

Get to know the sponsors personally. You will interact early on when drafting the project charter. Even though you and the PO are the likely *authors* of the charter, the sponsors are its only signatories, and they can single-handedly change the charter, even to the extent of halting the project. Later, they will defend the project in meetings or get you more time and resources if necessary.

Most sponsors are incredibly busy so they have gatekeepers. The team usually sees them only at the kickoff and the occasional iteration demo. The rest of the time, the sponsors communicate mostly with you. In the successful cases I've seen, though, every team member knew the sponsors in person, and vice versa. Even basic familiarity strengthens trust and goodwill, which are particularly helpful when the going gets tough.

Your interaction with the sponsors is similar to that in traditionally run projects. A sponsor may ask:

✦ Are we on track to meet our objectives?

✦ What are the risks?

- ✦ What can we do to increase our chances of success?

- ✦ What else is happening that I should know about?

- ✦ What do you need?

- ✦ How can I help?

I've met many ATLs who took these questions (which were posed to them rather frequently) as an unwelcome intrusion on the team's autonomy. A more helpful interpretation is that the sponsors need data so they can make informed decisions about the rest of the program, the project portfolio, or other IT investments. Maintain a trusting relationship with them: when the road turns rocky, you want them on your side.

2.2.5 With the Team Members' Managers

Most organizations implement Agile by grafting it onto their existing structure. If your organization is a siloed (functional) hierarchy, your team members have been assigned from various technical functions such as development, testing, and database design. Between them, they report to several managers, one of whom may also happen to be your boss. Those managers may be closely tied to the team or be fairly uninvolved with their daily activities.

This situation might not be news to you if you're used to matrixed environments, yet it's going to be extremely delicate nonetheless. The functional managers and you ought to have the same overarching objective: contributing to your organization's continued value delivery. You ought to have the same strategy: unleashing the power of self-organizing, collaborative teams. When that's indeed the case, you and the functional managers can forge delightful relationships that enable your team to shine. When it's *not* the case, you might encounter adversarial relationships, turf wars and politics, and frustrated team members. See section 5.6 for advice on handling this situation.

2.3 What Are My Responsibilities?

As an Agile team leader, you work at the tactical level with a certain team, helping them meet development objectives. You guide situational delivery, where the value systems of the team and their customers align. Your responsibilities fall into four broad categories: people, product, process, and project. In your particular context, and given your talents and career path, you will not carry out each duty to the extreme. In addition, as your team evolves (and anytime you move to another team), you will tailor your responsibilities to the specific needs in each category.

Note: If you are a functional or line manager as well as an ATL, you have additional duties (see Appendix). In small, tight-knit environments, it may be fine to play both roles. In larger organizations, though, that would be an antipattern.[2] These roles have different focuses — one is vertical, one is horizontal — while both demand your full attention. Choose one, as you are not likely to succeed in both.[3] If you prefer the ATL role, a collaborative relationship with your organization's managers may still see you sharing some of their duties.

2.3.1 People

Your responsibilities in the people category revolve around letting team members focus on doing their job as best they can.

Head off distractions. Your team works best with minimal interruptions and external obligations. The challenge is that many of those appear legitimate.

The most common type of distraction is the unanticipated task. Whether it is a customer support ticket, a production support issue, or someone's urgent request, a team member has to drop what he's doing and switch contexts. Rather than merely budgeting iteration time for "average" interruptions, work with the team to minimize their occurrence or their effect.

Aaron, a developer on a new Agile team, constantly received "extracurricular" tasks from his manager and from end users. He felt powerless to push back and feared the consequences of saying no. He was not feeling like a true team member, and the team stopped expecting his full contribution. Once we rerouted all those tasks through the PO to the backlog, he integrated well into the team.

Another type of distraction is when your people are poached, even part-time, for another initiative. The other initiative might benefit, but your team will suffer (see 4.5 and 6.1). If you can't prevent the departure of those members, strive to get their and the team's consent.

The third common type of distraction is pervasive inattention. Members' engagement with their project and team can run low when their affiliation or allegiance is focused elsewhere. This happens when functional managers continue assigning tasks and monitoring accomplishments at the individual level. It also occurs if your project proceeds despite having low value — staff will focus on more important or more visible work. Decide whether to keep fighting for your team or halt the project.

Protect the team from undue pressure. Unless your organization has bought into Agile, your team's conduct will worry certain people of influence. Matters such as short iterations and work-in-progress limits, sticky notes on whiteboards, and team room discussions instead of fervent typing might appear lax or unprofessional. Outsiders, especially senior managers, might feel compelled to "restore order" and "demand accountability." The iteration cycle, and particularly its demo, can also spell a regular, frequent opportunity for those managers to resort to traditional tactics, which can destroy Agility (see 10.6). Most teams can't handle such pressure on their own. Deflect the pressure and keep protecting your team (see 10.7). Allow them space to collaborate, experiment, and correct course.

Foster collaboration. Coming from command-and-control environments or used to working in cubicles, team members tend to work heads down on *their* stuff. If a person notices that she's stuck, she may hesitate to ask for help, and others wouldn't know she needs it. By walking around, observing, and listening, you can notice the situation and send for help. Get people talking and encourage them to work together. Park yourself next to someone for a pairing session, thereby leading by example and providing a reference experience for solo-work types.

Hold people accountable. Agile planning has built-in reciprocity. The team commits to certain deliverables in exchange for control over the design, the task breakdown, and the work budget (as approximated by velocity). If the team doesn't live up to their commitment, hold them accountable and help them learn to do better the next time (see 10.3).

Support personal growth and development. You have a good vantage point on the consequences of actions and decisions. Give respectful, timely feedback[4] to support both team and individual growth. In collaboration with their managers, help team members develop personally and professionally while maintaining balance with team obligations. Encourage team members to give each other feedback — and teach them *how* to do so.

Procure resources. The team requires resources such as new hardware, access to outside expertise, training, and even food for some meetings. Secure the funds and approvals, and make the arrangements on the team's behalf.

2.3.2 Product

Your next set of responsibilities revolves around keeping everybody focused on the right product to develop.

Ensure the flow of business value. Help the product owner keep the backlog stocked with valuable, ordered items, which are ready for the team's consumption. Help the delivery team and the PO find effective ways to collaboratively define the backlog's contents in support of the project's mission. Ensure that capacity is respected, that priorities are followed, and, ultimately, that the team optimizes its value delivery.

"Just last week, one critical piece of a spec got lost along the way. We built this export ability to append metadata to an offering, and the piece that was overlooked was getting that metadata from the internal system into a way it can be utilized. So we had engineers all weekend long working to try and fill in this missing piece... Somewhere along the way, I think it was a part of the original spec to have an export done that contained this stuff, but that piece got forgotten. It's not like it was deprioritized; that was impossible. The whole purpose of doing this feature was to get an export in some way; you can't use it if the data is just sitting in a system. It was like you make a cup of coffee but you forget to pick it up and drink it."

— A team's stakeholder

This team was not lacking in smarts or energy. An ATL, bringing a more detached perspective to the table, might have prevented this oversight or promptly convened a retrospective for discovering its root cause.

Maintain alignment between tactical execution and strategic intent. Check frequently that planned deliverables remain valuable. Keep reminding the community about the big picture, because short cycles and small stories easily engender team myopia and a hamster-wheel feeling. Maintain the charter, ascertain that the team still buys into its vision, and govern to the charter's parameters. If parameters have changed, announce the changes and make sure they are understood. (Don't assume that it is enough to update a document; people need to *pay attention*.)

> At a team kickoff, the product owner emphasized that time-to-ship was absolutely fixed and that scope, quality, and cost were flexible. However, a few months later, the importance of quality had grown until it became the fixed parameter — but only in the PO's mind. The last few iterations became strained as the team kept feeling they were late, but they were not: their *target* had moved.

Keep the stakeholders in the loop. The larger the project and the further it reaches in the organization, the more numerous the stakeholders are likely to be. Invite them to iteration demos and release planning meetings to get their input about the evolving product. Keep them informed about changes. And manage their expectations, since they will probably not see all their requests implemented.

Coordinate externally. If other software teams contribute to your team's solution, get the teams talking about plans, dependencies, and shared concerns — they won't naturally communicate much without your prodding. If the project includes more than software, be the point of contact to its nonsoftware elements, such as marketing, packaging, and third parties. Coordinate schedules and plans, and manage dependencies. Act as a translator to non-Agile teams for effective expectations management.

2.3.3 Process

When it comes to process, you help the community use their process, adapt it to circumstance, and get it unstuck.

Assume process stewardship. The *team* owns the process, which they inspect and adapt in retrospectives and on other occasions. Unfortunately, many teams don't pay enough attention to process or don't bother adapting it (or simply don't know how). Help your team follow their chosen methods and respect their agreements. Point out problems they may not have noticed. Guide the members to continuously improve and adapt their process.

From my interview with Eugene Kiel, vice president at Cengage Learning:

Gil: Who owns the process?

Eugene: Well, the teams.... We *all* own it.

Remove impediments. Impediments (obstacles) hamper a team's progress or productivity and occur almost daily. Monitor the situation constantly so you can proactively address issues. Any team member can attempt to resolve them, but it's your responsibility to help do so or at least to lead the charge. Removing a given impediment can take some time — especially when it involves reaching outside the team — so make sure to follow up. (For more on impediments, see 2.4.)

Manage knowledge, information sources, and artifacts. Establish repositories for easy access. Maintain the artifacts that need to stay current, such as plans, risks, and issues, and archive the rest.

Track progress, trends, and metrics. Because your role does not involve you in daily construction or definition of the solution, you can observe and analyze the path taken toward the solution. Collect information about it (with minimal disturbance to the team's focus), and make it visibly available. Bring emerging risks or trends to the team's attention. Some of those you will mitigate; some you will escalate. Be sure to measure usefully, because measurement tends to influence behavior.[5]

Lead meetings. Most Agile implementations have a standard repertoire of meetings, sometimes known as "ceremonies": planning, standup, demo/review, and retrospective. You schedule, host, and facilitate them. If you can't attend one, delegate the responsibility. When the community opts for additional meetings, help make them effective and efficient (see chapter 9).

Promote organizational Agility. Whether your team is one of several Agile teams in the organization or the sole one, increased organizational Agility will improve the team's results. A larger-scale Agile implementation requires support and leadership; as one of its active practitioners, your participation is instrumental to its success.

2.3.4 Project

Whether facing a single project or longer-term, continuous value delivery, you have an additional set of responsibilities: connecting the team's work to organizational needs.

Establish a suitable team and secure the sponsors' support. Set up a team that can deliver the goods (see chapter 4) and identify the entire community by name. Don't forget the sponsors! Without involved, supportive sponsors, your team's success is in jeopardy.

Kick off the effort properly. Even with the right team and sponsors, starting development by just filling up a backlog and jumping into the first iteration is irresponsible. Make sure the project has a clear, collaboratively produced and sponsor-signed charter — even if you write most of it yourself (see 10.2). Only then should you proceed to plan releases and iterations.

Provide data for budgeting and forecasting. Most organizations, Agile or not, need to know what they are getting into when they start a new endeavor. You can supply the relevant data, based on the backlog and other information from the product owner and the team.

Identify, manage, and mitigate big-picture risks. Most people on a team work heads down and may not notice nonimmediate risks. You have a wider-lens view, and a bit more objectivity, to detect those risks before they materialize. Make sure the entire team understands that continuous risk management is everybody's business — you just happen to lead it.

Report needed information. No matter how transparently the team maintain their plans and artifacts, such raw data rarely helps senior management in making high-level decisions. Translate or roll up progress information to answer management's questions, and do so regularly. Similarly, manage audit and regulatory information needs as appropriate. Collect all data with minimal disturbance to the team.

Supplementary resource: Download "Agile Team Leader Responsibilities Snapshot" from the book's companion website, **www.The HumanSideOfAgile.com**.

2.4 Which Impediments Should I Remove?

Impediments, also commonly referred to as roadblocks or obstacles, are anything that holds the team back from working effectively. They are *everywhere*.

You might see these obstacles for yourself as you perform your other tasks, or someone might point out an impediment to you. The regular opportunities for that are the retrospective and the daily standup meeting, and in both you will have the same difficulty obtaining useful information about impediments. People can be quiet in retrospectives or just share innocuous observations. The standup meeting easily turns into a brief status report ("Here's what I did yesterday…") with very little mentioned about roadblocks.

The reasons vary. Sometimes people don't notice that they are held back and what it is that's holding them back. Sometimes they don't admit it. Sometimes they don't care. For effective discovery, you need to design these meetings' processes (see chapter 9). Also, check in with individual members on an ad hoc basis to learn what may be standing in their way. (See chapter 8 for techniques to optimize these conversations.)

Some impediments are technical, such as:

+ The team is using an unfamiliar technology.

+ The team needs hardware, licenses, installations, or configuration changes.

+ Some equipment is malfunctioning.

Other impediments have to do with a suboptimized process, such as:

+ Work can't be completed or moved to the next stage.

+ Work can't be started due to missing information.

+ An artifact is waiting for rework.

+ Someone is waiting on another person, within the team or outside it.

+ A dependency is causing a delay that could have been avoided.

+ There are some long feedback loops, such as slow builds, heavy regression testing, and questions addressed to unavailable product owners.

Even though these impediments are process-related, remember that you and your team make your process. Together, you adjust or redesign it to minimize such impediments.

Impediments can arise simply from working within an organization. For example:

+ A sign-off is needed (e.g., expense approval).

+ There is time-consuming bureaucracy (e.g., procurement and timesheets).

✦ Another group is poaching your team members.

✦ Workspace is limiting certain activities.

✦ The team needs credentials for accessing certain environments.

Perhaps the hardest impediments to tackle have to do with the team's being human:

✦ Loss of focus (e.g., due to interruptions)

✦ Unclear, partial, misleading, or missing communication

✦ Commitments and decisions that don't get made on time

✦ Faulty assumptions

✦ Rush and haste that detract from the quality of the work

✦ Confusion caused by differing interpretations

> I was assessing a team's Agility once. The team had an unusual approach to pair programming: three of the seven developers worked alone, and the other four worked in two fixed pairs, which rotated every two months. One of the four used to come in to work at 8 a.m. As they were not allowed to work alone, the early bird spent one hour every morning doing nothing productive until his partner showed up at 9. Would you consider that an impediment?

You can tune your impediment antenna by constantly looking around and asking yourself, "Could *that* be slowing the team down?" For instance, suppose you see a developer hanging around the kitchen making coffee several times a day. You could assume that he really likes his coffee; you could also wonder whether he's idling while waiting on something, such as a slow build or someone's email reply.

2.5 What If I Can't Work Full-Time as the Team's Leader?

Nothing in your duties and responsibilities implies a full-time job or continuous interaction with team members. I've been around teams whose leader was kept busy only half the time, most days conversing with members only a few times.

The key to your being an effective ATL is making the team feel it can always depend on you. If other obligations now and then prevent you from resolving problems and addressing needs in a timely fashion — and time in Agile comes in small doses — the team can't use you at those times. Few ATL responsibilities are schedulable. Everything else depends on need and context, and blocking out time for those responsibilities is always difficult.

If you're an ATL part-time and a delivery team member part-time, at least you're around. You can observe the environment and respond to situations. But if you're leading two or more teams, you risk becoming a bottleneck for each one of them. You can alleviate the bottleneck by offsetting meetings and being available by mobile phone or email. Consider carefully, though, whether these solutions truly help the teams or merely shift the bottleneck.

"I am full-time on the team, but I'm not just the ATL. I'm also the product owner, overall architect, and lead developer — like the product champion at 3M or the chief engineer at Toyota — as well as the team members' line manager. On top of this, I evangelize Agile/Lean development across the company. Even though it's only a small team (peaked at seven, including contractors; now down to three), I don't have time to cover all the roles adequately, so I have to shift my focus, and there is usually an area which is suffering from lack of attention."

— *Ian, software ATL in a hardware company*

Your involvement may well change over the team's life cycle. In the early days, as they storm and norm (see 6.1), they can use a lot of your help. As the project progresses and the deadline nears, they can use more air-cover help. You will have to tune your role accordingly and notice how it changes over time. If you are not full-time with the team, that could become a serious impediment. The situation is exacerbated if you're not with the team from the beginning, or if you can't promise the team a certain amount of predictable, dedicated time; it just makes you look like an outsider. Focus your energy on building trust with the team so you can consider yourselves a single unit that self-organizes.

2.6 Can We Distribute or Rotate the ATL Duties Among the Team?

I have visited many organizations that adopted Agile only to discover that they lacked suitable candidates for full-time Agile team leadership. Those that didn't want to hire additional people tapped one member in each team (such as an analyst or a technical lead) to take on part-time ATL duties. In other arrangements, two or more team members shared the duties on a rotating or fixed basis.

In most cases, the results were dismal. Those employees had limited opportunity to grow as leaders of Agile teams, and often received poor training. Their existing obligations (e.g., coding) suffered, for two reasons: they no longer had sufficient time for them, and the asynchronous nature of ATL responsibilities meant that they could rarely focus on those obligations for a good, uninterrupted stretch of time. Many of those employees were neither suited to the role nor interested in learning it.

After using Scrum successfully for two years, a strong Scrum-Master suggested decentralizing some of her responsibilities. The team agreed, so at every iteration a different member would make sure the task board was current, lead the meetings, keep stakeholders apprised, and so on. After a few weeks, they gave up. "They really didn't like doing all that," the ScrumMaster told me, "but they've all expressed their appreciation for the difficulty of my role!"

It is not advisable to slice and dice the ATL responsibilities any old way, though one way works well: carving out the process stewardship component. The process steward can help the team keep their methodology alive and continuously improving, without worrying about execution details. A willing and able team member could assume this role effectively even part-time. This approach has a positive unintended consequence: it is how many people got started as Agile coaches.

2.7 What If the ATL Responsibilities Are Too Much for One Person?

If a development community numbers 15 or fewer people, and if they work fairly independently of other groups in the organization, a single ATL is likely to suffice. Depending on circumstance, and possibly with the team's help, a single person may successfully serve as the ATL in a larger community.

But if a project's development component is large and it touches many stakeholders or teams, a single person may not be able to perform all the duties effectively. Two people can then share the role. Both of them help the team deliver: one faces mostly outward and focuses more on product and project, while the other faces mostly inward and focuses more on people and process.

One company was migrating its platform to a modern environment. Since the project spelled changes in numerous business units, the entire community numbered 26 people, most of them stakeholders. The inward-facing ATL (dubbed "iteration manager") helped the programmers and testers on a daily basis, mostly by removing impediments. The outward-facing ATL (called "project manager") coordinated among the entire community and ensured continued alignment with senior management's roadmap. Both ATLs attended the kickoff and the iteration ceremonies, but the project manager was otherwise uninvolved in the day-to-day workings of the delivery team.

Some newly Agile companies assign leaders or ScrumMasters to teams because they've been told to do so. Others consider ATLs a luxury they can't afford. Some never bother recasting their classically trained project managers as ATLs, wrongly believing that their title and former responsibilities mean they are controlling, redundant, or even a hindrance more than a help. Yet savvy Agile companies know differently — their ATLs are astute servant leaders who help their teams deliver, and these companies ensure that every team has a dedicated ATL.

Supplementary Resource
Go to **www.TheHumanSideOfAgile.com** and download
"Agile Team Leader Responsibilities Snapshot."

CHAPTER 3

Be the Best Leader for Your Team

Imagine a hypothetical Agile software development team starting a project. Their competent Agile team leader (ATL) helps them deliver by taking on many duties that they will not, cannot, or should not perform. A few months into their project, you drop in for a visit and ask a random team member, "How do you like working with your team leader?" Without hesitation, he smiles broadly and says, "She's awesome."

In a parallel universe, the exact same team kicked off at the same time with *another* competent ATL. You're visiting them at the same point in the project and meet the same team member (after all, that universe *is* parallel). In response to your question, he shifts nervously. After a long pause, he says quietly, "She's OK, you know, but...."

What would it take for you to be like the first team leader? Which qualities and mind-set matter? This chapter looks at the human side of the role: how to be and feel useful as an ATL, how to align your actions with the team's needs, and how to apply your strengths and make the role *yours*.

3.1 What Are the Qualities of a Great Agile Team Leader?

Qualities are the talents and characteristics that make you *you* and the professional that you are. They are natural strengths, recurring patterns of thought and behavior[1] that you have, regardless of your chosen career.

Every role, performed to a standard of excellence, requires certain qualities. (Those for team members are listed in 4.2.2.) The following list captures important qualities that make great ATLs: facilitative leaders who help teams meet their goals. As you read the list, consider which qualities you possess so you can recognize and play to your strengths.

Attention to detail. This is the ability to notice, and the motivation to care about, the little things that make up the whole. "Did we end up testing the latest feedback form on Internet Explorer 7?" "Have we covered all the scenarios when we split story #42 into five distinct pieces?" "Which items have we deferred, and is it now time to take care of them?" Teams, business units, and senior management alike must know where their project stands — but team members generally prefer to *do* tasks, not track them. Many perceive tracking as boring or a nuisance, which is why the task board or planning tool often stops telling the truth. Moreover, since teams focus on only a few tasks at a time, it's not easy for them to notice any missed ones. Careful attention to detail throughout the project helps the team stay out of trouble and provides the right data for strategic decisions.

Big-picture thinking. This is the polar opposite — a vital counterbalance to attention to detail. Your big-picture thinking can save the product owner and the team precious time they might otherwise waste building the wrong thing or gold-plating a minor feature. Big-picture thinking is critical for chartering a project. In addition, it is often executives' preferred mode of operation and communication, so get comfortable using it with them.

Forward thinking. Looking ahead and considering implications are vital to Agile planning. I've witnessed many POs struggle to determine priorities, reduce scope, or make a commitment, and I've seen many teams keep quiet and just wait for someone, *anyone*, to make a decision. You can provide a valuable perspective on product evolution, explore possible scenarios, and facilitate the crafting of sensible plans.

Effective communication. Conveying information, requests, and feedback usefully is critical in a fast-moving knowledge environment. After years of technical specialization, many individual contributors struggle with their daily need to communicate status, decisions, and problems in terms that others can use. You can help distill, organize, and package the information for effective consumption. And you can save everybody time and distress spent on communication gone awry.

Attention to process. All Agile methods assume self-correction and adaptation to a team's reality. To make that possible, a team must notice the effects of their actions, dynamics, and procedures. Most team members I've met in my work rarely seemed to notice process or care much about it; they largely took directions from management and perpetuated their status quo. Because you don't have to worry about implementation details, you are well positioned to observe process *and* help the empowered team make improvements.

Sensitivity to risks. Few undertakings are guaranteed success. Even seemingly straightforward projects are exposed to multiple risks, such as personnel trouble, priority shifts, and misunderstood requirements and solutions. Chances are your team includes a few people who are just keen to run ahead and implement a solution; it also needs a few of those people who can smell trouble a mile away. The latter frequently reflect on the project's parameters, mingle with team members and stakeholders, and keep their ears and eyes open for signs of trouble. As an ATL, you have the perspective and can take the time to do these things.

Problem-solving leadership.[2] Some risks graduate into real problems ("issues"). Other problems just pop up in the ordinary course of product development: "How would we test credit card payments?" "What's the migration path for version 2.2 users?" "We thought this was a great checkout screen, but our focus group said it's incomprehensible!" You shouldn't have to solve the team's problems — they'll grow stronger by doing that themselves — but you *can* offer guidance and support. Help them notice their problems, teach them problem-solving techniques, and cultivate their courage to tackle challenges.

Dependability. Your team must be able to depend on you if you're to be their glue, impediment remover, and champion. One aspect of that is making yourself available even when you're swamped. Another aspect is follow-through; when you keep your promises, own up to mistakes, and take responsibility, you send the message that you're there for your team.

People orientation. Without motivated, engaged individuals on the team, the project will get nowhere useful (albeit in quick sprints). You constantly have to look and listen for changes in motivation and engagement. Don't just assume that a nice reward will do it (see 10.3) or that the functional managers will take care of team members. "Have we acknowledged and thanked Ella for working late on Monday on that weird cross-browser defect?" "Is Claudio's recent quiet demeanor nothing to worry about, or is something gnawing at him?" "Who would be most excited to pick up the specialized skills we're missing?"

Social sense. Are you used to teams whose members connect over food and coffee but not over their work? Great Agile teams are more social and collaborative than that. A friendly, facilitative, caring team leader can connect people at work, arrange social opportunities, and even help boost team members' sense of belonging. These changes translate into higher productivity and satisfaction, reduced stress, and greater team resilience.

3.2 How Do I Develop My Confidence?

Since the entire Agile team is responsible for delivery, it's sometimes hard to see which individual actions made a difference. As long as there's oil in the engine, nobody cares about the oil; it's when it's absent that it matters a lot. How are *you* being the oil? How do *you* grease the team's wheels so they deliver what's needed? Just as it is important for other team members to be motivated and engaged, so it is for you. If you are to be the best leader for your team, you first have to believe that. Anytime you want to develop your confidence and feel more useful in your role, try the following exercises.

3.2.1 Notice Your Effect

In years of coaching individuals and teams, I've noticed something uncanny: *People seldom notice the positive effect they have on others.* Some never have their attention drawn to it, and of those who do, not everybody believes it is so!

Have you ever heard people say, "I joined this team because so-and-so was there," or "Man, am I glad so-and-so isn't managing *our* project!" or "After so-and-so left, the team just wasn't the same"?

Two great questions to help you discern your effect are:

1. Suppose the team did *not* have someone in my role. What would happen, and what would *not* happen?

2. Suppose the team had someone *else* in my role. What would happen, and what would *not* happen?

For *you* to answer these questions clearly, you need a detached perspective on the team's progress and results. That's hard, since your personal biases and "internal critic" get in the way. So ask your team members: one on one, in retrospectives, or anonymously. You may be surprised!

Their answers will probably relate to your personality, qualities, or conduct, not to any of your *actions*. Even if your role has a high clerical content, even if the team could take over some of your duties, your greatest contribution could be the fact that *you* perform them, imbuing them with *your* personality and *your* qualities.

You could indeed be the glue that holds your team together. You could be the reason some key folks haven't left the team or the company. Your work may allow others to focus on what they enjoy and know best, which in turn makes them happier and thus more pleasant to work with. When new people are hired into the team and their "fit" is considered, it's also a fit *with you.*

3.2.2 Recall a Situation

Think back to a team or project situation where you felt *you* made a difference. It doesn't have to be recent. Take a few minutes to write down your answers to the following questions:

1. What three things did you do to make that difference?

2. What prompted you to do them?

3. What internal resources (talents, abilities, skills, experiences) did you apply in that situation?

Now look at the resources you identified. Can you think of other situations in which you've applied them with good results? As you consider those situations, tap into them internally and recall them in more detail. What are you feeling now about your effect and the results you achieved?

I had the following dialogue with Chris, a ScrumMaster:

Chris: There was a time, not long ago, when I was sensing a bit of divergence in opinion about the technical direction we should take for the product. The product owner and stakeholders were coming to us with technical solutions to the particular problem. There were starting to be divisions within the team: "Yeah, this is how we ought to do it," and "No, it's not." Eventually I called for a stop to figure things out. We got the business owners involved, we got technical people and architects involved, we hashed it out and came to an agreeable solution. We were able to move forward, whereas if we hadn't done something, it could have disintegrated quite quickly.

Gil: When you say "disintegrate," what form would that take?

Chris: Continued dissension, us-and-them, camps being formed — basically things grinding to a halt. That actually started to happen.

Gil: And if you hadn't called a stop and convened the subsequent meeting, would somebody else have done that?

Chris: It's hard to say.... It would have probably happened eventually, but I decided to step in early, and things worked out well in the end.

Gil: What resources did you have that enabled you to get everybody to come to a resolution?

Chris: Hmm.... Well, I was sensitive to the negative impact on our project community. I figured that while I didn't have to solve the problem, people needed a process with which to solve it. I kicked it off by getting everybody together in one place and kept it up until we had the solution.

Gil: Sounds like two great resources: sensitivity to the team and problem-solving leadership.

Chris: Interesting.

Gil: Can you think of other situations where you applied either or both?

Chris: Well, there was one time the team needed some highly specialized skills, something to do with database performance tuning. They did what they could without complaining, trying to be cool about it. But I could sense the struggle and frustration, so I asked if we should get a consultant in. They agreed, and I was able to get approval, and within a few days, we had a guy come in and teach them what they needed. Now that I think of it, they looked relieved!

As you repeat this exercise with more situations and more resources, you'll feel greater self-efficacy — and the feeling will increase even more in real life with actual feedback.

3.3 What Actions Will Build the Team's Trust in Me?

One of the prime catalysts of team performance is members' trust in each other. Another ingredient is their trust in you, their servant leader. By counting on your support, they can focus on their work and do it well. And when they treat you this way, your own work is more pleasant and rewarding.

Building a trusting relationship takes effort and patience. A popular metaphor is the emotional bank account: you have an account with each person, and, over time, your actions translate into emotional deposits and withdrawals.[3] The greater your balance, the more trusting, tolerant, and open your relationship with that person. You have to proactively grow your emotional bank accounts and constantly monitor your actions and behavior. Breaking trust is very easy, and restoring it is very hard. If you're new to the team, your starting balance is low. If they haven't met you in person, it's lower yet.

Even if members give you the benefit of the doubt, their default inclination would be to trust you only after you've proven yourself. And since you are just as human as they are, you would probably not trust them, either, until they've proven *them*selves. Trust builds gradually, and one of the sides must go first and act in a trusting way — and that side is you.

That means you will have to trust your team to deliver, even if you know very little about them. Most people naturally reciprocate kindly behavior; after you have given them the gift of your trust, they are likely to give back the gift of *their* trust. Reciprocation will continue with ever-greater gifts until a sufficient level of trust is established.

This can only work, though, if you are being authentic about trusting your team. You must look inside and ask yourself whether you truly do, and within what boundaries. If you're not sure how to answer this, reflect on previous experiences of working with teams. Do your actions reflect an attitude of "I trust you to do the right thing as long as I agree with it"? Or "I trust you to do X and will defend your performance of it"? If you are only putting on a show — if you are trying to make them trust you, but you have no intention of trusting them — that's asking for trouble.

When it comes to trust, actions speak much louder than words. You have to perform overt acts that demonstrate your support to the team. Here are a few, in rough order of their challenge to you.

Respect their decisions. For example, if they schedule ten points of work for the next iteration but you feel that 15 would be more appropriate, be careful what you say (if you even say anything). Don't give the impression that doing ten points amounts to slacking off; nobody likes to be perceived this way.

Let them complete their work in quiet. You might be anxious to know their progress or how you can help, but such questions can easily turn into harassment. Extend them the benefit of the doubt, *especially* if they work in other offices or you don't see them frequently. Make sure your process is set up for everyone to have access to current information about status and impediments without bothering people.

Allow your team the slack and flexibility they need for self-organization. This demonstrates that you know they are being team players even if you are not seeing them typing away.

Keep your promises. If you take on an action item or an impediment, follow through on it — and make sure the team knows you've followed through. Be timely about closing the loop with the individuals who rely on you. If you keep a personal queue of ATL tasks, consider your promises high priority. If others have reason to even *think* you've forgotten about them, you can easily lose their trust. (This is one of the most damaging pitfalls of being overburdened.)

Mentor and coach team members and the team as a whole. This demonstrates your willingness to invest your time and energy to help them grow. For individual mentoring, one-on-one meetings work best.[4] Well-timed, impromptu mentoring conversations are also effective. (For coaching, see 11.7.)

Have their backs. If the team slips an iteration or misses a show-stopper bug, treat it as a learning and improvement opportunity and protect them from the people who would use it as a flogging opportunity (see 10.6).

Bring weighty demands and needs to their attention, and obtain their consent. For instance, if overtime is needed, don't make a commitment to it on their behalf until they understand why it's needed. In a more far-reaching example, involve the team in the process of hiring additional members.[5]

Trust, like leadership, is tested in times of pressure. It means letting the team make decisions and possibly fail. It is then up to you to determine how to respond: step in or step back, declare failure or consider it feedback? This can happen on a small scale — for instance, implementing a certain feature with very low quality — or a large scale, such as slipping an entire project. Even if you are authentic about trusting your team, it might turn out to be harder than you thought.

Your actions flow from beliefs, and trusting leaders hold certain beliefs. Read each of the following statements out loud, slowly, and notice your reaction:

"My team is an asset to the organization."

"I'm here to take care of these people *and* serve the organization."

"I can trust someone and still give caring, useful feedback — without coming across as judgmental."

"I'm here to help the team turn out valuable work, now and later. I'm not here to catch people goofing off."

"I have *some* answers, not all. My way is rarely the only way."

"My team members are doing the best job they can with the tools and information they have." (This belief is also a necessary condition for useful retrospectives.[6])

Consistent behavior is critical. Nobody can trust you if two apparently similar occurrences result in opposite reactions from you; in particular, do not play favorites in public.[7] And if you break trust unintentionally or due to deep-seated fears, own up to your actions. Ask to start over. When appropriate, apologies go a long way.

On the receiving end of your trust are human beings. Even if they are generally trustworthy, they still employ defense mechanisms (see 7.2). They may hide a blunder or dress up a questionable decision. Choose your words and actions carefully; don't write them off completely.

Your team's trust in you will depend on your responses to situations. Before doing anything, catch yourself and try to understand why you want to act in a particular way. Is the story you are telling yourself true? Can you know that it's true?[8]

Supplementary resource: Download "Team Trust Tracker" from the book's companion website, **www.TheHumanSideOfAgile.com**.

3.4 How Can I Learn What the Team Needs From Me?

You can use the list of responsibilities in section 2.3 as a starting point for customizing your role and identifying value-adding tasks. To learn what else you can do, or how you can perform certain things differently, turn to your team. Just as Agile teams draw on *pulling work* to be effective, so you can pull ideas for your role.

3.4.1 Ask for Feedback

During a retrospective, or anytime as a special request, ask the team for feedback about your work. Use open-ended questions, such as these:

✦ "How do you think I am doing?"

✦ "What works well in terms of my interaction with you?"

✦ "What could I do more of?"

✦ "What could I do less of?"

Feedback is a sensitive matter. Unless your team has exceptional trust in you, ask for anonymous feedback. True anonymity increases a feeling of safety and thereby the likelihood of receiving useful information. Keep an open mind as you read their answers (which will probably be more positive than you expect!).

If you promise anonymity, stand by it. Teams are small enough that members might believe you'd recognize their handwriting, spelling, or choice of words. If you expect some to demur, look for simple online tools that enable untraceable feedback. Another option is to go through a trusted third party.

> The first iteration retrospective with a very large team was going to be sensitive. I had observed indications of mistrust among developers, as well as between them and their leads, and the program manager was not a forgiving person. The team seemed to trust me as their coach, so two days before the retrospective, I asked every member for input by email. I promised to collect all observations and suggestions in such a way that none could be attributed to any specific person. I received contributions from half the members, which exceeded my expectations.

3.4.2 Incorporate Appreciations

One particular type of feedback is the simple thank-you. Even if all team members, including you, do the work they're paid to do at its expected level of performance, an expression of appreciation can go a long way. By focusing on positive feedback and being an act of *giving*, appreciations are a powerful mechanism for boosting teamwork, increasing team cohesion, and strengthening the social fabric.

As the team gets used to offering them regularly, you will find yourself on the receiving end a number of times. You'll be able to identify and learn what in your conduct and activities works well for the team. If you hear too few appreciations, that can also be useful information.

> "Multiple team members greatly appreciated my restructuring and cleaning up of the Wiki — something that I considered to be a menial task."
>
> — *Gary Marcos, ScrumMaster*

Help appreciations become an acceptable norm, by making them the last step in retrospectives. Explain that appreciations are for specific actions, not for having a certain character. They look like this:[9] Raj turns to face Elena and says to her, "Elena, I appreciate you for helping me out with the build script last week. I was stuck updating it, and you showed me an easy way to do that." Whether Elena's actions helped Raj just this time or reflect an enduring quality of hers, they are worthy of appreciation. Elena may smile or say "thank you," but she is under no obligation to return the appreciation. When you first introduce the practice, Raj may turn to *you* and say, "I want to appreciate Elena for what she did...." Raise your hand gently and ask him to *face* Elena and talk *to her*, using "you" language.[10]

Anybody who wishes to offer an appreciation does so; there's no strict order or limit to the appreciations being offered. (They tend to run their course in about five minutes.) When you offer a genuine appreciation, choose your words carefully so it is interpreted as intended.

3.4.3 Ask What You Can Do

Ask the entire team at the standup meeting, or in one-on-one meetings, "How can I help you today?" or "What can I take off your hands to make your work easier?" Make sure you ask this authentically. If they interpret your question as an attempt to score points, you'll decrease goodwill.

Sometimes they will take you up on your offer. If you carry out their idea, you will have increased trust and goodwill — but *only if you close the loop* with results or feedback! Make sure they know you've done it.

If they answer your question with "I don't know; probably nothing," don't take it personally. Your genuine offer is enough to increase trust.

3.4.4 Watch for Opportunities to Help

Observe the team and their progress through their tasks. Be patient and open, and you'll see where balls are dropped. Pick them up, and report your results at the next team opportunity (e.g., the standup). Emphasize that you're looking for improvements, not assessing performance. The team will come up with additional ideas for you very quickly.

"On a recent project, I maintained my own ScrumMaster backlog/in-progress/done board in the form of Post-it Notes on the window behind my desk. Team members could add items to my backlog for impediments they'd like me to work on. It helped with transparency, and for the same reasons we use the team's progress board, also with visibility and engagement."

— *Rob MacGregor, ScrumMaster*

3.5 How Can I Adopt More Effective Behaviors?

Your patterns of behavior cause you to initiate many actions — some proactive, some reactive. Once you become aware of actions that tend to backfire, or fall flat, you can choose to change them. But merely telling yourself, "Next time, I'm not doing *that!*" or "This won't happen again!" is not enough. You have to consciously discover effective alternatives, apply them deliberately, and repeat them until they become habitual. You can use two processes for that.

3.5.1 Catch Yourself

Take a few minutes to ponder these two questions:

1. Which actions do I take that don't have desirable results?

2. For each of these actions, what typical situation triggers them?

Now, set yourself some sort of reminder to notice these trigger situations (a sticky note on your notebook might suffice). When you find yourself in a trigger situation, *before you act, pause.* Write down your answers to the following questions:[11]

1. What am I observing — in me, in other people, in the context?

2. What am I feeling about these observations?

3. What's the significance of these observations and my feelings?

4. How was I going to react?

5. What are three better responses?

Pick the option that looks best and apply it.

Here is an example of how this might run.

Imagine I'm the ATL. The team has just sat down for iteration planning, but once again, our product owner is a no-show. I know we can make little progress without her and we may have to call off the meeting.

1. I notice myself getting upset. A voice in my head rants, "Again! Doesn't she realize how important this is?! How many times have I asked her to join us?!" I notice some team members are getting bored, others are shooting the breeze, and others are playing with their phones.

2. I'm feeling angry — with myself for becoming a victim of circumstance, with the team for not seeming to care whether this meeting proceeds, and with the product owner. I'm also worried that this is another setback in our Agile implementation; management has been breathing down my neck for some time.

3. I guess I'm concerned about our next iteration, as well as the bigger picture of our project community and perhaps also the use of Agile. Even if we do figure out an iteration plan, we're likely up against bigger problems.

4. I was *probably* going to say something snarky about her, and I *was* going to text her "WHERE ARE U," and I was going to try to stand in for her....

5. Three other things I can do to get potentially better results are:

    a. Ask the team what they think we should do.

    b. Call her on the phone and be gentle — maybe she got caught up someplace.

c. Suggest that the team take on refactoring tasks. When I'm finally able to get hold of the PO, we'll reconvene for iteration planning. She'll clearly have fewer available points for new development in this iteration. Maybe that will cause her to pay attention to her behavior.

Hmm.... I like the "extra refactoring" option, but if I present it this way, I might sound defiant or retaliatory. That won't help our relationship. Here's another one instead:

c2. Let the team do some refactoring. The minute I get hold of the PO, we'll all gather in a retrospective meeting to discuss what happened — and maybe revise our working agreements.

Later, analyze the impact of your choice on you, on other people, and on the context. You'll need to repeat this process several times for the better behaviors to become more natural. And with them, your feelings about your role will improve.

3.5.2 Rehearse a Situation

Think forward to an upcoming situation (not a hypothetical one!) that might challenge the team and where you can help significantly.

1. What specifically would that situation be? What would be happening?

2. Imagine the situation in detail. What would you be seeing, hearing, sensing?

3. Which outcomes would be desirable?

4. What specific actions would you take to achieve those outcomes?

5. What would *that* feel like?

From another dialogue with Chris, the ScrumMaster:

Chris: I foresee a challenge coming forward, but I haven't yet figured out how I am going to deal with it.... It has to do with some new information coming down about the product itself, and where our owners want it to head. It will mean some pretty serious evaluations of some aspects of it. Its future is not in jeopardy; it's the look and feel that's being reconsidered. And we're not sure how to deal with the whole product being tossed up in the air.

Gil: How will this be a challenge to the team?

Chris: Well, the suggested ideas seem to be almost universally felt to be the right move. It's just that, in the short term, how do we move forward, what comes next? How do you rip it all apart, so to speak, and put it back together, while keeping what we have running in the meantime? That's the challenge I think I'm facing right now.

Gil: What will you be seeing or hearing?

Chris: Confusion. People will have a hard time making decisions. We'll see them struggle to write stories and, even more, to estimate them.

Gil: OK.... If you think about your responsibilities, which of them could be beneficial for the team as *they* figure out this technical challenge, of keeping everything running while changing the look-and-feel?

Chris: I guess it's mostly to keep the right people involved and to facilitate some fairly significant discussions and decisions that have to happen. Ensuring the discussions happen when they need to happen, making sure everyone has a clear vision of the risks of this change in direction.

Gil: Sounds like it might be useful also to imagine the various ways this might unfold, and to rehearse some of the statements or tactics you might use. Because this is really a team problem; it's not your personal problem. You're not technical and you're not part of the construction crew. It's not something you would actively work on, but you can help those who do work on it.

Chris: Yeah.... I kept seeing this problem in front of me, and I wanted to resolve it! Framing it this way — "it's the team's problem, and I'll help them resolve it" — definitely helps me feel more up to it.

Anytime you wish to change your behavior or your responses to situations, *mental rehearsal* strengthens the relevant neural pathways. Once the real-world situation unfolds, your responses may be different, yet you'll have a better sense of responses that work and ones that don't — and consequently greater confidence in yourself.

As with any other role, having the right qualities of an Agile team leader positions you for success. Previous experience in traditional project management can be beneficial, as long as your actions align with the Agile principles. A technical background can also be useful. Confidence and attention to your behavior will carry you far; but the strongest determinant of your contribution cannot be learned: It is your genuine desire to help your team succeed. When you have that, your role can have *outstanding value.*

Supplementary Resources

Go to **www.TheHumanSideOfAgile.com** and download "Effective Team Leader Behaviors" and "Team Trust Tracker."

PART II
Grow a Solid Agile Team

Two of the most significant distinctions between classic approaches and Agile have to do with the concept of the *team*.

In serial life cycles, functional teams work in sequence. First comes the analysis team, then the design team, then the programming team, and so on. Each team carries out their portion of the work chain in contract fashion: They receive input, do their work according to set expectations, and hand the output down. The teams are led (or rather, managed) by a person who divides the labor among members. One axiom is that *individual productivity* is a key success factor and that the manager needs to optimize the work breakdown and assignment.

Agile turns this concept on its head. An Agile team is intentionally formed with enough skills and abilities to take care of most of the chain of work: it is *cross-functional*. Once the team understands the problem to solve, they have autonomy over the activities for producing a working solution.

Thus, the first notable distinction is that, in an Agile framework, *the result-producing unit is the team, not the individual*. The other distinction is that, rather than being managed, such a team works best when its members self-organize to meet their objectives. With effective self-organization, collaboration, shared responsibility, and mutual commitment, *Agile teams are more productive than the sum of their parts*.

The Agile team's purpose of delivering value is your role's *raison d'être*. Their sustained effectiveness is the central measure of success — and you cannot control it! You can, however, be there for the team throughout their life cycle. Part II provides the tools you need to select the members and support their growth into a solid, productive *Agile* team.

CHAPTER 4

Select Members for a New Team

Of all your activities, setting up a new Agile team is arguably among the most infrequent — and quite possibly the most sensitive. When the need arises, it's unlikely to be a clean start: current product lines, staffing, and obligations limit your options. You may be inclined to give the greatest consideration to personnel expertise, knowledge, and availability, yet Agile teams need more than that in order to succeed. Anytime you have a choice in the matter of team composition — whether through hiring or internal moves — use this chapter's suggestions to select the people.

4.1 How Should I Form an Agile Team?

Four characteristics qualify a working group as an Agile team:

✦ Having the sole purpose of delivering value to their customers and the business

✦ Being cross-functional and having all necessary skills represented

✦ Having autonomy to meet their objectives

✦ Manifesting the Agile principles and values

When all four elements are present, the team is in a position to reap the benefits of Agility. They will have a harder time if they serve multiple organizational needs, if they are short on skill or ability, if members are prevented from exceeding the strict duties of their jobs, or if they can't (or don't care to) manifest Agile thinking.

For the team to quickly and repeatedly turn a list of valued ideas into working product — "get to done" — they cannot wait around. Therefore the team must be cross-functional, and, between them, the members need to have the skills and abilities necessary to turn ideas into deliverables. Don't stop short at programmers and testers; as necessary, include specialized disciplines such as architecture and database design.

Just as important as *value delivery* is *value definition*. The aspects of the product owner (PO) role are so varied that a single person can rarely perform all of them well. Giving the product shape often calls for both functional and "nonfunctional" requirements, user experience (UX) design, usability, and solution architecture. The product's evolution further requires the incorporation of various inputs from users, customer service, product servicing, market research, and focus groups. The *Agile customers*, led by the product owner, provide these specialized contributions on a continuous basis.

> Agile teams generally have more people in the developer role than in the customer role — although not always. In one project community, the delivery team numbered five people. Since they were building an innovative piece of technology and had to consider multiple aspects, their customer team was seven strong.

Agile teams often start out with clearly drawn roles and responsibilities. Over time, members may shoulder other roles' duties if they can help meaningfully. For instance, business analysts tend to be on the customer side of the Agile team, defining stories and acceptance-testing completed ones, but they may also join the delivery team in exploratory testing and documentation activities. In other cases, certain technical contributors have developed their talent and interest in business to the extent that they occasionally stand in for the product owner.

A good size for an Agile team is six to ten people. This range supports a stimulating social and professional environment, with the potential for powerful synergy. Members bring to the table more life experience, professional history, and perspectives than in a smaller team. At greater than ten people, human dynamics become more challenging, and the team requires stronger servant leadership and supporting processes. Don't lose sleep over the number; the particular individuals on the team matter more.

One Agile team included 13 people on the delivery side, two product owners working *as a pair*, and a ScrumMaster. Nevertheless, they collaborated and communicated well; artificially separating them into two smaller teams would have been harmful. On two occasions, a temporary subteam of three split off to focus on a specific piece of technical infrastructure. When the subteam had finished its work, it reintegrated with the main team.

You may not find ideal candidates for certain team roles. For instance, companies that build software for internal use often have difficulties staffing the PO role. As the Agile team leader (ATL), help your team and colleagues grow in their new roles, while customizing the methodology — including the roles — to their current abilities and inclinations. Don't try to force a dogmatic interpretation of Agile; remember that part of the Agile mind-set is flexibility.

4.2 Who Would Work Well on an Agile Team?

Choosing a suitable set of people for an Agile team is a sensitive affair. You may have to approach several functional managers and ask them to assign specific people. They might not agree with your choice. The folks you tap should want to work with you on the project and with the other members you pick. Naturally, they should also not object to using Agile.

As in the pre-Agile days, you still need to look for basic nontechnical skills such as communication, problem solving, and principled negotiation (striving for win-win solutions). And while domain knowledge and technical skill still matter, they are not the main determinants of suitability. In fact, fewer team members might require them, since colleagues can coach them.

If team members were "resources" — as they are sometimes called — their contribution would be merely *additive*. But being people, their *synergy* can amplify results. When you consider a candidate, ask yourself: "How can this person help the team become *more?*" Beyond adding capacity, how would this person's engagement increase the team's ability to meet their objectives? To answer the questions, consider diversity, preferences, and qualities.

The more complex and uncertain the development work, the more diverse the team should be. Look for diversity in talents, preferences, knowledge, problem-solving approaches, and work experience. Seek out pleasant, "social-glue" people as well as eager, driven, and decisive people. Leverage the tremendous potential of diversity in cultural background and life experience. Diverse teams have fewer blind spots and expert hang-ups. With reduced groupthink,[1] they are also more likely to come up with simpler solutions and thus be more productive.

The next three sections describe the desirable preferences and qualities of Agile practitioners. Since they are unlikely to be present in every team member, aim to have them spread as thickly as possible across the entire team. Every team member will also have a few weaknesses or *undesirable* characteristics; with enough diversity, the strengths of some members ought to balance others' nontalents.

Preferences and qualities are invisible, so how can you tell whether your candidate has them? Even if he genuinely believes he has some of them, self-descriptions are never objective. Instead, watch his behavior. Consider holding an audition.[2] If you have neither the opportunity to observe the candidate nor access to trusted colleagues' opinions, then interview him. Develop a set of behavioral and follow-up questions that can predict or indicate the characteristics you're looking for. The best questions distinguish between people who repeatedly demonstrate those qualities and preferences and those who do so only occasionally.[3]

4.2.1 Preferences

Everybody has preferences, or tendencies, in the context of work. Some preferences are good predictors of performance in an Agile environment. Agile-friendly preferences include:

Collaboration. Working together on a task and being collectively responsible for the outcome defines "collaboration." Does your candidate prefer to join forces with others, or would she rather be the sole person responsible for a deliverable? (Caution: Many people will say that they collaborate with others when they really mean "I work alone, but I don't mind asking someone an occasional question.")

Quick feedback on partial work. Agile people want useful feedback on their work, they want it early, and they want it often. They are unafraid to demonstrate partial results and check their understanding. They realize that their ideas, assumptions, and preconceptions might not be correct or complete and that others might have something useful to contribute.

Learning from others. The Agile environment is rife with learning opportunities. Does your candidate leverage opportunities to learn *from others*? Does he accept feedback willingly and allow himself to be coached? One can have an ego and still be willing to absorb knowledge from others. When that happens, the team experience becomes symbiotic and engaging, as opposed to an informal competition.

Being part of a team. A lot of people want to work in teams for the companionship, mental stimulation, and occasional support. Agile practitioners have an additional reason: together, they can build something much larger than they can on their own.

4.2.2. Qualities

In addition to preferences, your candidate will also have noncontextual qualities (traits or characteristics). The following qualities work well on an Agile team:

Dedication to one's profession. A person will do a great job only when she has the passion for it. She will naturally learn, grow, and improve her methods. She resists being considered a plug-compatible "resource."

Self-discipline. Can the person motivate himself to do whatever is needed? Can he handle the ups and downs of a team experience? Can he moderate his responses in tough situations? A knowledge-work team environment requires self-discipline for sustained success.

A questioning mind. Instead of a team of order takers, you want people who ask "Why?" "How can we simplify?" and "What if...?" By asking probing questions and not taking anything at face value, they enrich the solution space and increase effectiveness.

Ability to handle ambiguity and unknowns. Even with careful planning, teams will encounter ambiguity and missing information. Can team members make just enough progress for securing pragmatic feedback, or will they freeze and wait?

Focus on execution. Agile practitioners strive to minimize all activities that delay execution. Does your candidate frequently ask herself questions like, "How much should I plan before I start doing?" "Am I stuck?" "Is this a good time to get help?" "How do I get to 'done'?"

Responsibility. If your candidate becomes unhappy with something in the team or their work, would he bring it up and strive to find a good resolution, or would he engage a defense mechanism such as blaming or justification? (See 7.2.)

Initiative. Does the person get and keep things moving, or does he wait to be told what to do?

Adaptability. Team members need to continually adapt their behavior to their teammates in the protracted dance called "teamwork." They may have to adapt their roles if some functions are underrepresented or underperforming. Will your candidate adapt, or will he just stay within a prescribed role description?

4.2.3 Qualities for a Dynamic Team

Before you form your team, ask yourself: How dynamic must the team be? To what degree of change will they need to respond?

Agile processes first emerged in the early 1990s as a way to embrace change in product development. Using built-in inspection and adaptation mechanisms, the Agile team responds to change as a normal part of working life. However, the *degree of required change* varies wildly from organization to organization, from team to team, and even in different points in a team's life cycle.

I have guided Agile transformations at companies working on mature products. For the most part, their teams' work was incremental. The technological landscape was fairly static, and staff turnover was low. Since those product teams had obligations and deadlines to meet, they needed to be *efficient* — to figure out a minimal-waste way to carry out their work productively.

I have also worked at and guided organizations whose products were novel, whose business model was in flux, or whose clients varied from year to year. Those companies didn't work on stable solutions; they were discovering their solutions. A few were startups, some developed software for internal use, and others developed custom software. Being efficient was less important than being *effective* — discovering and doing the right thing. The teams had to be extremely *dynamic* to support product, staffing, and technology changes.

If you determine that the team needs to be highly dynamic, look for the qualities of openness, flexibility, and resilience in your candidates.

Openness. Is the person receptive to new options and different perspectives? Does she explore them? Does she give new ideas a chance, even if she has already produced a solution?

Flexibility. Does the person approach problems with a fresh perspective or merely perfect a known procedure? Does he consider feedback or just run ahead with preconceived solutions? If the team agrees to make a change, will he go with it? Will he leave his comfort zone?

Resilience. The challenges of a dynamic environment can be taxing, even for open and flexible individuals. Does the candidate have sound emotional responses to setbacks? Does she maintain her stamina?

In my experience, having these qualities in half the members was sufficient to create a highly dynamic team. Often, that half led by example.

Make sure to consider the team's horizon. If they evolve a successful product, eventually it will stabilize and require mostly incremental work. If the same team members remain on the product, they will not have to be as dynamic — their balance will shift from effective to efficient. Will they modify their process accordingly? Will they want to?

Supplementary resource: Download "Team Member Attribute Matrix" from the book's companion website, **www.TheHumanSideOfAgile.com**.

4.3 Can Specialists Be Team Members?

This question comes up in most Agile transitions and classes. The answer is, "Yes, but it's not so simple."

Great Agile teams ignore titles, self-organize, and collaborate as peers. That does not make them a mass of faceless, fungible resources; they are still individuals with myriad abilities and inclinations. However, *individual accomplishments* matter less than the overall result: delivering value to their customer. Therefore, they should contribute where the needs are, and statements such as "I'm a UI developer," or "I don't do databases," or "I'm a test automation specialist" are not acceptable. Work flows more easily between generalists, avoiding unnecessary delays and bottlenecks.

Nevertheless, the complexity of software development requires specialization. Developers need to know the assumptions, design, construction, and quirks of particular modules. They need to master arcane technological details (such as the perennial nemesis: making a particular Web interface appear and function correctly on all browsers). Different parts of the product require different testing sensitivities (e.g., testing the experience of using investment modeling software is rather different from testing its computational engine). The absence of specialization can thus give rise to inferior results, as well as other sorts of delays.

A popular solution to this balancing problem is to include a few generalists and a few specialists in the team. The specialists take care of "the hard problems" while the generalists deal with the nonspecific work. Where I have seen this solution at play, however, it fragmented the team, perpetuated a pecking order, and retained bottlenecks.

A more powerful solution is to populate the team with *specializing generalists*. Every member contributes competently to multiple areas of development — probably not all — while also cultivating a few specialties. This solution allows full self-organization while respecting people's natural desire to develop expertise. The specializing generalist pattern works synergistically with pairing to enhance team skill and adaptability (see 6.6). It affords flexibility, too. Rather than being limited to *task experts*, each task has more *task naturals* who can carry it out meaningfully. This flexibility translates into higher ability and greater likelihood to finish each iteration's commitments.

If only specialists with complementary skills are available to populate the team, hope is not lost. As long as they can turn out valuable work regularly, they should be able to use many Agile mechanisms successfully.

4.4 What If My Team Can't Be Co-Located?

One criterion for team selection is member co-location. Whether working in nearby cubicles or in an open space, short distances between members contribute to communication and collaboration. The ease of casual interaction, the ability to observe facial expressions and body language, and the immediate sharing of artifacts facilitate team evolution (see 6.1). When a co-located team experiences conflicts, they are more likely to manage them healthily, rather than to pretend they don't exist.

Depending on your office layout, you might be able to secure a team open space, also known as a "bullpen." If your office is all desks or cubicles, and members work in various parts of a single office, see whether they can switch locations to be within walking distance of each other. See section 5.5 for effective arrangement ideas.

A new Agile team was spread all over one huge floor, with no hope of desk switching or dedicated space. When I suggested that they take over the windowless, cramped classroom in which I taught them the Agile fundamentals, they were excited! Their project manager obtained the right approvals, and for several weeks they worked happily and productively in this otherwise-dismal space. In the meantime, other arrangements were made for them.

If team members' locations are fixed, hopefully they are not too far apart. A 30-foot distance (about ten meters) suffices to deter people from leaving their chairs to engage colleagues in face-to-face conversation.[4] In closer quarters, your team may be more inclined to communicate in person and use phones and chat software the rest of the time.

But what if your team cannot all be in the same place? Industry experience shows that, despite the extra challenges, the increased overhead in time and money, and the loss of productivity, dispersed teams can nevertheless be quite Agile.

The alternative to direct communication tends to be technology. Nowadays, person-to-person video calling costs next to nothing, works reasonably well, and is fairly easy to set up. Group conference calls are still at the shared-screen and conference-call evolutionary stage. More powerful, almost-in-person solutions are becoming more commonplace, but they are not immediately and constantly available at the individual team level.

However, once a team cannot make do with visual and presence-based communication, they must rely on tools to capture and track their plans and artifacts. These tools make some parts of planning and tracking easier, and some harder. They might also have the following negative effect: even when many of a team's members *do* inhabit the same space, they may gravitate to the tools, email, and chat to converse among themselves, rather than leveraging the potential of closer in-person communication.

Teams are quite vulnerable to "out of sight, out of mind." If you see a teammate — on screen or in person — for only two hours a week, you're less likely to feel the bond of shared purpose and mutual commitment. If most of your communication is on the phone, that's another discouraging factor. Most team members are likely to process information visually rather than auditorily,[5] which makes concentrating on a phone conversation difficult for them. And the remote people participating on speakerphone usually have a rather poor experience; for the most part, they struggle to hear and identify speakers.

Their temptation to disengage and multitask during a conference call is huge. They might tell you "I can't hear," but they *won't* tell you "It's hard for me to focus and be on the phone for so long."

Geographical team distribution has three common forms:

1. Most of the members are co-located; one or two are remote (probably at home).

2. Half the team is in one site; the other half is in another site.

3. The entire team is distributed (for instance, they all work from home).

If you have the choice, avoid form 2. Such a team naturally devolves into two subteams that work largely independently. The situation is even worse from the perspective of team growth and collaboration when one of the halves is the obvious "home team" and the other one is known as the "offshore team."

Distribution form 1 is less susceptible to the clique problem. It might work well with highly engaged people who already have a previous working relationship. Since onsite folks can easily make progress and decisions, the constant risk is that they don't remember or care to pull remote ones in and involve them. It's an effort they don't always wish to make.

The best option is form 3, since it puts all team members on an equal footing. They will invest in communicating and coordinating with each other. They will set up their technology effectively and adjust their process and practices to their reality. Many successful open-source projects operate this way.

A company in downtown Boston allowed every employee to work two days of every week at home, to reduce their commute time. One of their teams was a hybrid of the co-located and the distributed. All its members chose to work from home the same two days, and the rest of the time they were co-located.

If your team has even a single remote member, one technique to strengthen the entire team is pair programming. Block off several hours every day during which the entire team is available and pair programming is the norm. Help the team make this an explicit agreement (see 6.2). Make sure technology is not an issue: everyone should have personal headsets, fast computers, and fast screen-sharing software. If the pairs switch around at least once a day, this pair-wise way of growing a team will strengthen team bonds in a matter of weeks.

4.5 Why Should I Insist That Members Be Full-Time?

Most Agile experts recommend dedicating people full-time to their Agile team. Developers, testers, and other professionals should only deal with items in their team's work stream — the backlog. This minimizes the cost of switching between unrelated activities and enables the team members to concentrate on their work.

Management usually frowns on this advice, for two reasons:

1. They want to maximize people's output. If someone is only needed 80% of the time on one project, what happens with the rest of his time?

2. The workload usually includes more than net new development. It also includes production support, some training, fixing older versions, roadmap planning, or merely smaller one-off projects. These activities are often managed separately and, to staff them, individuals are "sliced and diced."

Many individual contributors also embrace this thinking. They consider it reasonable that they be 60% on project A, 25% on project B, and 15% on project C.

Both management and line workers are well aware that, in most software development efforts, the largest cost item is the team's pay. So, naturally, they follow the factory logic of maximizing *utilization*, which goes hand in hand with referring to people as "resources." Many of them don't realize the cost of context switching and don't know that utilization is not the right measure to look at. The useful indicator isn't that people are kept *busy*; it's their contribution to the company's overall productivity and business.

> At one standup, I heard a developer report to the Scrum-Master, "I just finished that task I'm working on, so I'm a free resource now."

Consider Alex, a highly skilled database analyst. He is only needed half the time on the Blue Team, so he spends the other half helping the Green Team and the Red Team.

This approach implicitly assumes that the return on Alex's time — his usefulness or productivity — is proportional to the time he spends on projects. After all, he's competent, he's motivated, and he wouldn't waste company time. So, every minute he's on a task, he's being useful. Makes sense, right?

Sure, if Alex were a computer.

Because Alex is human, though, he will *not* be all that productive, and *neither will his teammates.* Here are just four reasons:

1. When Alex switches from the Green Team's project to the Red Team's, he needs time to catch up on Red's developments. This isn't like synchronizing a smartphone; it takes time and often involves asking people questions, thus lowering *their* output.

2. Inevitably, his bonds with the Blue Team members (and the Red ones, and the Green ones) are weaker. He's simply not

around enough, and when he is, he's this "expert" they should all listen to. This often translates into reduced collaboration, trust, and knowledge sharing.

3. Alex has no slack time in which to come up with new ideas or simplifications. He lacks the bandwidth to consider that perhaps they should be building *other* product features.

4. The Blue Team needs him for 50% *on average*. What happens the week he's needed for 80%? Either he becomes the bottleneck and Blue suffers, or he spends that time with Blue and then Red and Green both suffer. A flurry of management activity ensues to coordinate his time, none of which gets deducted from anyone's "productivity."

What about the costs you see only much later? A few months of this, and Alex burns out, or asks to be reassigned, or even leaves the company.

What can you do? Stop the "maximizing utilization" madness. Even your computer's operating system avoids 100% CPU utilization (and that's a machine!). Serve your team by fighting to have full-time members on it. Keep pointing out that what matters is overall team throughput — a steady stream of value — not the productivity of individual Alexes. If you absolutely must share certain people, then fight to share them with only one other team and make sure they are being *useful* and *effective* when they are on *your* project. You can rotate your specialists among the teams every few months for increased knowledge sharing, solution consistency, and personal satisfaction.

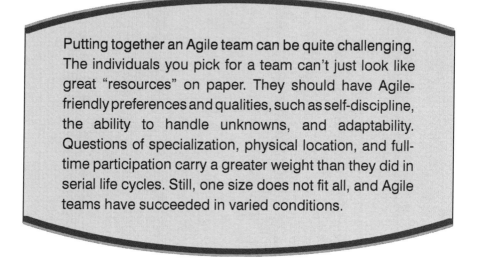

Putting together an Agile team can be quite challenging. The individuals you pick for a team can't just look like great "resources" on paper. They should have Agile-friendly preferences and qualities, such as self-discipline, the ability to handle unknowns, and adaptability. Questions of specialization, physical location, and full-time participation carry a greater weight than they did in serial life cycles. Still, one size does not fit all, and Agile teams have succeeded in varied conditions.

Supplementary Resource

Go to **www.TheHumanSideOfAgile.com** and download "Team Member Attribute Matrix."

CHAPTER 5

Fulfill Preconditions for Teamwork

Once members are selected for the team, they need to agree to cooperate and commit to delivering completed items. Certain elements catalyze their evolution into a successful team, while other elements handicap their growth and result in a "team of one" situation. You can help them pull together, jell, and become *a team*.

I facilitated a review meeting for a successful, year-long Agile project. As the participants were identifying patterns and lessons from the timeline they had reconstructed for the project, the product owner suddenly spoke up. "Don't take this the wrong way," he said, "but when we started, I didn't think we could do so much so well, given the product's complexity and our constraints. I've worked in several product development environments before and, coming into this project, I couldn't see how we'd be done in a year."

This is exactly the kind of admission that makes team meetings, particularly reviews and retrospectives, incredibly valuable. So I asked, "What would you say was a critical ingredient in achieving this success?" He started answering, but before he finished, another participant chimed in with another answer, then another one. I quickly captured this spontaneous outpouring in the flipchart shown on the following page:

Not a single one of the 13 contributing elements listed here is related to process, tools, or management of the work. These elements have to do with teamwork, shared leadership, and responsibility. Even though the core team experienced 30% turnover, and on average half the members were contractors, these folks saw themselves as a *team*.

WHAT AM WAS CRITICAL FOR SUCCESS
COLLECTIVE WILL + "CAN DO" ATTITUDE
SPONSORSHIP
PEOPLE WERE AVAILABLE + READY TO HELP
WENT OUTSIDE THE ORG FOR
                              INFORMATION
GENUINE BUY-IN
DELIVERY TEAM IS VERY DISCIPLINED
VISION + TARGET MODEL
CONSCIOUSLY DEFINED AS A PROJECT
NO NATURAL ENEMIES (NO THREATS OR DISPUTES)
DEDICATED SUPPORT FROM CORE SERVICES
                    ONCE WE WENT LIVE
"WE" THINKING

TOOK THE WORK SERIOUSLY
(DIDN'T TAKE OURSELVES TOO SERIOUSLY)
NO EGOS/HEROES/DOMINANCE

5.1 What Encourages Team Members to Pull Together?

One defining characteristic of any team is their shared purpose. I always ask about it when I meet a new team. The answer is usually beige, something like, "We do the social media component." Stronger teams have an identity, a vivid purpose, or an inspiring vision. Such teams ask themselves, "What must we do together that is larger than any of us, requires all of us, and for which none of us can claim individual victory until it is done?"[1] In some cases, a team will reflect their identity in a name.[2]

Basic affinity between the members is necessary for them to *want* to be with each other. Some common background and shared interests are helpful, although shared values are much more powerful. Imagine you and I are on a team writing medical software. You were attracted to your job because it improves people's lives, whereas I joined for the outstanding pay, which allows me new luxuries. We are both motivated and willing to work together, but would you *care* to work with me? Would you go the extra mile on my behalf, or have my back, when you know I'm really just in it for the money?

Another powerful catalyst to team growth is success. If a team follows through on a valuable commitment, they will grow stronger. As each member considers that, together, they have hit a significant target, their success becomes a reinforcing feedback loop. Agile coaches rely on this loop to get teams started on the right foot by helping them secure "quick wins."

You don't have to wait for big team commitments, since those can take several weeks to materialize. The same principle operates on a smaller scale. Every time a person makes and keeps a small promise to a coworker, the mutual trust level goes up.

If you and I are on a team, we are not joined at the hip. There will be situations in which I will have to make decisions and promises *on our behalf*. You cannot control what I say, but you *will* have to live with the consequences. How do you like that? This worry is the highest hurdle to teamwork — and to lower the hurdle, you need trust. Trust is the foundation of teamwork, and if I am a member of your team, it is my responsibility to demonstrate my trustworthiness to you. Here is what I would do:

Share relevant information promptly. I would share meaningful updates and new developments in a timely manner. In particular, if I no longer thought I could keep a promise, I would tell you as soon as possible.

Be authentic. Speaking the truth is only the beginning. I would not pretend to know what I don't know, or say "yes" (or "maybe") when I mean "no." I would work with you, but I would not pretend to be your friend unless I meant it. I would treat you as I would want to be treated.

Pull you into conversations that affect you. If I am about to make a decision that determines your work or limits your choices, I would delay it to the last responsible moment to allow you to join the decision-making process. (Examples include iteration planning and defining our meaning of "done.")

Strive to be a dependable colleague. If my job pulls me in different directions, one of which is our team, I would arrange my other obligations as best I can so you know when and to what extent you can depend on me. If my schedule causes me to disappear on you unpredictably, and that hurts you, I would rather leave the team.

Caution: extremely challenging advice ahead. **Address issues directly.** When something about our work together upsets me and impedes our progress, I would hope for the nerve to have the uncomfortable conversation with you. It would demonstrate how important our relationship is to me, and I hope you would take it in that spirit.

5.2 How Can I Help the Team Buy In?

A common challenge with Agile adoption (and other instances of organizational change) is team members' buy-in. "Buying in" means being convinced and willing to work a certain way. As the team's leader, you will need to help them buy into the Agile way and the particular work being undertaken.

Buying into Agile means accepting, and agreeing to, the mind-set and the process:

+ Short cycles as opposed to months-long projects

+ Less detailed up-front planning; working with incomplete information

+ Being members of a whole self-organizing team, possibly in an open space

+ Having freedom and responsibility to make rules, decisions ... and mistakes

+ Delivering features as opposed to developing blocks

A CTO decided to switch his department to Agile for the next major undertaking: a product rewrite. Once his management staff and the product managers returned from an Agile fundamentals course, they divided the department into teams of programmers and testers. They established iteration planning and reviews, daily standups, and a product backlog with user stories.

The product definition team loved their new "powers" but did not balance them with the requisite negotiation and collaboration. The delivery teams had trouble buying into the "getting to done" concept; since the database group's boss wanted no part in Agile, the database would be developed on a separate track. The expectation of hardening sprints allowed developers to keep their coding habits, thinking they would fix defects before the release. The managers controlled the planning and retrospective meetings; some team members would drop in just to make an appearance. Even their brightest developers realized that results meant demonstrated stories, regardless of the underlying code's quality — collaboration was nonexistent in the rush to collect story points. When reality didn't agree with the planned schedule, the CTO's solution was to work evenings and weekends.

Buy-in is a voluntary choice to spend one's energy a certain way. A person is not guaranteed to buy in merely on account of working willingly for the organization. Without sufficient buy-in, Agile will not stick, and motivation will be low. Your support is needed both at the individual member level and at the team level. The critical period for your efforts is the first few weeks of a team's life cycle.

5.2.1 Individual Buy-In

For someone to buy into Agile and the project, she must know what she is getting into. Therefore, basic education in both is an absolute prerequisite for buy-in. If team members are new to Agile, arrange for proper training. (Unfortunately, too many teams receive only a one-hour PowerPoint presentation.) If people were dropped in without prior exposure to the project, allow them the time to find their footing.

You need to understand and speak to each person's motivators (see 10.4). Why should the person buy into Agile, or this particular development effort? What's in it for him? If he and the team are new to Agile, expect a somewhat different set of drivers to be satisfied than in the pre-Agile environment.

For greater intrinsic motivation, have one-on-one conversations with each individual. Specific, personalized answers from you will counteract the weak effect of such blanket statements as "Agile will be good for you and for the company" or "This project will help us catch up to the competition." Don't just list out deliverables; express *why* they have been chosen. How will they make a difference?

Let each team member have a say in determining the project's direction and customizing the methods for it. An effective way to do this is to include the person, along with the entire team, in the project's kickoff or in chartering sessions.

Developing new software, or using new methods, involves risk. Most software professionals realize that some risk is necessary for progress. What they won't do, however, is commit career suicide. Unless a person is educated or experienced in proper Agile practice, she might fear that it is unsound or reckless, especially if her familiar, pre-Agile methods felt safe (or at least organizationally sanctioned). The following fears are prevalent before starting an Agile rollout and even during its first few iterations:

"If we always do quick work on small stories, we'll produce low-grade code." This fear is the unfortunate reality of many teams that misunderstand the iteration concept, underdefine "done," or just want to pass a demo unscathed. Help the team put measures in place to avoid this trap, including proper Agile engineering practices, a strong definition of "done," and true-capacity (not wishful) planning.

"We can produce small working features, but there's no time for enough system-level and regression testing." Testers as well as business people share this fear of experiencing an increase in nasty surprises.

"The iterations are so short, we can't demo anything valuable." This fear stems from inexperience in decomposing large features and from the mistaken belief that every story must have a visible, demonstrable element. Left unchecked, this fear gives rise to stress, haste, and an improper prioritization of work.

"Management says they support the new process, but it's still business as usual." In other words, if management still expects to nail ship dates, scope, quality, and cost, the Agile planning mechanisms become moot.

You will see these fears play out and also hear them stated. With practice, patience, and support, they are likely to dissipate.

Buy-in trouble may stem from several additional concerns:

Working with incomplete information. No one had complete knowledge in the pre-Agile environment or could predict every detail — but everybody proceeded to plan as if they did. The Agile thought process is more relaxed: "You will *not* know enough, and we can't wait forever to gather every possible detail. Run with the information you have, or wait just until the last responsible moment to proceed." That makes some people very nervous.

Having to choose what to work on next. While it's less motivating, having an authority determine your next steps feels safe and comforting. Greater Agility, however, comes from greater autonomy and personal responsibility.

> Adriana, a new product owner and designer by training, created new backlog items with ease. When it came to prioritizing them, her trepidation almost paralyzed her. She would privately ask the team lead to do the prioritization, and then she would indicate her agreement with his suggestions.

Being swallowed up into a faceless team. The old regime's system of conferring status and distinction helped people feel important. While folks recognize the potential of teamwork, they do not want to be generic team members; they want to be noticed for their individuality. Agile teams do recognize individual contributions but don't translate them into formal status.

Since professionals avoid admitting these concerns, you can't address them directly. Instead, have regular one-on-one conversations with your team members, coach them, and be highly supportive and patient until, hopefully, those concerns disappear.

5.2.2 Team-Level Buy-In

Before a team will buy in as a group, some interpersonal foundation is absolutely required. It has three elements: professional trust, respect, and basic capability to work through conflicts.

Members need to *trust* each other enough to buy into a methodology that is predicated on teamwork. Even if they don't expect to collaborate or cooperate with each other, do they assume others would at least do their parts? Do they trust that they have the necessary skills and would apply them?

Beyond professional trust, do team members *respect* their colleagues as people? They do not need to feel admiration or subservience, although an absence of respect will hamper team buy-in.

Not all *conflict* is confrontation, and not everybody knows or believes that. Evolved teams respect conflict and use it for personal growth, for team evolution, and for heightened involvement.[3] The team would benefit from having at least one person who can help resolve conflict usefully when it arises; that person would be you, by default. Just as in marriage, team members share the same roof for hours every day, and they can make each other happy or miserable. The team should rely on rules and agreements — even implicit ones — to know what is acceptable and how to deal with conflict.

Do *you* believe that all members are required for successful project completion? Do all team members share this belief, or do some consider themselves heroes who could shoulder the load on their own? The Agile philosophy attracts people who can pull their weight together and understand that "all alone" is not an option. Moreover, this interdependence applies across the entire team, not within functional subgroups. From the very beginning, reinforce that team members are in it together.

I always gather entire project communities together for their kickoff. Some spend two or three days together in structured activities that draw everybody's participation — even if some folks remain mostly quiet. Without exception, the mere presence and engagement of the full community results in palpable excitement and buy-in.[4]

You may have been the first one to bring Agile into the company or the team, but if people can offer suggestions to tailor the implementation, they will feel it's their idea. Allow them to do so, both in individual conversations and in team settings where ideas build on each other.

Do you remember the old saying, "Seek forgiveness, not permission"? It is synonymous with autonomy, which is a core intrinsic motivator also at the team level and thus a catalyst to buy-in. Instead of creating a system of approval rules and workflows, build a loose framework in which people are free to experiment, informed initiative is welcome, and risks (even mistakes) are permitted.

Even though you have access to more project information than most members, don't keep it all to yourself. Every team member should have access to information that affects the team. Establish an atmosphere of transparency and sharing so people know what they are buying into. Involve the whole team in significant discussions. Even when they know their input has limited influence, they will feel valued and important, and thus more inclined to participate.

Always remember that you may not be the only leader. Most groups have a number of people who are fairly dominant and influential — whether their formal title implies it or not. Make sure that they are on your side and that they comprehend the Agile concepts and why they work. Tread carefully around overly dominant people (see 7.6).

5.3 What Does the Team Need in Order to Commit to Deliverables?

Commitment is the willingness and agreement to deliver something and to account for shortfalls. In our context, once the team has bought into Agile and the project, are they also committing to producing certain deliverables?

This commitment usually takes place in iteration planning. After the team has identified, negotiated, and understood a set of stories and tasks, they are asked to commit to delivering them in a potentially releasable, "done" state at the end of the iteration. Similar commitments can happen at the release level prior to the first iteration and at the project level as part of chartering.

Some Agile teams don't bother committing to particular deliverables, working instead on a best-effort basis. This might be good enough, or not. Other teams are never asked to commit — instead, they are told that they've committed.

I observed an iteration planning meeting of a team (three developers and two testers) who were expected to deliver ten points per developer per iteration. Once the development manager and product owner had identified stories totaling 30 points, their iteration planning was complete. They told me afterward, "They will deliver those 30 points — no ifs or buts."

The commitment mechanism gives members the impetus to pull together as a team. They begin with the end in mind: "What's our iteration goal? What do we want to accomplish?"[5] It works synergistically with the mechanism of disturbance-free iterations: a commitment applies only for a week or two. Moreover, it reinforces the concept that the *team* produces deliverables, not individuals.

Commitment is a powerful mechanism when it's voluntary, not compelled by positional authority (say, if you're the team's manager). Furthermore, if you impose obligations that they have trouble meeting, you're courting danger. They are part of a bigger system, and anytime you apply pressure, its force may propagate or dissipate differently than you expect. As pressure on people grows stronger, its intended effect becomes more temporary.[6] When a team doesn't commit (or falls short of their commitment), your honest and constructive feedback — rather than exhortations, threats, or punishment — goes a long way.

Commitment builds motivation and engagement because most people like to be consistent in their conduct. If they make a promise on which they don't follow through, they are being inconsistent, which makes others doubt and mistrust them. On the flip side, commitment strengthens people. Once they apply themselves, their minds come up with good *new* reasons to justify their new behaviors. These reasons stick around, as do the behaviors.[7]

Commitment requires empowerment or autonomy. Can your team make significant choices and binding decisions? Does commitment even make sense for them? They need enough data on their capacity, their abilities, and the work at hand to properly commit. Do they have the prerequisites and tools to succeed? Even if the team is effectively staffed and protected, could they still run into situations where commitment is impossible?

One team was building a data system on top of an immature third-party product. That product crashed repeatedly, lacked functionality, and didn't perform suitably. They slipped several iterations because the vendor didn't get back in time or wasn't able to fix up the product in time for them to meet their iteration goals.

Another condition for commitment is shared accountability. If a team misses a few iterations, will someone account for that individually, or will the entire team have to answer for it? Are members accountable to each other? Several factors usually interfere with shared accountability:

+ Individual rewards for merit and exceeding expectations (see 5.7)

+ An informal pecking order among members

+ Recent changes in team composition (see 6.1)

+ A powerful formal hierarchy

+ Processes that parcel out work to individuals based on specialty

One Scrum team planned sprints using task breakdowns, complete with individuals' names and hour estimates. The implicit understanding was that each person owned a list of sprint tasks, with little flexibility or sharing. They never committed as a team; instead, individual members would indicate whether they could finish their tasks.

A similar challenge affects many teams that make a genuine, capacity-based iteration commitment, only to get sidetracked due to production support, customer support, and other true urgencies. Even when these teams account for an average overhead of interruptions, their asynchronous nature and occasional spikes might derail the teams' commitments. Again, they must tailor the process to their situation so they can make viable promises.

5.4 What Can We Do to Break Down the Silos?

For an Agile team to deliver value effectively, they need to self-organize and collaborate. All members are allowed to do anything, and as far as possible, they become specializing generalists. This framework prevents members from becoming bottlenecks. It also increases the team's flexibility and resilience.

But what happens when your reality is different and your team members are siloed? Are you therefore not Agile?

Team members differ on several professional dimensions:

A. Seniority and background

B. Main activity (such as programming, testing, or technical writing)

C. Subject matter expertise (such as trading systems, graphics, or quantitative analysis)

D. The technologies they work with (such as .NET user interfaces or Java-based enterprise architectures)

E. The system components they've come to know well

Most Agile teams handle dimension A gracefully. Senior folks help junior ones integrate and grow. Teams that self-organize well don't necessarily blur distinction B, but they continuously collaborate across those main activities.

The silos you're likely to encounter are along the C, D, or E dimensions, and they do in fact reduce the team's ability to self-organize. So don't announce, "We're using Agile. From now on you will all work on all the components, across all technologies, even on stuff you don't know yet!" If you do, you'll be laughed at and subsequently ignored.

The subject matter expertise (C) barrier is real, as it usually requires degree courses or extensive experience. Other than in rare cases, you have to hire for those skills.

Mastering new technologies (D) takes weeks or months. Developing component expertise (E) can take substantial study and practice. Despite the beneficial effect of versatility on technical contributors' careers, not to mention continued employment in your organization, you will encounter considerable reluctance and push-back if you enforce it without their agreement. The two common objections are:

"It's not worth it." (I couldn't get past "mediocre" quickly enough.)

"I couldn't learn it anyway." (I'm too old/young/busy/experienced/ inexperienced.) This is the adult's fear of taking up something new and maybe appearing incompetent.

If you believe that the team member has the talent and that the learning is worthwhile, make the investment. Three popular means of promoting such learning are books, study time, and courses. While many software professionals are used to building valuable skills through self-study and experimentation outside of work, their motivation grows considerably if their employer makes a comparable investment of time or money.

Two less-common techniques that achieve superb results are *pairing* and *mentoring*.

In pairing, the learner joins an experienced colleague as he carries out current tasks that have some teachable value. In each session, the two collaborate on the task. The learner asks clarifying and challenging questions. Her colleague puts the conversation on an equal footing — he doesn't pull rank or assume that he has all the right answers. Where possible, the learner is actively involved in the task, not just talking about it or watching her colleague type. Pairs switch every few hours, so the learner gets the benefit of multiple viewpoints and styles.

In mentoring, also known as the buddy system, an expert is assigned to the learner. Accessible on demand or on scheduled occasions, the mentor answers questions, challenges the learner, reviews progress, and directs the learning.

Most professionals I've met in the past 20 years have believed that their team or organization simply couldn't afford the expense of breaking down the silos. Since reality dictated that, sometimes, someone would have to learn something new, the attitude was "Let's try to minimize the time investment," while the rest of the team was busy doing their own stuff. The backdrop of a sophisticated knowledge industry only underscored the widespread belief that competent software professionals ought to be able to learn anything on their own — from books, documentation, and experimentation. The unfortunate result, for many learners, was heightened performance anxiety and a fear of looking incompetent. Both pairing and mentoring are a "You're not alone" antidote to this.

An XP team comprised two subteams: eight C++ developers working on the application's user interface and logic, and two Java developers working on a database compiler. A few weeks before the deadline, the compiler had to be modified considerably. The application developers agreed to participate in compiler work but were clearly apprehensive due to the unfamiliar language and technology.

Two of the application developers stepped up first. Each one paired with a compiler developer throughout the first week, modifying and adding code, writing unit tests, refactoring, and learning the compiler's inner workings. The second week, two additional application developers joined the rotation, sometimes pairing with colleagues who had studied the compiler only the week before. During the third week, all developers were active on the compiler. All the while, the original two compiler developers participated in each design or review session.

Even though the newest compiler developers were still novices in that component — and not all of them liked it — in pairs they became effective. And the team made their deadline.[8]

5.5 What Are the Elements of Effective Co-Location?

Co-location is intended to facilitate team-wide collaboration and communication. For effective co-location, members ought to be within earshot and, if possible, have lines of sight to each other. The simplest arrangement that achieves that is having team members sit around a single large table (like a boardroom table).

Collaboration happens in front of a computer, a whiteboard, or even a coffee machine. Once people get infected with the collaboration bug, they will adjust to all sorts of conditions. Until that happens, their environment might discourage them from working together; it takes considerable energy and goodwill to foster collaboration, and very little to impede it. Remove all obstacles, including:

✦ Not enough chairs, keyboards, or mice for impromptu paired work (many people will avoid using others' keyboard and mouse for hygienic reasons — but they won't admit that)

✦ Desks configured for a single person, like the typical L-shape

✦ Insufficient space for informal meetings

✦ Inability to post information visibly

✦ Being separated by partitions, or having their backs to each other

Two senior developers occupied adjacent L-shaped desks, as in Figure 1. They rarely paired up at a single desk, but each one felt comfortable starting a conversation with the other several times a day.

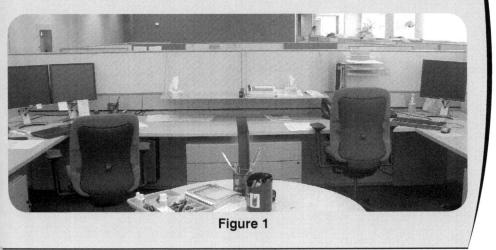

Figure 1

A week after their team was moved to the area depicted in Figure 2, where a low partition separated the two developers, both of them told me, "We used to talk ten times as much as we do now!"

Figure 2

Some sounds and sights can disrupt concentration in the team space, such as nonteam foot traffic, a paging system, and shared meeting rooms. If the product owner or other people spend a lot of time on the phone, have them sit just far enough from the delivery team so their voices don't disturb them. Team members' voices (in paired work or other conversations) do not usually disturb other colleagues — as long as they're all focusing on related deliverables.

Sadly, too many corporate offices can be best described as sterile. Let the team personalize their space so they *want* to work there. Personalization helps the team take ownership of their work and build a shared identity. Although this freedom usually translates into a few free or low-cost actions (such as putting up a traffic light to indicate build status), it's apt to draw attention from other groups in the organization, including the facilities department. You can provide the team with needed air cover so they don't feel somebody is trying to standardize them.

5.6 How Can I Support Team Members Who Report to Functional Managers?

If you are an ATL in a siloed organization that has adopted Agile, every person on your team answers to two entities. On one hand, they collaborate with colleagues on work they pull from the team's backlog. On the other hand, they report to a manager, such as a development or QA manager. That person is responsible for their evaluation, compensation, retention, promotion, or termination. How can you help your team reckon effectively with this highly loaded situation?

The first thing to take care of is *education*. Still wanting to perform their role, functional managers may unwittingly compromise Agility by taking such actions as:

+ Providing story estimates or overriding the team's estimates

+ Shifting people between teams

+ Assigning nonbacklog work to individuals

Help these managers acquire basic education in Agile and accept its underpinnings. If arranging full-day training for them is difficult, coach or teach them in frequent one-on-one meetings. This is well worth your time.

Second, make sure your team members *respect* their functional managers as fellow members of the community. The team, newly self-organizing and now negotiating work with someone else (the product owner), may start questioning the functional managers' role and value. The managers, having to adjust to unfamiliar expectations and relationships, may have similar doubts.

Yang was a development manager. During the Agile fundamentals course and the project kickoff, he felt perplexed and apprehensive about his place in the upcoming Agile implementation. He was receiving no support from his developers. In my readiness assessment interview with his two senior full-timers, they spoke dismissively of him, describing him as redundant and "clueless."

During the first week after the kickoff, I coached the entire team and paid particular attention to Yang. He quickly hit his stride as the team's primary impediment remover on all technical matters. He was busy coordinating activities and resolving issues. The large project community, spread across six offices and not used to direct communication, found Yang very helpful. The developers told me the following week, "We don't know what you did to this guy, but he's turned around 180 degrees. He's actually fun now!"

The third matter is *team allegiance*. Members must realize that their higher calling now is to deliver the right product in a team setting. That can be scary. If their boss asks them for something, they may find it hard to say no, even if it disrupts the team's plans. While they respect their team, the boss can do them damage. Team members must place their allegiance in the team first — and that can only work if their managers and the company culture respect this arrangement. As a sign of this respect, managers should not attend iteration retrospectives unless they truly support and serve the team.[9] You can heighten the members' awareness of their allegiance by asking them to report nonbacklog activities at the standup and by tracking those efforts on an information radiator.

For most hierarchical organizations, adopting an overarching value-delivery mind-set is a tall order. Assuming you've brought

Agile into an otherwise receptive environment, one good way to foster team allegiance and avoid surprises is to establish clear rules of engagement. For instance, all special requests for work must be funneled through the backlog.

5.7 How Can I Mitigate the Damage of Performance Reviews?

Unless your organization is young, it subjects you and your team members to annual or semiannual performance reviews. If it doesn't, it probably hasn't gotten around to implementing reviews yet. Quick, stop them!

The word "review" sounds fairly neutral. Shouldn't managers review and manage their subordinates' performance? Sadly, the other words by which this technique is known, "evaluation" and "appraisal," depict its essence more accurately. It is an opportunity to *judge* performance, if not the people themselves.

Despite their prevalence in the corporate landscape, performance reviews cause far more harm than good.[10] They are one-sided, even when the employee starts the process with a self-assessment. They can never be fully objective, since humans conduct them. They strike fear in employees' hearts worse than exam anxiety. They force managers to rate staff on a contrived linear scale. As the review period draws near, employees consciously resort to safe or placating behaviors reminiscent of political parties before elections. The potentially useful elements of performance reviews — feedback, recognition, the employee's introspection — are diminished when done infrequently and in a fear-based atmosphere.

In an Agile context, performance reviews cause still-greater harm. Functional managers have little firsthand data about their reports, who spend their time in cross-functional teams. Then these managers compress the data into a "meets expectations" and "exceeds expectations" scale, which is a meaningless comparison if their subordinates work on separate Agile teams. Their data rarely accounts for team members' interdependence and mutual support. When tied to merit pay and increases,[11] performance reviews send the message that one should be better than one's teammates.

In some places, performance reviews are tied to individual objectives. These may be meant to encourage personal growth (such as improving one's time management skills) or be part of a larger technique known as Management by Objectives (MBO). Individual professional development is certainly welcome on Agile teams, but formally managing it sends the wrong message. Ultimately, the individual's contribution to his team and company is the primary variable of interest. If personal objectives are tied to deliverables, it's better to put those deliverables on the backlog. And if they are strategically important, they may deserve a dedicated team.

> "We have quarterly MBO goals. People put in their goals every quarter, saying, 'I'm going to do x, y, z,' and they get paid on them. These goals are not always tied to the particular product release that everybody is working 85%–95% of their time on. It's just assumed they are stretch goals, and that people just find a way to get them done. After all, you have a whole quarter, right?"
>
> — *Mike, test manager and ScrumMaster at a large company*

You may not be able to abolish performance reviews in your organization. I know of some who have stopped them — but that's only because they were so busy they forgot to keep doing them (or they stopped giving bonuses or raises). If you *must* conduct your team's reviews, you can do this:

✦ Set the expectation that performance corresponds both to team contribution and to Agile-friendly behaviors (see 4.2). Make those expectations explicit and fully transparent.

✦ Focus your review conversations on the employees' pride, joy, satisfaction, and engagement — not on the inane attempt to improve them.

✦ Try to disconnect reviews from pay increases and bonuses. One possibility is to divide increases and bonuses equally among team members.

✦ Conduct reviews less formally and more frequently, even once a month. This injects meaning into the feedback loop and avoids election-time behavior.

Make honest, caring feedback a normal part of your interaction with team members. Build trusting relationships with them, whether or not you conduct reviews. If there *are* reviews, these trusting relationships will drive out the fear.

Some environments are a natural fit for Agile teams. Engaged professionals form teams and make shared commitments. They overcome various handicaps and grow stronger. In this scenario, your role is largely supportive and straightforward. But even if your starting point seems challenging, take heart. Use your positional authority and influence to establish and maintain team-friendly conditions. Keep supporting your team in overcoming their hurdles. Your dedication to the team's success will bear fruit.

CHAPTER 6

Cultivate Team Agility

With the suggestions in the previous two chapters, your team is well-positioned for success. They are a good mix of skilled, bought-in, committed professionals, and they will work nicely together. Your work is not done yet, though. Certain factors — and your involvement — catalyze the team's evolution into a strong *Agile* team.

6.1 What Are the Stages of Team Evolution?

Almost half a century ago, the American psychologist Bruce Tuckman published a theory of team evolution.[1] Agile software development teams did not exist at the time, but Tuckman's Group Development model applies well to them. According to the model, a team has to proceed through a certain sequence of stages on the way to the desirable stage, *performing*.

In the initial stage, *forming*, members learn what the team is supposed to accomplish. They get to know each other and their first-draft idea of roles and responsibilities. In this stage, most of the work is still individual, and some members try extra hard to look good. The forming stage is generally short-lived, overshadowed by the realities of the next stage.

In the second stage, *storming*, the team experiences conflict and difference of opinion. Some of the decisions they need to make draw out tensions and emotions. There might be some jockeying for influence and leadership. In a new Agile team, the first several iteration planning sessions tend to include disagreements about estimation approaches, the extent of detail in user stories, and task assignments.

If the team can pull itself out of storming, whether on its own or with your guidance as the Agile team leader (ATL), it reaches the third stage, *norming*. Members understand the rules of engagement. They establish, follow, and adapt agreements. Everyone understands the team's goals the same way and cooperates to achieve them. They know and follow their process.

The fourth stage, *performing*, is the big deal. A performing team doesn't just hum along — it *buzzes*. Its members are motivated and delighted to be there. They don't have to speak with the same voice, but they don't let conflict turn into confrontation. Consensus and self-organization are easy for them. They don't worry about making their team work anymore; that has been taken care of, and now they focus on results. They don't merely cooperate, they collaborate.

The following diagram[2] shows the change in the team's effectiveness in the various stages. Note that the qualitative effectiveness level in norming is similar to that of forming. In forming, they are a group of individuals who apply themselves; in norming, the added value of their teamwork may still not compensate for the energy they spend on being a team.

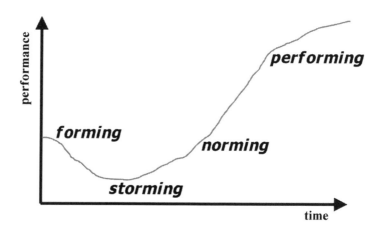

This model has several important implications for you. The team is at risk of never reaching norming. Team growth is *evolutionary*, and success is not inevitable. Even with the most suitable people using the best methods with good support, there is no guarantee they will graduate from the storming stage. Some teams may appear to have normed, but in reality they put on a happy face, stifle all conflict and differences, and defer to their product owner and managers.

Three teams were working on a single program. To be cross-functional, each team had been formed with half of the Batch Team (back-end) specialists and half of the Online Team specialists, in line with the main technological divide. Each half was further divided into programmers and testers, working in handoff fashion. Iteration planning sessions were muted and ineffective; retrospectives were louder but resulted in little traction. After a year of using Scrum, they struggled mightily to figure out roles and collective ownership — self-organization was all but moot. Few people seemed happy.

Expect conflict. If you put intelligent, capable people together and ask them to share responsibility for a goal, how likely are they to agree on the means to get there? How likely are they to exhibit a healthy balance of leadership and followership? Conflict is necessary for the elaborate dance of team growth. It is not inherently detrimental, unless it is allowed to devolve into confrontation and one-upmanship.

The road to low performance is paved with good intentions. Whenever you add people to a team, even temporarily (such as contractors), you knock the team down a stage or two as they adjust to their new composition. New permanent members require an investment of time, energy, and goodwill from veteran members. If you redeploy a valued member to seed or help another team, the remaining members will restorm to fill the void and adjust their leader-follower patterns. (You can mitigate the effect by seeking their agreement to the move.) If you remove a noncontributing member, the team will have to adjust the norms they had established to accommodate that person. All these changes in team composition spell a drop in performance, which might last longer than you intend, even indefinitely.

> "Our team was originally bolstered with several contractors, who stayed for differing periods. Only once the last contractor had left and we had settled into a stable team — well over a year after the team was first created — did I feel the team really started to jell."
>
> — *Ian, software ATL in a hardware company*

6.2 How Does the Team Customize Their Process?

Since continuous improvement is a core Agile principle, Agile methods are inherently adaptable. A team that embraces Agile is expected to customize the methods, practices, and techniques within the framework of the Agile principles and values. By modifying the methodology to their particular makeup and context, they increase their ownership and quality of the results.

This kind of adaptation is rarely static. If you're picturing an early-stage Agile team holding a marathon meeting to produce a detailed rulebook or an SDLC document, that's not it. As a typical team forms, it will pick an established method and supplement it with a few operating norms. These usually include their definition of "done," the initial slate of roles and responsibilities, and a few standards and agreements. As the weeks go by, the team modifies the adopted method and these norms, often during the retrospectives. (That's one reason they should hold retrospectives as frequently as every two weeks. They spell a predictable opportunity to pause and reflect.)

An element of process adaptation is the *team agreement* or *working agreement*. Agreements cover anything the team wishes to codify, such as:

+ Relationships: "Give help when asked." "If you're not learning or contributing in a meeting, feel free to go do something else."

+ Behavioral expectations: "All meetings start on time." "All production code to be done in pairs." "Core hours are 10 to 4."

+ Standards (e.g., for coding, API documentation, and user story format)

+ Temporary arrangements: "Work an extra hour every day until <critical date>."

+ Decision rules: "At least three people must participate in making high-level design decisions."

The rationale behind Agile team agreements goes like this: since members want to be part of the team, they will naturally apply themselves to the work. They don't require policing, because a shared understanding of their environment and objectives, a sense of professionalism, and common courtesy ought to take care of most interactions and situations. Still, gaps will occur — areas that they never considered or valued behaviors that occur inconsistently. Whenever the team stumbles into a gap, they should close it with an agreement. Agreements are typical Agile decisions: they remain in effect until they stop working, at which point they are revised or removed.

Agreements should be written down, since human memory can be rather plastic and misleading. The act of writing an agreement down is a chance for clarification and refinement. Written agreements should be posted visibly. That makes them a nagging-free, accessible reminder, something they could never be if buried in some electronic tool.

Notice that the foregoing description makes no mention of *you*. You don't own the agreements, change them, or put forth new ones. As the team's servant leader, you can contribute your observations and suggestions. Since you're their process steward, the team might also rely on you to help them enforce the agreements — for their sake.

> "One of our teams came up with a 'wheel of shame' to deal with the inevitable violation of working agreements. The transgressor would have to spin the wheel of shame and carry out whichever 'punishment' the dial landed on, which usually involved having to do something silly like wear a silly hat or treat the rest of the team to ice cream. It was a surprisingly effective and fun way to defuse problem behavior and enhance the team's sense of cohesion."
>
> *— Pat Reed, senior director, Gap, Inc.*

6.3 What Does Self-Organization Mean?

Agile team members check their individual titles at the door. While their organizational titles might still convey position and specialty (e.g., Senior Web Developer), on the team they are all equal members. They may speak about "our developers," "the tester," or "the architect," but effective teams don't sort themselves into "the development team" vs. "the testing team."

During the time between committing to goals and delivering results — whether that's a release, an iteration, or something else — the team makes its own decisions collectively.[3] Members find out *together* how they want to develop, collaborate, divide tasks, track progress, handle feedback, and do everything else that supports meeting their objectives. They determine the best way, based on their understanding and within the organizational framework, to achieve their shared purpose of value delivery. No authority, such as a manager or a team leader, makes those decisions for them.

Self-organization underlies having team goals, team commitment, and team achievement. The individual member is no longer the unit of value production, a "resource" — the team is. If the team can in fact accomplish valued results ("get to done"), self-organization acts to maximize those results. That is why Agile methods ascribe velocity to teams, and why effective Agile teams eschew both individual performance measurements and individual rewards.

This self-directed division of labor and responsibility permeates the community's spirit. Don't hurt it by endorsing story or task assignments at the beginning of the work cycle — even if you believe their ownership is obvious. For example, if during iteration planning Mircea says, "Hey, I'll pick up Story B," or you say, "Mircea, why don't you take Story B?" for the remainder of the iteration Mircea will *own* story B and not easily "trade" it or give it up.

A developer told me once, "I shouldn't test. I am paid too much to be doing testing." Yet Agile teams work differently. Every member's ultimate goal is for the team to ship valuable working software, regardless of his specialty or focus. As a developer, for example, he might program most of the time; the rest of the time, he would do whatever the team needs to reach their goals. He is a team member who specializes in programming.

Self-organization accounts for reality on the ground, which is another reason that preassignment is suboptimal. If a team member develops a fever at 2 p.m. and goes home, the rest of the team stays behind and figures out how best to continue without her. They might take over her task, or assume she will finish it later, or find other creative options.

Early on, a team felt that their technical decision making was lacking and expressed a wish for technical oversight and leadership. So, during their second retrospective, they elected a technical leader. This happened in a corporation where managers normally designed leader roles for teams without consulting their members, but this group resolved their aching need by modifying their own structure all on their own. Interestingly, the chosen candidate — an architect, already a part-time member of the delivery team — wasn't exactly thrilled; he was already too busy. The team made an agreement to experiment with this arrangement for four weeks. Later on, someone who enjoyed the entire team's backing was promoted into this position.

Another aspect of self-organization is that a team reaches consensus and makes decisions using mechanisms that fit *that specific team*. Some teams require unanimity; some are fine with majority vote. Some teams only make changes during retrospectives; others make them continuously. The key is that the team chooses their own decision-making process and uses it to set further decisions.

6.4 How Can I Help My Team Self-Organize?

Many well-meaning managers operate under the assumption that teams will naturally self-organize once they are freed to do so. In some environments, granting the permission — or setting the expectation — to self-organize is indeed akin to breaking the shackles of a former regime. However, a team may have limited motivation or ability to apply this new freedom. Several conditions must apply for self-organization to take place.

A basic condition is for *the entire team* to rally behind meaningful targets, goals, or outcomes. When working toward something worthy of a team, something only a team can do, every member is more inclined to exceed official duty. But that has meaning only in an empowered team, which doesn't need to vet decisions with management or wait for instructions. When the path to the outcome is not prescribed, and the team has the autonomy to make decisions and set a tactical course, self-organization will be a natural result.

Even if the team has shared goals, in most organizations the members don't rise and fall as a team. There must, however, be team rewards for pulling through and team consequences for not doing so. Company rewards or sanctions for individual behavior can be your biggest hurdle to self-organization. Until you can get them changed, shield the team from their effect.

In many newly Agile teams, technological and product specialization poses a high barrier to self-organization. Legacy codebases, in particular, tend to correspond to having experts and silos. Tasks that do not require specialties are few and far between, and making them available to the entire team can feel contrived. Consider carefully whether the team can break down the silos over time and whether doing so is worth the investment (see 5.4).

The roles and responsibilities that a team settles on should be suitable for their specific work, preferences, and situation. While responsible members contribute where they can meaningfully do so, they are human beings and will prefer to retain their distinction. For instance, many Agile developers are glad to backstop functional testing and documentation activities — although only as a temporary measure. I have met few developers who would consent to having those become a regular part of their work.

Help your team make clear agreements and set behavioral expectations that match their unique situation and culture. By doing so, they reinforce their identity and shared motivation to work together.

Explicit rules and agreements establish an operational framework that tells members, "You can be flexible within these parameters."

A critical element of self-organization is continuous feedback. Whether received from peers, customers, code, tests, or management, feedback helps people tune their actions and behaviors. Just as individuals need it, so do teams, which is why most Agile frameworks incorporate a review and a retrospective at the end of each cycle. The more continuous, actionable, and respectful the feedback, the more easily the team can learn what works and what doesn't.

6.4.1 Encouraging an Early-Stage Team to Self-Organize

Many Agile teams start out with little understanding or reference experience for self-organization. Their tendency or habit may be to continue working individualistically. Since people take behavioral cues from their peers, they might infer that having individually determined tasks is not a problem and is the right course to take.[4] Give them an early taste of the alternative, using facilitative group techniques, including simulations, as well as stories and videos.[5]

Your guidance and support can be golden when the team is still forming or storming — generally speaking, the first few months. There are several actions you can take.

First, make the team boundary crystal clear. Clarify to the team where their work fits in the grand scheme of the product portfolio. They should understand where their part begins and ends and what they are accountable for as a group. A good occasion for that is the project or team kickoff.

Next, *underorganize* the team. Play up their shared purpose — the overall deliverables and their parameters — and downplay the expectations from each individual. Make sure they understand the Agile principles and process mechanics, and let them figure out who does what. They might ask you to tell them what to do; resist that temptation. Help them discover how to proceed rather than jump in with answers.

Ensure that supporting process mechanisms are in place. It should be easy for team members to communicate, know what's going on, and understand what's urgent and/or important. Common mechanisms include the daily standup meeting, inhabiting a shared space, and having an easily accessible and visible task board. You need to continuously evaluate whether these suffice. All too often, I find members in new teams do not know how to ask for help, or float risks, or pick the next task, or determine that they're done with something. When this happens, some folks improve the process, using Agile principles; others may freeze or fall back on old habits. You can help the former establish the mechanisms, while taking the latter along for the ride.

Help your team discover their patterns of thought and behavior. Behavioral research has classified common patterns, such as analyzer, persuader, and relater.[6] Models also exist to identify people's psychological preferences, decision-making modes, and perceptual filters. Not everybody is aware of their patterns, and fewer still can accurately identify those of their teammates. These patterns play out in conversations and daily existence; the mere awareness of them can prevent many unnecessary confrontations and hurt feelings. Arrange for your team to take self-assessment tests together, then discuss the significance of those findings. However general the models are, they provide useful information (see 8.8).

Make sure to run proper iteration retrospectives, where everybody is free and welcome to talk, there's time to delve into valuable and/or difficult topics, and team members own the action items. Functional managers (bosses of any team member) should generally stay out of these retrospectives, unless they have a genuinely supporting relationship with the team. If your iterations run three weeks or longer, consider an additional, shorter reflection meeting midway through the iteration.

Besides actively encouraging self-organization, keep looking for factors in the team's environment that inhibit it. Ask yourself the following questions:

+ Is the group under any undue pressure? Have any temporary "crunch period" measures become the norm?

+ Are people demoralized?

+ Does the workspace hinder sharing, movement, or communication?

+ Do members have insufficient time to figure out their teamwork and process?

+ Are challenging attitudes and behaviors playing out (see 7.4, 7.5, and 7.6)?

+ Are team members' contributions not treated respectfully?

In its early stages, self-organization calls for reflection, discovery, experimentation, and introspection. It takes time, focus, and motivation. If you answered "yes" to any of the above questions, your team will probably *not* self-organize, but at least you'll know where to aim your efforts to get them started.

6.4.2 Encouraging Self-Organization on an Ongoing Basis

Self-organization is a process. It doesn't *end* even when the team graduates to the performing stage. You can still support this process, but now you need to *do* less and *notice* more.

Consider team sociology. Watch and listen carefully: How do people work with each other? How do they speak? How do meetings run? Where do people congregate? Pay particular attention to subgroups. Are there cliques? Who doesn't talk with whom? Are some people constantly shut out or left to handle simple tasks? Do a few people run the show while others acquiesce?

Well-functioning Agile teams have a *buzz*. The buzz is akin to a protracted dance or an ongoing conversation. It is the excitement of progress and the thrill of purpose. Storming and norming teams have no buzz yet. So what's missing from your team? What are you not seeing or hearing?

> "We take self-organization to the max. On good days, my job *rocks*. Sometimes, my favorite thing to do is just walk around, and you can just feel the energy; it's unbelievable. That's because it's so self-organizing; people care deeply about the product we're creating."
>
> — *Eugene Kiel, vice president at Cengage Learning*

Self-organization thrives when people take responsibility. Conversely, it suffers when coping mechanisms such as blaming (see 7.2) kick in. A coach told me once, "This team seems to *like* to have a manager to blame things on." If team members lay blame or offer justifications, what in their environment stimulates their actions? What is amiss in their dynamics?

Are you worried that if you allow self-organization, your team will make preventable mistakes? (They will.) This is a normal concern. When the inevitable happens and something goes wrong, you will probably feel quite anxious about *not* intervening or regretful about not preventing the error. If you believe that self-organization is worthwhile over the long term, acknowledge your feelings; don't fight them or beat yourself up. Notice your immediate response: Will it move you forward, or are your personal defense mechanisms kicking in? Both for the team's sake and for yours, develop the powerful habit of reframing "mistakes" or "failure" as opportunities for feedback that allow growth.

> "What if we allowed everyone to do something really stupid once a year and just forgave them? If we have 50 people, that averages out to one really stupid thing every week...."
>
> — *R. A., a manager*

> ***Supplementary resource***: Download "Help Your Team
> Self-Organize" from the book's companion website,
> **www.TheHumanSideOfAgile.com**.

6.4.3 To What Extent Can a Team Self-Organize?

If the above gives you the impression that every team can self-organize effectively when given enough support and freedom, it's time for a reality check.

Every team is naturally limited by their talents and abilities. A team can be perfectly suited for the work and still prefer that you tell them what to do and how to act. They might be content with whatever process you suggest or consider their cubicle farm to be a normal, sane arrangement. You might believe that moving to an open space would be a breath of fresh air, but they could see it as a source of angst and feel overwhelmed by it.

Every team is also limited by the organization in which they operate. For instance, an Agile team producing a complete stand-alone product can be more flexible than a team whose functional testing environments are never stable or one that has hard dependencies on other groups. Human dynamics in the organization, such as politics and dysfunction, can limit self-organization even more.

The extent to which every team organizes itself changes over time. With successes and failures, with natural and involuntary turnover, with changes in direction and technology, their adaptation will take different forms. If your team stands low on the self-organizing scale, take heart. If it's high on the scale, don't assume it will continue forever.

One result of self-organization is an increase in specializing generalists (see 4.3). While that's desirable from the perspective of team resilience and capability, members can feel conflicted. If everybody can contribute everywhere, they become less special and possibly perceived as interchangeable. If the company experiences financial trouble, the generalists might feel more expendable than the specialists. Help the team understand that extreme specialization is not the path to job security. Instead, it's their talents, competencies, and conduct that are important, because those give rise to *team* results. Play up opportunities in which someone holds the fort, speaks reliably for the team, or rises to the occasion.

6.5 When Should I Step In, and When Should I Step Back?

In self-organizing teams, even ones that have nominal leaders, it's *everyone's* responsibility to participate in leading the team: this is the essence of shared leadership. It is not the exclusive duty of the formal ATL or the coach. Moreover, it is not the manager's role to fix all the problems; many problems belong *to the team*. When teams willfully own their problems and solve them, they grow stronger. That is your motivation for stepping back.

If you're a parent, you have seen this. If you regularly intervene on your kids' behalf, they either come to you with issues before trying to solve them on their own, or they resist your help and resent you for it. However, if you allow them room to resolve their issues with your optional guidance, they will develop personal responsibility and healthy learning habits. Your team is not a bunch of kids, and you are not their parent, but they *are* human beings. As such, they like to have a safe framework with understood (or understandable) rules of engagement.

As their leader, set the framework — the envelope for their work — and let them get on with it. Make sure everybody knows that you're there for them if they need you but that you won't tell them what to do. That designates you as their servant leader.

You need to monitor the goings-on and pay particular attention to their decisions. If you think you must intervene, ask for permission to make a suggestion or act on their behalf. Some teams will welcome a lot of help when figuring out how to move forward, whether due to technical disagreement, process immaturity, or team dynamics.

If the situation turns bad, you might fly in and save the day. Before you do that, *pause*. Ask yourself two questions:

1. "Is winning the battle worth possibly losing the war?"

2. "Am I worried that their results mean bad leadership or performance on my part?"

If you feel confident about your team and trust them to do their work, they will sense that and respect you for it. If they understand that you step back *deliberately* in order to help them grow, they will respect you more than if you just solved their problems. However, if your confidence and trust are not genuine and you swoop in at the first sign of trouble, you will lose their respect, and they will lose the chance to learn and grow.

Many issues are not truly urgent or critical. A mistake may result in learning that improves long-term results.[7] Both teams and individuals grow stronger and more resilient as they work their way through problems. If they sailed smoothly through the first few months of a project, they would probably be less prepared to respond well to later disasters or upheavals.

Ten years ago I was leading an in-house development team. One afternoon, I was checking a data migration script and accidentally ran it on the production database instead of the test database. I spent the evening cleaning up my mistake. The next day, I got the team together, and we made a rule: "If you're going to touch any database, someone from the team will pair up with you." (Notice how this rule obliges a second person to act in the team's interest.) It was *our* process and *our* decision; no external manager told us how to mitigate our risk.

If the team experiences a problem and you let them work it out, take these three actions:

1. If they (or others) perceive a failure, help them reframe failure as an opportunity for feedback.

2. If they are taking corrective action and appear to learn from the problem, play up their response. If necessary, make sure they are forgiven.

3. Follow up on their responses and learning.

As an ATL (or any type of manager) who is serving the team while being beholden to higher-ups, expect to feel uneasy stepping back. That's how it is for servant leaders. If you do step in, do so gently. Do not immediately fix the problem for the team. Coach them by asking questions that ignite discovery and creativity. Give caring feedback and avoid judgment or evaluation.

6.6 Should Team Members Work in Pairs?

The first Agile method to include the practice of *pair programming* was eXtreme Programming[8] (XP) in the late 1990s. The practice remains controversial to this day, and it is among the reasons XP has enjoyed limited popularity. In its generalized form, *pairing*, team members pair among themselves on most project work. It is an extreme form of collaboration — a core Agile principle — intended to expand options, foster creativity, and yield better solutions.

Pairing means two people collaborating on a task and being equally responsible for the results. Sounds simple, but it is widely misunderstood. Individual contributors have told me, "I don't want to work with someone watching over my shoulder." Managers have asked me, "Why should I have two people do work that one person can do?" Both falsely assumed that if a single competent person can perform a task — true for much of software development — adding another

person is a waste of the latter's time. This thinking is a natural corol-
lary of the attitude that people are resources and that maximum team
performance results from maximizing individual contributions.

The point of pairing is to *mitigate the risks of being human,* even
bright and competent ones. As long as we have people — not
robots — developing software, we are exposed to *human risks.* These
include fatigue, tunnel vision, and misunderstanding objectives;
not realizing the effect of actions; having preconceived solutions;
missing details; and getting stuck. When those humans are experts,
the risks also include idiosyncratic artifacts, reduced innovation
and communication, solving a bigger problem than necessary, and
limited sharing of expertise.

> "Pairing is the most powerful managerial tool I've ever
> discovered."
>
> — *Richard Sheridan, CEO, Menlo Innovations*

One notable risk mitigated by pairing is that people avoid certain
tasks or quit them prematurely. For instance, most programmers practice little or no test-driven development (TDD) and barely refactor
their code. Yet if they regularly work in pairs, programmers are less
inclined to cut corners on good practice. They want to look good to
their pairing partner, their partner encourages them, or they feel more
confident working together.

In many teams, I have observed developers sometimes "sit" on a
task, unsure of how to proceed or making little progress. After a while,
they would muster the courage to ask a teammate for assistance. The
two leading reasons for their reluctance to ask for help were fear of

looking bad and insecurity about their competence. *Making pairing the norm eliminated the unease about being helped.*

I no longer consider pairing an obligatory practice. I help *all* my teams build the collaboration muscle, but for many, regular pairing is simply not in the cards. They might make a half-hearted attempt, but the struggle and frustration are not worth it. If they ask me, "Can we just agree that we'll consult each other when we see the need?" I just let it go. I can safely assume the team will not embrace pairing.

However, if your team is open to close collaboration, the team-wide, daily practice of pairing can take their performance to the next level. They will realize substantial and sometimes surprising gains in satisfaction, skill mastery, individual growth, and team resilience. They might also benefit from reducing activities that don't add customer value: pairing often abolishes code reviews and facilitates code integration.

Before you raise the subject with them, consider probable resistance and plan accordingly. Typical grounds for push-back include individual objectives, silos, uncomfortable working arrangements, and a misunderstanding of the value of pairing.

Help your team realize that pairing is a conversation about a task, not code syntax checking in real time. Explain the etiquette of pairing. Instead of giving a presentation on pair programming, do short stints of pairing with various individuals to give them a reference experience, after which you debrief them. Remind them that pairs are not joined at the hip; "alone time" is still fine for some tasks or for some hours in the day.

Pairing spells a substantial change to daily experience. Expect the chaos period of the change curve (see 11.1) to last several weeks. Unless the team is enthusiastic about the prospect, treat it as an experiment (see 13.4).

Have pairs switch at least once daily. According to my experience and some research,[9] results are better with even more frequent switching. However, that's cause for another kind of resistance: programmers have an almost-universal belief that describing their progress and thoughts to others takes at least an hour. You can vanquish this largely unfounded belief if your team is used to small tasks.

Remember: pairing is a *team* practice. The team will need to establish agreements about switching, the type of tasks that require pairing, and availability in order to integrate it. If someone is uncomfortable with pairing, that's a team issue. If it's not fully practiced, use alternatives for risk mitigation.

Even when pairing is a team norm, people naturally pair up with those they are more comfortable or familiar with. Before long, cliques may form: subgroups who only pair among themselves. If you can't break up the cliques gently, get the team to make an agreement that has the same effect.

Supplementary resource: Download "Pairing Booster" from the book's companion website, **www.TheHumanSideOfAgile.com**.

6.7 Which Tools Should We Use?

Agile pioneers promoted simple solutions for noncoding needs: index cards and sticky notes for planning, hand-drawn posters for radiating information, sitting together for easy communication. These days, teams have access to a staggering array of software for any project-related need. Tool vendors are quick to describe amazing productivity gains.

All my clients have asked me, "Which Agile planning tool should we get?" and "Where should we store artifacts?" These questions presuppose acquiring a software tool and that you only need to compare options. Even when you must use some tools (for instance, in geographically distributed teams), know that they affect their users more deeply than you think. Ask yourself the following questions before acquiring them.

How will our users respond emotionally? Professionals get emotionally attached to their tools. (Just observe hard-core Unix programmers react to the suggestion that they replace "vi" with a modern editor.) They are comfortable with their tools and use them effectively. Replacing a tool with a supposedly better one might evoke discomfort, fear, or even a sense of betrayal.

Can we adapt the tool to our needs, or will we need to adapt our process to the tool? Many new practitioners discover that their process adaptation doesn't sit well with the planning tool they rolled out to great fanfare. The result: complaining and grinding teeth, changing the process to make the tool happy, or ditching it for another one. Agile testers report similar misfortunes with testing tools.

Will folks use it enough to justify a rollout? I've observed several teams go from paper-based to software-based planning, only to revert soon thereafter. The reason? After iteration planning, nobody bothered using the software! Team members simply didn't want to click multiple places and wait for screens to load. I've observed similar recalcitrance with tools requiring complex setup (e.g., Java profilers). And many users don't bother learning their tool's productivity potential: some Java developers use Eclipse only as a text editor, and some Outlook/Notes users use those tools only for email.

What effects will the tool have beyond immediate productivity increases? The best tools increase productivity as well as improve habits and open up possibilities for further improvements. For instance, I'm a big fan of certain Java and C# development environments because they automate away much of the repetition, waiting, and mechanical work involved in TDD and refactoring. These tools allow me to focus on the important and interesting elements of my code and design, which facilitates solving the right problem. Other tools have the opposite effect. In many teams, story management tools have become the de facto communication medium between the product owner and the delivery team, to the detriment of conversations and human contact.

Can we use simpler means? Some tools solve your problem and then some. For instance, many co-located teams merely need a whiteboard and sticky notes to plan and track their work. A notebook and pen still work well, even for people who tote smartphones and tablets. And sometimes, people turn to tools to solve the wrong problem.[10] Remember, Agile advocates simplicity.

Is now a good time? The new tool's users will experience a temporary drop in productivity until they master the tool sufficiently (see 11.1). You might need to delay the rollout if you can't afford that chaos period quite yet.

6.8 How Soon Can the Team Become Really Good?

As the Tuckman model predicts, the team needs to go through three stages before you can expect high performance from them. Along the way, their performance will drop for a while, which might make you wonder whether the Agile team thing was a good idea. Or you might not even notice. I've heard people say they got better performance from unnormed teams using a mediocre Agile implementation than from teams using their regular plan-driven process.

Suppose you have established a proper team (chapter 4), they play well together (chapter 5), and they experience no difficult behaviors (chapter 7). They grow as an Agile team. If you are a great servant leader and performing your responsibilities well, expect the path to high performance to take at least a month, more likely two.

The previous paragraph made many assumptions. Your reality is probably not so rosy. Many teams spend far longer in the storming and norming stages. If they are under the pressure of an aggressive schedule, they are likely to revert to nonteam behaviors, each person doing his or her own thing. They might spin and thrash in norming. Reaching the performing stage — if it even happens — can take a year or more.

And ... there is a catch. Over the course of 6 to 12 months, the composition of the team may change. Perhaps another manager has dire need of your star developer. Perhaps you added people to the team because they were not moving fast enough (after all, they never made it to the performing stage). Or maybe some team members wanted to try their luck with a better-functioning team elsewhere. All these changes can knock a team down to storming or norming, where they may stay for weeks.

For that reason, Agile and Lean methods emphasize the stability of teams. Rather than *push* a project onto a specially formed team (in matrix management style), have standing teams that *pull* work from a central prioritized queue. Not all teams can select any piece of work, but this approach forces them to become more adaptive and generalist, which builds organizational muscle. And when team members stay together, starting and finishing whole pieces together, they have the time — and the chance — to reach the performing stage and reap its benefits. This in turn increases motivation and staff retention rates, which improves aggregate staff performance.

True Agility remains an elusive target for many teams. Some managers, unaware of the nature of team evolution, attempt to rush it. Unfamiliar with, anxious about, and possibly leery of self-organization, they do not let their teams experience necessary growing pains. But with continuous, diligent, and sensitive action, you can help your team evolve into a strong *Agile* team.

Supplementary Resources
Go to **www.TheHumanSideOfAgile.com** and download "Help Your Team Self-Organize" and "Pairing Booster."

CHAPTER 7

Manage Behaviors
That Derail Teams

A s an intelligent, capable person, you appreciate working with others who are also intelligent and capable. But the picture is not always so simple or rosy — every person has quirks, behaviors, and attitudes that can be challenging. The highly collaborative, people-first Agile framework may magnify their effect to the point of derailing the team.

7.1 What Can I Do About Emotional Behavior?

Observe any meeting or conversation in the workplace, and you'll notice that people talk about more than their work. Colleagues who share goals and responsibilities often reveal some of their personal history and aspirations. However, the one topic most folks avoid discussing is emotions. Unless they feel safe, they are not likely to express private hopes, frustration, passion, confusion, or guilt, or admit that they are feeling overwhelmed. The same avoidance extends to providing feedback to another person who is behaving emotionally.

You cannot afford to ignore your emotions or other people's. Everybody has them, even those who don't appear to. No matter how rational we believe people can be, feelings drive most of their actions. Emotions kick in both when people's needs are satisfied and when they are not — in other words, constantly. People have emotional reactions in any life cycle and methodology. While Agile makes these emotions harder to hide, it offers mechanisms to help address the problems: standups and retrospectives, coaching and facilitation.

Emotions play a role in an internal process:

stimulus ➡ emotion ➡ action

First, you sense something internally or receive an external stimulus: you hear something, such as an alarm going off or your phone ringing, or you see something, such as your frowning manager. Subsequently, an emotion is triggered inside you. Your subconscious mind takes in the emotion and automatically chooses your action based on your state, the context, and your entire self (preferences and patterns of behavior). In some cases, that choice will be to transfer control to your conscious mind for a deliberate decision.

Some folks don't acknowledge their feelings effectively, which can lead them to out-of-range reactions. Long ago, I was managing a team in which two members didn't get along. Both considered themselves highly intelligent and competent. Each one constantly interpreted the other one's actions (the stimuli) as one-upmanship or personal affronts, and each felt slighted. The resultant behaviors included avoidance, extra competitiveness, and even a screaming match.

The following are the four negative emotions that I detect most often in software development communities and that explain some of the behaviors we see:

Inadequacy, triggered by difficulties in performing tasks. Feelings of inadequacy are the inner critic saying, "I'm not up to this job" and "What else will I discover that I can't do?!" A person who is feeling inadequate might keep silent, complicate matters, or avoid sharing until their part is done.

Frustration, triggered when expectations or needs are not being met. Expectations can include anything from leaving work early today to receiving a bonus next month. The frustrated person closes up or overcompensates, choosing other ways to satisfy the unfulfilled expectations.

Insecurity, triggered by a perception of vulnerability. A person might consider himself adequate and competent and still feel that others (team members or managers) are judging his actions and performance. The insecure person will surround himself with invisible walls to avoid stepping on others' toes, stay away from conflict, and not allow himself to look stupid or be hurt.

Fear, triggered by a perceived threat. Even if you take the best care of your team and protect them like a mother hen, they might still experience fear. The most common fear is of losing one's job and not finding another. Members of jelled teams might be afraid of their team being disbanded. Fear gives rise to playing it safe, which suppresses risk taking and innovation.

All emotions are valid. A person's emotions are part of his or her makeup and you cannot, and should not, attempt to change them. Advice like "Don't be afraid to…" or "You should feel happy that…" or "There's no point feeling frustrated about…" cannot help unless the listener is truly open to changing and has invited such assistance. Stronger exhortations, such as "Shape up!" and "Others are doing it, why can't you?" are likely to backfire.

Not all behaviors are valid. Expect people on your team to behave within an acceptable range. The range is a matter for the team and the organization to decide, although they rarely articulate it explicitly. For example, my team didn't have a rule about screaming matches, but our conversations after one happened clarified that they lay outside the range.

You can and should ask people to manage their *emotional reactions.* The best way to do that is to offer feedback and teach them how to take feedback.[1] This is *hard.* Not only is effective feedback on emotional reactions difficult to give, but you may have never seen someone do it well, and you don't get many chances to practice. Be extremely sensitive to the other person and how she would take your guidance. Provide only high-value feedback and let some things slide, otherwise you'll engender resistance.

Although you may have the best intentions or the positional authority to do it, never attempt to change or "fix" someone. Even if you could, it is not your responsibility to change someone's character, and it is socially irresponsible to do so. Emotions are too ingrained; they belong to their owners, who need to work through them on their own. You can, though, coach those who welcome your help to manage the transition from emotion to behavior, because they need to function effectively on the team.

Emotional behavior does not have to be loud or unsettling. I was transitioning a team to Scrum, and they seemed to take well to it. Planning sprint 4 took a long time, and at the end I asked them, "The tally of the stories' point estimates seems to be in the ballpark of our assumed velocity. Can you commit to that?"

I didn't hear a yes. I didn't hear a no. Absolute silence. People looked down at their shoes. Further prompting resulted in continued silence.

What would you do in this case?

When faced with counterproductive behavior that requires your feedback, you can address either the symptom (the behavior) or the underlying cause (the emotion and its supporting set of values and beliefs).

Addressing the symptom is the more obvious, familiar, and seemingly safe way to go. The team is silent? Remind them of the rules. Address each person individually. Say, in your best Scrum headmaster voice, "Well, we'll have to restart planning!" Remind them of their empowerment and that, before Agile, they wouldn't even have been consulted. Be warned that these approaches are not always helpful.

Addressing the underlying cause is something else entirely. People won't readily admit to feeling insecure or inadequate. Even when they do, their admission won't solve anything. They need to shift internally, to adopt empowering beliefs and values, in order to behave productively. That takes time, courage, and motivation. Coach them gently.

> I sensed some anxiety in the team and guessed that it had to do with the number of planned stories. So I turned to a member who had demonstrated leadership before and asked, "Do you think this plan is too big?" She nodded. We reduced the plan, and the team went back to work quietly. Their mood picked up as the days passed, and they were on track to achieving the sprint's goal.

When a person or a team undergoes change, they pass through a period of confusion and chaos (see 11.1). You can expect all four emotions — inadequacy, frustration, insecurity, and fear — to be present during that period. Even though its duration is limited, the strength of the emotions (and their contagious nature[2]) might derail the change.

Unhelpful emotions can also be triggered occasionally and briefly. When that happens, the remedies are fairly straightforward: get help from a team member, air those feelings in a conversation, or switch activities.

It is when some of these unproductive feelings are constantly present that you have a serious problem. This is the time to consider the person's fit with the team and the organizational culture.

7.2 How Should I Deal With Coping Mechanisms?

For every person, sooner or later, something will go wrong. For instance, someone may be extremely reluctant to take a needed action. His modes of navigating social interactions might land him in hot water. He may not be able to adequately handle a situation. The best thing he could do is *to take responsibility*: to *respond* to the situation with an action that moves him and the situation forward.

Unfortunately, not all people do that all the time. What you will see more often are attempts to absolve oneself of responsibility. These habitual mechanisms kick in to help the person *cope* with the situation. Here are the coping mechanisms a person is most likely to exhibit:[3]

Denial (repression). The person pretends the problem doesn't exist. Shockingly, intelligent adults do this all the time.

> In a consultation once, a development manager told me, "We have no schedule problem here. We ship most of our versions on time." His VP, also present in the conversation, retorted, "Where have you *been*? Our last release was a year late. *A year*. We just kept pushing the schedule back!"

Blaming (displacement). The person identifies something or someone else as the source of her trouble: "We couldn't even start testing that user story for a whole week. There were build failures all week, and the developers did nothing to get the continuous integration server back on track."

Justifying. The situation is to blame: "It was like this when I got here. Why are you picking on me now?" Or, that's just how other people are: "Of course we were late, we knew we couldn't trust so-and-so to keep up his end."

Being super-reasonable. Relying on logic and objectivity, the person approaches the situation like a litigator, removing herself and others from the equation: "Given our backlog and the expectation of ten story points per developer, we won't ship on time. To meet our May 2nd deadline, everyone will have to work 70 hours per week until then."

Shaming oneself. The person beats himself up: "I should have known that this construct wouldn't work on Internet Explorer 7. I'm such an idiot." Or, "I can't be the ScrumMaster again. I messed up badly last time." To make up for the perceived deficiency, he might overcompensate: "My tests didn't expose this showstopper defect in the Analyzer module. Next iteration, I'm going to attack the Analyzer a hundred different ways so *nothing* will escape me!"

Obligation. The person attributes her actions to someone else's decisions: "As a developer, when a customer support ticket comes in, I have to drop everything and address it. I don't have a choice." Whole teams can feel obligated: "One day, management came in and said we're starting to do Agile." A feeling of obligation can lead to compulsive behavior.

Diffuse these behaviors quickly because they are contagious. When someone pretends to be obliged to act, blames others for omissions, or checks out, it is easier for others to behave that way as well. One "bad apple" does spoil the bunch, because people take behavioral cues from their social environment. Nip it in the bud.

As you were reading the list, did you find yourself self-assessing? Do *you* also employ those coping mechanisms in some situations? You do, because you're human. You can never be evolved enough, *ever*, for them not to apply to you. However, personal growth and increased self-awareness will reduce their incidence (see 8.8).

A simple, quick way to reduce your defensive or coping behavior is to *catch yourself*. Notice when you are behaving in unhelpful ways, then trace the behavior back to your emotions. Are your buttons being pushed? Are you feeling less than useful? What's going on? Then, in your own private space, come up with better responses, which you can then practice or rehearse before the next time (see 3.5).

Once you have raised your awareness and established your internal feedback loop for responsibility, help your team the same way. Both in a team setting and one on one, guide them in discovering the meaning and manifestation of responsibility. Show them the list of coping stances, play with examples, and help them grasp how those stances are less than helpful. Discuss Christopher Avery's Responsibility Process[4] with the team and then hang a printed copy in the team space to serve as a constant reminder.

7.3 How Can I Get Through to Quiet People?

Almost every team I've ever coached included one or more quiet members. Those are the people who work at their desks all day and rarely strike up a conversation with others; who answer the three questions at the standup when their turn comes but don't engage others as they speak; who provide data and observations during planning meetings only if asked.

The quiet people I've met tended to be solid contributors. They were generally introverts — people who derive energy from internal rather than external dialogue.[5] Having one or two quiet people on a team isn't necessarily a problem. After a few months with their team, they are likely to be well integrated.

When several team members are quiet and prefer working solo, though, many Agile mechanisms start breaking down.

I once observed a retrospective that lasted all of three minutes! The dominant product owner spoke first, soliciting the development manager's agreement that the iteration had gone well. The database specialist disagreed. The development manager signaled the end of the retrospective by saying, "No, I think it was just fine." The rest of the team was silent during this exchange, apparently just waiting it out.

The team in this story missed an opportunity to improve their process and relationships; planning is affected the same way. In several Agility assessments I've conducted, I observed a few programmers and testers sitting quietly through meetings, speaking only when they were spoken to.

You need to assess whether and how the withdrawn members pose an impediment to the team's performance. Are they affecting the sociology, the well-being, or the resilience of the team? If so, the best technique is to have one-on-one conversations with them. Even though the team is affected, this matter does not belong in a retrospective. You must respect their privacy and never embarrass them. Another technique is to persistently call on them in team meetings to offer their opinions. For instance, the manager in the story could have polled the members, asking each one, "How would you characterize this iteration?" This technique is useful only to the extent that members feel safe expressing themselves in this forum, however.

Some people simply talk very little. Others are extreme introverts, preferring to be mostly on their own and to gather energy from their inner world. For others, the quiet demeanor is *contextual* behavior: it can be changed, if only in specific contexts. In your one-on-ones, use techniques from chapter 8. Consider the following as you hold these conversations:

Is the behavior a response to not fitting in? First check whether they want to work on the team. What motivates them to be on the team, to use Agile, and to work on the particular product? Then be discreet, patient, and respectful as you explore their fit with the team. What has been their experience with the team and the organization so far? Are any disempowering emotions (see 7.1 and 7.2) causing them to withdraw from the team?

Is it a holdover? A nonparticipating attitude might be a holdover from many years of working in an environment driven by detailed plans and controlling managers. You may have to reiterate that successful Agile teams are empowered and self-organizing, so waiting to be told what to do next is in neither the person's nor the team's interest.

Is it their background? Today's teams include people with vastly disparate cultural heritages. Even when operating within an atmosphere of openness, some people defer to senior colleagues or avoid appearing contrarian. But is that response helpful in the team? No person is merely a victim of his upbringing; a supportive environment can do wonders to ease people out of their shell.

Is it a matter of language? Is English — or your team's official language — not their first language? Expressing oneself sensibly and fluently and understanding fast-talking natives are often the highest hurdles in language acquisition, which is already hard enough for adults. Your quiet team members, who are likely talented and accomplished professionals, might feel extra self-conscious about expressing themselves in team forums.

Can they afford to make mistakes? If the organization makes them pay for mistakes — especially in reputation or stature — any initiative would be high risk. Do they play it safe by agreeing to whatever you or the rest of the team decide?

Do they feel valuable and important? Each team member is important and necessary. But with Agile's emphasis on team commitment, team consensus, and team responsibility, it is easy to make the opposite interpretation. If members don't believe they add value or don't feel important, keeping quiet and withdrawn would be an expected behavior.

Do they appreciate the consequences? The team may produce great product and value, show progress, and celebrate accomplishments, but the quiet, withdrawn folks can be left behind. Suggest to them that the more they contribute to discussions, planning, reviews, and teamwork, the more their mark will be felt.

7.4 What If a Talented Team Member Treats Colleagues With Contempt?

A product was a few weeks away from release when management decided to have the client and server teams merge and use Agile practices. The server code was in good shape, but the client code was a buggy legacy mess. Since considerable work remained, their manager announced they would increase the iteration budget (velocity) by putting in an additional hour or two every day. The star server developer got very upset and blurted out: "You mean I should work longer because my team is stupid?!"

The move from a manager-driven, individual-based process to a team-based, collaborative Agile one implicitly assumes that the team can work through their conflicts and challenges. Perhaps with a lot of guidance, perhaps taking longer than hoped for, they will eventually graduate to the norming stage (see 6.1) and even get as far as performing. This expectation, in turn, relies on another hidden assumption: that the members *agree* to be part of the team.

This assumption held for most of the teams I've coached to date. Having joined their companies voluntarily, these professionals naturally accepted the need to work together. Yet they had no say in determining their team's composition, nor did they necessarily agree with management's decision to hire some of the members. A few teams had members who didn't want the "responsibility" of being teammates with others, whom they considered inept.

All employees have opinions about their colleagues. They might share those opinions with you in order to improve the team's and company's performance, or they might do so to appear in a better light. Discussing their observations with you privately and respectfully is acceptable. If they are pointing out a true area of concern, that information can be useful.

It's another matter, though, if one team member harasses or bullies another. If she pretends he doesn't exist, disparages his contribution, or dismisses him, you must resolve this problem forthwith. You must block uncivil behavior to ensure the safety of the team environment. This isn't just a conflict between two people; the entire team is aware of it, and their performance suffers for it. The problem belongs to you and to the parties' managers, and you should all work together to resolve this situation as early as possible.

7.5 How Can I Handle Negative Attitudes?

Have team members ever told you that one of their colleagues "has a negative attitude"? Or have you perhaps had that thought yourself? Negative attitudes on Agile teams include the following:

✦ The **cynic** never quite appreciates the positive and the authentic.

✦ The **hostage** does the job but clearly doesn't want to work on the team and play by the Agile rules. She wants to be left alone and gives off a feeling of being a hostage or victim of circumstance.

✦ The **fault-finder** finds fault in everything and everybody (but doesn't stoop to harassing or bullying specific people).

✦ The **naysayer** shoots everything down, doesn't hold much hope for the future, and isn't willing to experiment.

Negative attitudes pose a high-priority impediment to the team's performance. Since a team's performance correlates to its level of collaboration, self-organization, and communication, the effect of one bad apple is much stronger than in a traditional, manager-run environment.

One team's members were fairly tolerant of their gruff, cynical, passive-aggressive senior colleague. One iteration planning day he was working from home and didn't dial into the meeting. That meeting turned out to be a smooth and pleasant exercise in collaborative planning, quite different from their usual experience. They kept marveling about it a few days thereafter.

If someone says that a colleague is a *negative person*, let that be a red flag for you. This act of labeling is very risky, because most folks only need to observe a behavior two or three times before they generalize from it. As a leader, give the person the benefit of the doubt and assume that his negative behavior is situational: Is he having a health problem? Is he experiencing problems at home? Is he negative only in specific situations? If all the answers to these questions are "no," and if the negativity is a recurrent pattern of behavior, the person might not be a good fit with the team. In that case, the relationship with him needs to change.

One of the determinants of behavior is a person's emotions. The behavior you observe stems from underlying negative or disempowering feelings. If you've established the fit between the person and the team or the organization, then his feelings indicate a problem in the team or the organization. So don't just tell him to act all cheery; he feels what he feels, and denying those feelings is pointless — and probably a bad idea.

Use the techniques in chapter 8 to explore the situation and uncover the improperly manifested grains of truth in an authentic and helpful way. You'll discover valuable information for the project and possibly help the person realize what has been going on with him. For instance, in a conversation with an analyst who'd been finding fault with his team, I uncovered a deep dissonance: "We've built our brand on high-caliber results, but on this project we don't walk our talk. We keep producing poor code because we just never say no to our client's demands."

Once you understand the person's underlying concerns, point out the effect of his behavior on his teammates, and ask him to moderate it. You should also help design the environment and team situations so the feeling isn't triggered anymore, and consequently the behavior goes away. Depending on the attitude, that might happen at the team level (as with naysayers), the personal level (as with hostages), or at the management level (as with the aforementioned analyst).

7.6 What Can I Do About Overbearing or Aggressive Team Members?

Jay has been on his team for two years. A skilled developer, he has participated in the product's early design. Whenever the team starts planning or designing, Jay makes his opinion heard. He dismisses others' input, always seems to know what's right and what's going to work, and is particularly short with new members. His colleagues consider him a valuable team member, but they are quick to describe him as a know-it-all who gets in their face.

An Agile team that's all Jays is most unlikely; such a team would be a reflection of a corporate culture that's probably ill-fitted for Agile.

The more common case is to have just one or two such Jays on a team. If your team is like that, ask yourself: How is this a problem for the team? Are their performance and resilience degraded somehow? In other words, don't deal with this situation before making sure that the overbearing, aggressive, or dominant behavior is a true impediment, not simply something that disturbs you personally.

If you decide to deal with team members who act like Jay, separate their content from delivery. You might bristle at their delivery; for instance, if they speak their minds with brutal honesty. But is their content — the substance of their message — valuable? Does it open up opportunities for improvement?

You should nip aggressive behavior in the bud, because it can alter the team's culture undesirably. The easiest tool for that is neutralization tactics. For instance, if a loud team member dominates meetings and doesn't let others talk, use a "talking stick" — only the person holding the talking stick may speak. Or incorporate more silent work (see 9.4) in the design for team meetings. Neutralization tactics address the symptom in the short term, but I doubt their long-term value. They do not change attitudes or motivation, and they do nothing to channel the person's energy.

As in other cases of unhelpful behavior, the better approach is to have one-on-one conversations with the offender. Prepare yourself for these conversations and use the techniques from chapter 8. Be ready for the case where the overbearing or aggressive behavior is aimed at you.

You might discover that the offender is not aware of his behavior. Since almost all behavior is subconscious and rooted in patterns, people stop noticing it (even more so when the behavior has a cultural background).

As you think of an overbearing team member, you probably imagine the underlying reasons for his behavior. For instance, you might assume that dominant behavior results from a drive for power. If you're correct, that person will probably not work well in an Agile environment. But if you approach the person with an open mind and empathy, you could discover other reasons:

+ He doesn't feel valued or heard, and he makes up for it by being aggressive.

+ He is masking his own insecurities and fears. (What does he stand to lose?)

+ He wants to belong, so he positions himself centrally in important discussions.

Accepting another person's reality (or "model of the world") goes a long way. If you come into the conversation truly welcoming the other's truth, whatever it might be, you may defuse the behavior.

If none of this helps, you may just have to reassign the person to a different team or facilitate his departure from the company.

7.7 What If a Member Doesn't Fit With the Team?

Agile development is not right for all software professionals. If you are bringing Agile into a siloed company accustomed to plan-driven methods, expect that 10% to 15% of the people will not fit.

In my experience, individuals might not fit with their newly Agile team for one or more of these reasons:

+ They strongly prefer to work alone, not as team members.

+ They would rather develop their specialties than shoulder miscellaneous team activities.

+ They prefer to implement other people's plans and designs and don't want to make any high-impact decisions.

+ They feel that the Agile methodology sets them up for failure because it doesn't mandate the detailed planning and up-front design they associate with responsible development practice.

+ They are willing to go along with the Agile methodology but feel that their particular team is not up to the job, which will reflect badly on them.

Some of these folks express their displeasure quietly, doing their best to mitigate the risks they perceive. They work hard, intent on demonstrating their own performance according to pre-Agile criteria. Others resist openly, advocating a return to the trusted old ways. (Some might even act up, like the senior developer in section 7.4 who exclaimed that his team was stupid.) Some attempt to influence their managers to modify the team's process. A small percentage — sensing the company's new direction — may even quit.

If someone doesn't fit in a siloed team, you could assign special work to her, have her sit separately, or have her communicate mostly with you. However, in an empowered, collaborative team environment, the fit problems affect her and the team a lot more. The team struggles to self-organize, to make commitments, and to hold each other accountable. As the Agile team leader, you have to be involved a lot more. It doesn't take much for team members to become rancorous about the "problem child" getting special treatment while they are expected to do whatever it takes to succeed.

You might have some success educating, encouraging, or cajoling these folks to make the effort and play on their team. If they are good performers and have integrity, and if you do not want to lose them, you should give them a chance. Their resistance might be temporary, an artifact of the chaos period of the change curve (see 11.1). Still, be watchful, and don't let it drag out.

"Let's say that we have somebody who has a performance issue and is unable to carry his own weight. The team carries his weight; everybody assumes that they *have* to carry his weight because they work as a team. That can go on for months before anything is done about it. Maybe Agile does not work for everybody, yet those for whom it doesn't work still remain on the team, and the team is supposed to still self-organize. Then we have morale issues. What ends up happening is that team members stay around eight to nine months longer than they ever should have. All the input others and I have for management appears to fall on deaf ears, because people strongly believe that since they are in an Agile team, *they should stay in that team.*"

— *Brenda, a project manager*

As Brenda's story shows, toughing it out may not only fail to work, it can even hurt a lot of people. Apart from reducing the team's performance, unresolved fit problems demoralize them. Sometimes, redeploying people can be a win for all involved, which means management must be part of any response.

All too often the person in question has highly valued skills, domain knowledge, or technical expertise. You and the team may feel that removing the person would hurt the team's ability to produce required deliverables. In the short term, that might actually be the case. However, when the teams that I've known had such a member depart, they quickly regrouped and made up for the loss. The combination of relief, improved interactions, and rapid cross-training helped them improve performance beyond expectations.

You may be tempted to give people a second chance, and a third chance, and even a fourth. If you are like most of the managers I've met, you don't want to hurt the person or lose their contribution. You must clearly realize the detrimental effect on the team of having that person there, or that the status quo may not be good for the unhappy person, either. For your own peace of mind and a level-headed decision, seek someone to coach you or discuss possible courses of action with you.

Your team is made up of *people*. Unlike resources, such as pencils and computers, they do not behave dispassionately and predictably. You probably wish they did (but then your role would be redundant). Since individual behaviors can derail an entire Agile team, you cannot afford to limit your role to process control and mechanics. You must support all members in managing their conduct for greater team synergy. That takes considerable skill, willingness, and confidence. While the necessary conversations are never easy, the effect on the team's eventual success is priceless.

PART III
Engage People in Powerful Conversations

With Parts I and II under your belt, you have a solid Agile development community where work is progressing nicely. Unfortunately, this is not a stable state. A development community is made up of people, whose constant communication is critical for sustained results and teamwork. Their communication is not always effective, and in fact some aspects of it tend to go awry in predictable ways, causing suboptimal results and souring relationships. Part III introduces practical communication skills —in both one-on-one and group settings — that you and your team ought to master. Studying and practicing these techniques takes time, which is well worth your investment. They will help you engage people in powerful, effective conversations that strengthen relationships and get results.

CHAPTER 8

Master Your Communication

Your smartphone dings to signal the arrival of an email. Upon seeing its title, "Build #452 failed," your stress level doubles. You approach Rae, a talented developer, and say, in a slightly ticked-off tone, "I notice the build broke."

Rae: "I know. It broke many times this week."

You: "Well, aren't you guys doing something about it?"

Rae: "We tried to fix it, but it's due to an ugly dependency. It will take some time."

You: "Failing builds are not cool; you know that. They make us look irresponsible."

Rae, not sure how to escape the situation, mumbles, "OK."

This brief dialogue, a possible one of hundreds taking place daily in the workplace, is an example of ineffective communication.

Workplace communication is vital for progress. It supports information sharing, decision making, collaborating, teaching, coordinating, and the like. Instead of being direct and effective, many instances of communication are fraught with misinterpretation and discomfort.[1] But you can change that. You are responsible for your end of the conversation, and in order to carry it effectively, you'd do well to build your *communication mastery*.

8.1 What Are the Levels of Communication Mastery?

Basic communication is an exchange of messages over a medium. Since you exchange those messages *with another human being*, there are multiple levels of communication mastery above the mere uttering or writing of words. Each level builds atop previous ones and enriches the exchange. As your mastery grows, you and the other party draw ever more value from the exchange and strengthen your relationship. The good news is that each level involves the application of fully learnable tools and skills. Indeed, whole bookshelves and courses are dedicated to this subject. This chapter introduces the tools that have served me well at each level, such as rapport, deliberate language, and precision questions.

Level 1: Respect the interaction and the other person. If you do so, you reduce the chances that the conversation will get off track. Great tools for this level are active listening and rapport.

Level 2: Communicate on the same wavelength. Even if you share the same cultural background and language, you don't necessarily have the same mental representations of the same objects. While you don't need to bend your mind to the other person's preferences, you do need to choose your language deliberately and phrase your messages carefully so she hears what you mean.

Level 3: Collect precise information. Think back to Rae's words, "The build broke many times this week." While not a lie, the statement is not an accurate verbalization of her underlying thoughts or beliefs. She could have meant:

✦ "The build broke more than once this week."

✦ "I'm tired of trying to fix the build."

✦ "Other people aren't careful with their check-ins."

Furthermore, if you heard those same words from a colleague of Rae's, he would probably mean something different. Taking such statements at face value might cause ill will, misunderstanding, and conversational dead-ends. To collect precise information, use precision questions.

Level 4: Accept the other person's truth. If Vlad tells you, "We can't pair program all day long," or Gillian says, "We've increased our Agility considerably since last year," those are not facts, such as gravity or taxes. They are statements of Gillian's and Vlad's beliefs — things they hold to be true, which you might hold to be false. Dismissing the message ("You call that Agility?!") or dismissing the person ("You can't sit down with someone else for a few hours? What's wrong with you?") is not a winning proposition. Instead, move the interaction forward by *accepting* that such is their perspective, even if you *don't* agree with it. Be patient and open-minded. If you'd like to help the person communicate more clearly, explore his or her position, or feel better about the content, use tools such as precision questions, empathy, and reframing.

Level 5: Take full responsibility for both sides of the conversation. The meaning of your communication is not in what you uttered; its ultimate measure is the response you get. If the other party reacts unfavorably to your message — shuts down, becomes defensive, or acts aggressively — you didn't communicate effectively. You need to have enough rapport with and empathy for the individual to anticipate his reception of your message, as well as the maturity to respond effectively if it is not what you expected. Your best tool in this situation is self-awareness. When you understand your emotional reactions, defense mechanisms, and thought patterns, you can craft your message suitably.

Supplementary resource: Download "Communication Mastery Levels" from the book's companion website, **www.TheHumanSideOfAgile.com**.

8.2 Active Listening: How Do I Check My Understanding?

Think back to a time when you observed two colleagues in an important conversation. Did it appear like a true exchange of information and ideas, or was one person:

+ Interrupting the other?

+ Putting words in the other's mouth?

+ Raising her voice if the other did not seem to understand something?

+ Checking her mobile phone?

+ Giving her planned answer, regardless of what her colleague said?

The two sides probably didn't gain anything useful from this exchange. In fact, they likely hurt their relationship somewhat, because the impatient listener was not respecting the interaction. Her conversation partner might have felt frustrated, ignored, looked down upon, or annoyed.

The active listening technique is much more than basic manners (e.g., don't interrupt, don't raise your voice). With active listening, you demonstrate that you're listening and verify what you think you heard. Use it to improve your conversations' results, to enhance your ability to influence and negotiate, and to sustain long-term relationships.

In active listening, you focus attention on what the other person says, with both his words and his body language. The central tactic is that of *feeding back the message*. It comes in three degrees: repeating (using the exact words you heard), paraphrasing (using similar words), and reflecting (using your own words).

Suppose you are having a conversation with Vijay, a team member:

Vijay: "Our defect count has been trending up this year. I don't think it's a matter of testing better and discovering more defects; we're simply introducing more than we're fixing."

You (*repeating*): "So you're saying we're introducing more defects than we're fixing, and that makes our defect count trend up?"

You just demonstrated that you've paid attention to Vijay's words, which invites him to contribute further:

Vijay: "I *think* that's the reason. The code we develop each iteration is not perfect, but we're so busy building new features, we don't dedicate enough time to fixing defects from that iteration or previous ones."

You might respond to Vijay's concern at this point. If his argument isn't clear to you, or you have doubts about its validity, you could feed it back to him:

You (*paraphrasing*): "Let me see if I understand. We're paying so much attention to coding new features that we don't have time to clean them up, which makes the defect count go up. Right?"

Or:

You (*reflecting*): "Hmm. So you're saying that new development is out of balance with defect fixing, which is why our quality is going down?"

Repeating retains the most of Vijay's original intent, while paraphrasing retains less, and reflecting may even lose it entirely. When you reflect a message, you inject your beliefs into it. In this case, you've posited that defects trending up means quality going down, and that maintaining quality requires a balance between new development and fixing. This might be quite different from Vijay's intent, which is why it's so important to voice your interpretation of his words before responding to them.

Active listening is suitable for many kinds of conversations. It is particularly powerful in emotionally charged situations, where it is extremely important that the other party know you are engaged, that she feel heard, and that you know what she is saying and thus are not responding to the wrong message.

To get the best results from active listening:

Minimize distractions. Your phone, email, and open door are obvious invitations to interruption. If something repeatedly tugs at you (such as your mobile phone vibrating), turn it off *and say that you're doing that.* If it's the other person's, ask him respectfully to turn down the notification.

Face the speaker. Eye contact (not staring) is best. If it makes you uncomfortable, at least have your body roughly angled toward the other person. Move away from your computer or other electronics. While looking downward or averting your eyes is hardly an optimal response, at least she will feel less slighted than if you were still typing on your computer.

Stay focused on the conversation. If your mind keeps trying to pull you toward other mental pursuits, don't just check out mentally. Either force yourself to focus or gracefully back out of the conversation. You could say, "I'd like to give this matter the attention it deserves, and I'm having trouble concentrating right now. Can we resume this conversation in <a specific period>?"

Supplement your words with simple acknowledgments. Nod for acceptance. Smile. Talk with your hands. Say "Uh-huh," "OK," "Hmm...," or "Right." Use "Interesting!" and "Really?" sparingly, since they have the potential to sound fake.

Use preambles. Before you feed back the message, say something that signals the feedback. "What I'm hearing is...," "So are you saying that...," "Sounds like you're referring to...," "If I understand you correctly...."

If you don't understand what they said, slowly repeat it word for word. That will help you comprehend what the other person said or it will encourage him to rephrase.

Don't prepare your counterargument before the other person has finished talking (even if she says more than you think is needed).

Otherwise, you're clearly showing that what she says isn't all that important to you.

Offer the occasional recap. It can be quite useful to summarize your understanding of the conversation to that point. Don't worry about taking longer to interact; making sure that you're both agreeing to the same thing can be more valuable.

8.3 Rapport: How Do We Get in Sync?

Picture us having a conversation at your desk. I'm facing you, sitting at about the same height. You're leaning forward a tiny bit, and I am leaning at a similar angle. We're speaking at similar tone and pitch. You occasionally pause in your speech, as do I. You sometimes wave your right hand to emphasize a point. I sometimes wave mine when I'm talking.

As you imagine this conversation, are you getting a good feeling?

If you are, that's an indication of being *in rapport* with me. By providing similar visual cues (notably posture, angle of spine, and use of hands) and auditory cues (specifically in tone, pitch, and pauses), we subconsciously indicate to each other that we're engaged in the conversation and having positive feelings about it. By being like each other, we also *like* each other.

Now imagine the conversation is continuing. You still wave your right hand occasionally, but I just have my hands in my lap. In fact, I've sat back. My eyes aren't meeting yours as much anymore. You say something nice and smile at me, yet I'm not smiling back.

How are you feeling now about the conversation and about me?

Even though we're still talking, I've broken rapport. I haven't stopped liking you, but I'm no longer engaged in the conversation as before. How long will you continue talking with me? Or will you perhaps shift your posture and mannerisms to match mine?

An interaction without rapport might work out well, but more likely it would be pointless and boring. If you start a conversation and you are highly vested in the outcome, the absence of rapport can suck the life out of you. Do your best to establish rapport in order to increase the likelihood that the conversation will be productive, satisfying, and enjoyable.

The most important element of establishing and maintaining rapport is matching intonation and body language. Doing that is possible, though harder, when you are not in proximity (for example, talking over the phone) or when interacting with a group. Next in importance is using similar content. For instance, an executive and a programmer are more likely to stay engaged in a fruitful discussion of customer success if they have similar mental models of "customers" and "success" or consciously attempt to understand each other's model.

The rapport mechanism is present, to different extents, in the subconscious minds of all human beings. You have probably been using it since early childhood without being aware of it. Now that you are, you can leverage it in several ways.

First, consciously start complex interactions by attempting to establish rapport. Otherwise, if you're preparing for a difficult conversation or a new situation with your team members, you might start it on the wrong foot. By consciously creating rapport with the other party before getting to the heart of the matter, you'll lay the groundwork for a healthy exchange that will make both sides feel better.

Next, notice when the other person breaks rapport. Your subconscious mind will register the change, but its reaction is sometimes unhelpful: you might get a queasy feeling, as though the space in front of you has shut down or moved. You can now recognize this as a signal of broken rapport and choose whether to try to restore it or gracefully end the interaction.

Also, catch *yourself* breaking rapport. If your attention wavers, or you lose interest, your subconscious mind will break rapport. The result will probably not be pleasant for your conversation partner. So catch yourself doing that and, as above, decide whether to restore rapport or end the interaction — while still leaving the other person with a good feeling.

If you establish rapport consciously, you must be authentic about it and use it in good faith. If you don't, count on your conversation partner to notice your actions and interpret them as manipulation. Even with pure intentions, you will need to practice the conscious use of rapport, otherwise your partner will sense awkwardness.[2]

8.4 Deliberate Language: How Should I Phrase My Message?

Communication involves sending and receiving messages. Anytime you have a message to send, you need to put it into words. Ordinarily, your mind does this automatically, based on habits and preferences. Still, you can deliberately choose other wordings.

8.4.1 Avoid Extreme Language

Every word you use carries associations and baggage, which are specific to you. Once you utter those words and they enter another person's ears, he will interpret them based on his own associations and baggage; this interpretation is automatic (subconscious) and rapid. The communication suffers a setback if he simply misunderstands you; it can go downhill fast if your words hit a nerve. You must choose your words carefully to limit the risk of achieving the wrong result or other unintended consequences.

As you read the following story, note your feelings:

"On one project we had a manager, let's call him Dave, who got more excited as our project progressed. We noticed Dave's language shifted from deadline dates and features to expressing how we'd be 'killed' if we missed a deadline and we'd 'die' if certain features weren't implemented. If a developer failed to deliver, Dave said he would 'murder' them. At one point, Dave likened our team to a special forces combat unit.

"One time, Dave wanted a way to motivate our team. Jokingly, we told him that shooting a developer in front of the team might have the desired effect. Dave, with a completely serious face, said he liked the idea."

— *Rob MacGregor, ScrumMaster*

Are you feeling motivated? Indifferent? Aghast?

Dave had a genuine intent of motivating his team to action without resorting to actual violence. He wanted to articulate the consequences of failure; like many people, he used extreme words and analogies to get his point across. Scrum pioneers, wanting to clearly distinguish those with skin in the game from those who are merely involved, succeeded by using the words "pigs" and "chickens."[3] To make the biggest impact on the greatest number of people in your audience, you need to choose the right strength of wording, and that is not likely to be the extreme. For instance, consider the following "grades" of the same message:

✦ "We will totally blow it!"

✦ "We will miss the deadline!"

+ "We won't meet the deadline expectation."

+ "We won't have everything ready by the deadline."

+ "We might have to defer delivery."

Remember to vary your words. With repeated use, some words lose their edge. If you want to prod your team a bit, you might say, "This iteration is a critical milestone." However, if you regularly describe iterations as critical, "critical" becomes a synonym for "normal."

8.4.2 Ask Open-Ended Questions

As the release of one team's product was coming up, the director of engineering would come to the team's planning sessions, saying, "We need to work weekends," and the team would agree reluctantly. One time, the director was away, and the ScrumMaster related the news differently: "We've been asked to put in more time. What can you do?" One developer brightened up and said, "Weekends are really problematic for me, but I can come in early on weekdays. Would that work?"

Asking an open-ended question, unlike making a statement or asking a closed-ended question, has three related effects that combine powerfully.

The obvious effect of open-ended questions, such as "What can you do?" in this story, is to generate possibilities for the subject of the conversation. The developer in this case could suggest a solution more in line with her needs.

A less-obvious effect is that the listener now has to *engage her mind*. Rather than tell the director "yes" (or possibly "no"), team members had to come up with an answer. If your conversation with someone appears to be losing focus, or if his answers sound mechanical, ask an open-ended question. He will be forced to increase his involvement in the conversation.

The third and sometimes most valuable effect is the subtle empowerment of the listener. Suppose we're midway through an iteration, and nothing is going right. You and I have been talking about the problems, and then I say, "I guess we'll have a lot to cover at the retrospective." I have effectively shut the door on our discussion. Instead, I could say, "Can you see a way to make *something* go well in the next few days?" That would put you in temporary charge of a problem-solving effort and probably make you feel more empowered and hopeful.

8.4.3 Use Softeners

If you think that the listener might react unfavorably to your message, you can preface it with softeners such as:

- ✦ "Isn't it nice that ..."

- ✦ "Have you considered ..."

- ✦ "I wonder whether <the topic> is ..."

Softeners turn your message into a question *and* deflect attention from you as its sender. By lengthening the message, softeners induce a slightly tranquilizing effect on the listener. However, they may dilute the message more than you intend and trigger a reaction like "Can't you just say what you mean?!"

8.4.4 Consider Modality

People's minds represent information using the five senses. When I describe a system's architecture, I draw a picture; I'm visual in that context. You might prefer to give a verbal account, perhaps of the names of components and how they relate; that would make you auditory. Another person may describe it in terms of emotions or sensations ("the database layer is the heaviest; the presentation layer is rather thin..."); that would make her kinesthetic.

When you talk with someone, his preferred representation (modality) for the subject matter will come across in his words and gestures.[4] If you pay attention to his choice of words, you can glean clues about that preference. Formulating your response using that modality's vocabulary will help the listener process your message more smoothly. For example:

Melina, a team member: "The plan is not so clear to me."

Her use of the word "clear" gives away her visual representation of the plan. To reply using the visual modality, use visual language:

You: "I understand. Let me *draw* you a *roadmap* for reaching our goals."

If you use the vocabulary of another modality, she could get confused or have to mentally translate your words.[5] For instance, the following reply is in the auditory modality:

You: "I *hear* you. It didn't *resonate* with me either initially. Let me *tell* you how it's going to work."

8.4.5 Keep It Positive

Although you are not in charge of others' emotions or well-being, your words and deeds affect them. For instance, if you make a request of someone, and he comes back with a less-than-perfect result, consider the impact of "Thank you. <These parts> are useful, and <those parts> aren't quite what I needed. Let me explain that differently," versus "Ugh, you spent all this time on the wrong thing! That's not what I asked for!"

The key is to keep most of your comments positive, or at least to have them mention the positive. According to social psychologist Barbara Fredrickson's research,[6] people need to experience positive emotions at least three times as frequently as negative ones in order to lead healthy lives. Their workplace — where they spend a good deal of their waking time laboring and interacting — can be a significant source of both positive and negative emotions.

Positive emotions at work include *engrossed, interested, hopeful, proud, excited, grateful,* and *calm.* Negative emotions at work include *apprehensive, disgruntled, indignant, alienated, ashamed, burnt out, miserable,* and *overwhelmed.* You would do well to promote an environment where the positive-to-negative ratio is 3-to-1 or better. That will help others feel better, as well as make them see you as a person they want to communicate with.

A low-cost and fulfilling way of building up to the 3-to-1 ratio is to give targeted, positive, and encouraging feedback (not vague praise) where it is due. Don't be one of those managers whose approach is, "If I don't tell you anything, that means you're doing well," because then your team hears only the negative from you.

8.4.6 Avoid the Question "Why?"

"Why" is an extremely powerful question. It explores motivation, challenges decisions, and seeks to understand behavior. It comes in handy in project situations ("Why are we doing this project and not another? Why does this story have high value?"); process situations ("Why did we say we were done with this story, when it's clearly full of defects?"); technical situations ("Why does this class have four constructors?"); and team situations ("Why are some people always quiet during iteration planning?"). By unearthing reasons, you can improve the system rather than just address symptoms.

The trouble with "Why?" is that it easily triggers unwanted reactions. Since a true answer might uncover an error in judgment, an area of incompetence, or an unflattering motivation, the listener's defense mechanisms quickly kick in. This human mechanism dates back to early childhood, when common responses to "Why did you do that?" included a mumbled "I don't know" or a defiant "I didn't do it!"

Instead of using "Why," ask other questions that don't sound blaming and get to the heart of the matter without triggering defense mechanisms.

You could ask these questions about a current behavior or past action:

+ "What was your intention in doing that?"

+ "What are you trying to do?"

+ "What did you want to achieve?"

Ask these questions about a decision or intention to do something:

+ "What would that do for you?"

+ "How are you going to use that?"

+ "Where would you apply this?"

+ "After you complete this, what will you/we have?"

A popular Lean technique for uncovering systemic issues is called "the Five Whys." The idea is to ask why something happened and then feed the answer into another "why?" question, asking recursively five times. Even though this is a well-intentioned, well-known technique, I've found that it falls victim to the same trouble as a single "Why?"

When is "Why" useful? When you're engaging an individual or a group in a true improvement effort, and you're all clearly taking responsibility for the situation and the results.

8.4.7 Replace "But" With "And"

Suppose you have a bright idea. All excited, you approach me and tell me about it.

I reply: "I like your idea, but I don't think it's going to work."

Notice how you're feeling about me and about your idea now. Are you crestfallen? Frustrated? Annoyed? Indifferent?

Now take a quick break from this book and look around you. Rest your eyes on the largest object in the room. Then come back to the book. Seriously, do that. Now.

Suppose you have another bright idea. All excited, you come and tell me.

I reply: "I like your idea, and I'm seeing some challenges in making it work."

How are you feeling *now* about me and about your idea?

The word "but" has a different effect on people than most speakers intend. In the first case, I truly meant that I liked your idea. Your subconscious mind probably heard just the second part ("it's not going to work"), because "but" erased the preceding statement. In the second case, chances are your mind heard and processed both.[7]

If you'd like to improve collaboration, empathy, and relationships, catch yourself before saying the word "but." Sometimes it's precisely the thing to say, and often it's not. If you have to use a conjunction, choose "and" instead.

8.5 Precision Questions: How Do I Recover Missing Information?

Your mind constantly takes in enormous amounts of sensory information. Its way of processing such amounts within a reasonable time frame involves three mental filters:[8]

Deletion. Your mind pays attention to certain input elements and ignores others. For instance, it probably didn't notice this book's font — until I called your attention to it. What your mind deletes at any moment depends on context and need.

Distortion. As powerful as your senses of vision, hearing, touch, taste, and smell are, your subconscious mind distorts some of their input. For instance, it's a safe bet that what you understood and retained from the last one-on-one meeting with your manager differs somewhat from what actually happened. The distortions are based on your beliefs, values, abilities, experience, and identity — everything that makes you *you*.

Generalization. If you see me smile at you once, and the next couple of times we meet I smile again, your mind is likely to generalize this data. Depending on your experiences with me and with others, you might conclude that I'm friendly, that I enjoy your company, that I like smiling, or something else. The generalization mechanism helps you form beliefs, sustain your values, and respond in unfamiliar situations.

These filters are constantly running in every person. They change over time as the person matures and changes. As useful as these filters are to existence, they can be inaccurate and fallible. They manifest themselves both in behaviors and attitudes, and, for our purpose here, also in communication.

Imagine you are in conversation with someone, whether written or face to face. The other person's deletion, distortion, and generalization filters operate two ways. On the inbound, they modify what she sees and hears from you. On the outbound, they affect the stream of words she utters or writes. There are patterns to these filters: consistent ways in which they modify what she truly means and reduce the quality of her outbound communication. About 20 patterns have been classified.[9]

Just as in software development we refer to design antipatterns as "code smells," I refer to these ubiquitous communication antipatterns as "conversation smells."[10] If during a conversation a "smell" is impeding your ability to make a decision, help the person, or learn something, you can challenge the pattern — refactor that smell — by asking a *precision question*.

Precision questions target information that your conversation partner hasn't presented. He may have intentionally omitted it, perhaps thinking it redundant; in other cases, however, he may not even be aware of that information. Your questions will exhort him to identify his thoughts and words precisely — undeleted, undistorted, and ungeneralized — so you can work with the right data.

Most precision questions are simple, building on such basic building blocks as "How?" "Who?" "Which" and "What?" But no matter who the other person is, you must establish rapport with him before asking them. He must feel that you value the interaction and that your questions are genuine. Without rapport, he might interpret them as interrogatory, manipulative, or even aggressive.

In deletion patterns, some information is vague or missing. For instance, "We welcome changing requirements, even late in development" contains a *vague action* ("changing") — a process word with an incomplete description. Clarify that description by asking the precision question, "**In what way** do they change?" In a *missing comparative*, such as "XP is better than Scrum," a comparison or relationship is asserted without stating the basis of it. To elucidate that information, ask, "**Based on what?**" "**What makes you say that?**" or "Better **how?**" (Notice how these questions avoid asking "Why?," as suggested in section 8.4.6.) Other deletion patterns include *vague object, vague reference, missing reference,* and *value judgment.*

Distortion patterns appear in conversations as faulty logic. The faulty logic can exist on both sides of the conversation; the speaker may be drawing unjustified inferences or meanings, and the listener may be making unjustified assumptions about what's going on in the speaker's mind. For example, "We can't get anything done because of these two-week iterations" contains a *cause and effect.* It implies that one thing (two-week iterations) causes another (not getting anything done), without sufficient logical support or evidence. Challenge the argument by asking "**How** are two-week iterations preventing you from finishing something?" Other distortion patterns include *meaning, presupposition,* and *mind reading.*

Generalization patterns make the statements in which they appear sound absolute. They present a black-and-white view of the world and apply subtle pressure on you to agree or disagree with them. Precision questions let you challenge the validity of a generalization without having to disagree with it outright. For instance, if you hear the *necessity* pattern in "Business people and developers must work together daily," you can ask, **"What would happen if they didn't?"** Another common pattern is *nominalization*. In "Our teamwork is so-so," a dynamic process (the team working) has been frozen into a thing or event (teamwork). You can tackle this abstraction or generalization only by asking about specifics; for example, **"How** is the team **working** right now?" Other generalization patterns include *universality* and *possibility*.

> ***Supplementary resource***: Download "Refactoring Conversation Smells" from the book's companion website, **www.TheHumanSideOfAgile.com**.

8.6 Empathy: What Is It Like for the Other Person?

A few years ago, I was leading the first iteration retrospective of a very large distributed team. I was in the room with the American half of the team, while the overseas half were on speakerphone. At the end of the hour, the client's Agile champion pulled me aside for a chat. "I don't know if you noticed," he said, "but the phone was very quiet."

"I opened each topic for discussion, and we had a conversation going for each one," I replied. "Anytime I asked whether the folks on the phone had anything to add, nobody answered."

"You have to realize," he said, "our guys there aren't usually asked for their opinion. You need to call on people by *name* and ask them to comment on what they heard. As a group, they are not treated like we are. Sometimes I feel that it sucks to be them."

These four little words, "sucks to be them," shook me to the bone. They have stayed with me as an example of the power and importance of empathy.

Empathy is often referred to as "putting yourself in other people's shoes." When you are empathetic, you ask yourself: "What is the situation like for them? What memories, fears, and hopes does it trigger for them? What are they experiencing that makes them speak or behave the way they do?"

Once you have answers to these questions, you acknowledge their emotions. A simple statement usually suffices, something like "You must have really put your heart and soul into that." Or even a simple "Doesn't that feel great?"

Empathy is *good for the other person*, who feels supported, recognized, treated as a human being, and/or appreciated. If she is experiencing a problem, by bringing a clear mind to the situation, you may help analyze its roots and identify resources that helped you in similar instances. Empathy is *good for you*, making you better aware of and connected to your own feelings. And empathy is *good for your relationship*, since it injects caring and trust. Empathy strengthens every type of relationship.

If you've identified the emotion correctly, you can lead the interaction in a beneficial direction. The more you empathize with someone, the more you can get immediate feedback on what she is experiencing during your interaction. Consequently, you can deliberately choose words and actions to help her experience more helpful feelings.

But how can you know what another person is going through, and how can you respond?

She may tell you, or you may see or hear direct evidence. I once saw a senior developer go home in tears after spending her first day of pair programming with her friend, the opinionated team leader. I approached her privately and said, "I can see you're quite upset about this experience. It probably wasn't what you expected, was it?"

You may recognize the situation and its associated emotional experience. For instance, if two of your developers recently vanquished a particularly pernicious bug after spending a whole day, you could say to them, "Feels great, doesn't it? High five!"

Other times, you just have to make assumptions based on the evidence and the context. Suppose the team worked 20 hours of overtime this iteration. Now their program manager is telling them, "That's great, but next iteration I'm expecting you to put in 110 percent." You can safely assume they are feeling dejected or disheartened. After he leaves, you might say, "That probably felt like getting the wind knocked out of you, didn't it? After all the hard work you put in."

Be aware that empathy is distinct from sympathy. Empathy involves relating to the other person's emotions; sympathy is offering your support, pity, or commiseration. When you're empathetic, you are a fellow human being who identifies with her experience. When you're sympathetic, you're sending a subtle message that *you* are in a better place.

When empathizing, don't say how a similar thing happened to you. If someone is experiencing a negative emotion, she wouldn't care about yours, and it takes away from the attention she deserves. You need to acknowledge *her* feelings, but be careful about taking empathy with a negative emotion too far. You'll feel bad yourself and have trouble resurrecting the conversation or helping the other person.

8.7 Reframing: How Can We See Things Differently?

Imagine that your team is contracted to develop custom software. The contract is up for renewal next month, and the final production deployment is this week. Your client said this morning that the team must fix the 30 outstanding bugs before deployment — or else. You've just announced this news at the standup meeting, and the team has grudgingly agreed to work extra hours over the next few days. After the meeting ends, Laurent — one of the developers — wants to talk to you.

Laurent (in a belligerent tone): "I don't mind the occasional overtime, but this one is outright annoying. Those defects have been around for *a while*. We shouldn't have to fix them in a crunch like this."

What would you do?

The first thing to do is accept that Laurent is annoyed. Faced with this situation, he is drawing a disempowering meaning from it. He is probably upset over two things: the imposed dictum of fixing those defects right now, and having to go along with the team's agreement to overtime. You can use active listening to check these assumptions, and you can use rapport and empathy to help him vent and feel heard. However, these responses probably won't help him cope with the situation.

If you're in rapport with him right now, you could try *reframing* the situation. By putting a new frame, perspective, or interpretation around it, you can help Laurent see the situation differently and feel more empowered. Use one of these questions to produce reframes:

The meaning question: "How can this situation (or behavior) mean something positive?"

In this example, working overtime is a fact. What can be good or valuable about it? Can it have some interpretation other than its current negative one?

You might say to Laurent, "Yeah, I don't like the overtime either, but after the client sees our level of commitment to their success, perhaps they'll extend our contract."

The context question: "In what other context would this situation (or behavior) be valuable?"

In this example, another way to ask the context question is: "Where or when would a late, concentrated, bug-fixing effort be a good thing?"

You might say to Laurent, "If we had fixed all those defects sooner, we would probably have had less time for new feature development, and the client would have been even less thrilled. At least this way we focused on what they feel to be important."

Instead of offering your reframe, you can weave the meaning question or the context question into the conversation. If the other party discovers the reframe on his own, it is more likely to have an impact. You might pose the meaning question as follows:

"I hear you, Laurent. Well, we're going to be putting in that overtime anyway, so maybe we can find something positive in this experience?"

Be silent at this point. Wait for him to process this question. He might brighten and pursue your idea. Even if he rejects your idea and merely mutters, "Oh well, I guess I could use the overtime pay," there it is: he found his own meaning reframe. You have helped him cope with the situation.

A reframe is an intervention, which the listener doesn't always welcome. Asking for permission ("Would you like me to help you see this situation differently?") is rarely a winning proposition. You have to have rapport and lead your listener gently through the conversation. Good ways to do that are to:

+ Lead with empathy ("You're probably not enjoying this…").

+ Use preambles and softeners (see 8.4.3).

+ Speak at length. Notice that the sample answers provided above are not brief. A longer utterance is more likely to lull your listener's mind into a receptive state than a compact, precise statement.

8.8 Self-Awareness: How Can I Make My Style Work for Me?

At first glance, the concept of self-awareness might appear puzzling. Wouldn't you know yourself better than anyone else? And wouldn't you know everything there is to know about you?

Even if the answer to these two questions is yes, your knowledge would be largely subconscious. It's wired into you and you *don't notice it*; you can't immediately put words to that knowledge. As you go about your actions and interactions, your subconscious mind expresses that self-knowledge, without pointing out what it's doing.

For example, if you're an outgoing team leader and one of your testers is withdrawn and often stone-faced, you're likely to spend less time in her presence than with others, because her interactions with you don't supply you with the feedback and mental stimulation you prefer. Chances are you're not minimizing these interactions *knowingly*; your subconscious mind — your autopilot — is in charge.

Your level of engagement with this tester will not change unless you start noticing it. The trigger can be external: someone draws your attention to it, or perhaps you read a text about human interactions and it gets you thinking about your team. You will also have an internal trigger once you have achieved greater awareness of your preferences, beliefs, and motivators in the context of workplace interactions.

Increased awareness of your inner workings doesn't take away from the magic of being human. It doesn't turn you into a machine. Rather, it opens possibilities for you and expands your choices. It can occur at the levels of environment and behavior: "Where am I at my best? When I talk with so-and-so, what's my body language?" Look inside and ask, "What's really important to me? What do I value and believe? What drives my decisions and responses?" You can look deeper inside and ask, "What role am I playing? Why have I chosen this role?" The more deeply you probe — the more abstract your observations — the more diverse your choices become, and ultimately you'll experience better interactions and results.[11]

Here are some simple techniques for raising self-awareness.

Take self-assessment tests. Two popular tools for analyzing personality and preferences are the Myers-Briggs Type Indicator (MBTI)[12] and the DISC.[13] Take these tests at least once to get a sense of your overall preferences and patterns. They will also open your eyes to the spectrum of preferences that other people have.

Keep a journal. During or after an activity, take a few minutes to write down your thoughts and observations. For instance, if you are improving your facilitation skills, make note of participants' behaviors during review meetings. Counting helps: you might count the number of times a difficult attendee acted up. Frequently review your journal for patterns.

Reflect on actions and results. After a significant activity or a predetermined time frame, such as a week, take 15 to 30 minutes to reflect on it. Focus on your actions and thought patterns. What did you do "as usual"? What did you do differently? What were the results?

Catch yourself. Some time will pass between your decision to eliminate a behavior (or a thought pattern) and succeeding in doing so. Minimize that time by catching yourself behaving that way and noting that it happened. Some people like to move a colorful rubber band from one wrist to the other to indicate that they've caught themselves in a particular behavior. The more visible and accessible the signal, the quicker you'll develop that accurate self-awareness.

Seek feedback. After an activity, approach one of the participants and ask for feedback. Make your request specific to the awareness you'd like to develop. For instance, after leading iteration planning, you might ask the product owner: "Could you offer an observation about the meeting's setup?" or "Did you feel that the whole team contributed? What did you see me do to increase or decrease their participation?" Depending on the openness and degree of trust in your relationship with the team, feedback from a peer at the same level of the organizational hierarchy might be the most genuine.

Get buddy coaching. If access to a professional coach is not in your cards, a simple alternative is to find a colleague or friend who's also interested in raising self-awareness. (Look for people who already read leadership, business, or self-help books.) Make an agreement about the types of feedback you'd like to provide each other and how long you want your buddy-coaching agreement to remain in effect. (In other words, don't overstay your welcome.) After an event in which you both participated, meet for a few minutes and share feedback with each other. Decide which improvements you'd like to make, then promise them to your buddy coach. When you meet again, he or she can hold you accountable to them and help you reflect on their effect.

Discover what makes you tick. When you are feeling contemplative, take 15 minutes to sit alone and reflect. Use the following questions as a starting point:

+ What kinds of pursuits make me happy and satisfied? What kinds of pursuits make me feel disgruntled and depleted?

+ What scares me? In past conversations, what did someone say that immediately rang panic bells in my head? And did my fear guide my answers, or did I respond to the facts?

+ Do I prefer the big picture, or do the details matter a whole lot more to me? Or do I balance these out as needed?

+ Am I excited by solving a problem or by helping others solve it? Do people come to me with a problem and just wait for me to solve it for them? If we decide on something together, do they proceed excitedly with implementation, or do they feel as though they are following my command?

+ Whom do I like to be around, when, and how? Whom do I *not* like to be around?

+ What kinds of messages from others push my buttons? In past situations, what did someone say or do to cause my anger to well up?

+ Am I seeing myself as equal to others, above others, or beneath them?

Discover how others perceive you. Since you can't ask people directly, "What do you think of me?" an alternative is to observe how they respond to you. When you're calm and able to take a detached perspective, ask yourself the following questions:

✦ When I bring up a concern, what do I sound and appear like? (Typical options include: confident, authoritative, open-minded, whiny, miserable, desperate.)

✦ When I move around our workspace, what impression do I leave on team members? (Typical options include: hurried, stressed, confident, engaged.)

✦ What words would others use to describe me?

✦ When do people avoid me? Which types of problems do they avoid discussing with me?

✦ When others give me feedback — negative or positive — what approach do they take? (Options may include: frank, brutally honest, evasive, complaining, gushy.)

> Can you imagine what the world would be like if everyone was a masterful communicator — self-aware, empathetic, able to reframe experiences? Can you envision just a single *team* of master communicators? I've had the good fortune of collaborating with such people, and so can you. The path to this delightful experience starts with you. Learn more about each level of mastery, and practice, practice, practice. The results will amaze you.

Supplementary Resources

Go to **www.TheHumanSideOfAgile.com** and download "Communication Mastery Levels" and "Refactoring Conversation Smells."

CHAPTER 9

Make Meetings Matter

Teams meet frequently in order to reach some decision or information objective, such as to plan an iteration, evaluate a design, or reflect on an activity. Since Agile methods promote more frequent meetings with more participants than traditional methods, the cost and value of these meetings are a common cause of concern.

Almost universally, people love to hate meetings. Have you ever attended a meeting that wandered aimlessly, detoured off its agenda, or got hijacked by its loudest or highest-ranking participants? Even though all the standard Agile meetings have well-defined processes, I've witnessed several where the process was ignored midway and the meeting meandered, or where tight enforcement squelched all options and creativity.

As more people attend, as more opinions and options are explored, and as the stakes get higher, the more guidance and process meetings require in the form of *facilitation*. Facilitation involves assembling the right group, helping it set objectives, crafting a workable process for meeting the objectives, and taking the group through the process.

Team time is expensive. A well-facilitated meeting respects that investment and moves the team forward. Badly run meetings don't just waste time; they cause the team to proceed with subpar decisions — or no decision at all. They cause resentment and rancor among team members. When they are the norm rather than the exception, participants avoid them. But since a self-organizing team has to make decisions regularly, they will have to meet — a lot.

Master facilitators focus on people first and on the process second. They handle emotional behavior empathically. They "feel the room" to funnel energy and innovation in valuable directions. And they ensure that participants leave the meeting feeling empowered and important, not ignored, second-class, or given lip service.

More art than science, facilitation is a sophisticated skill (as well as a profession). However, Agile team leaders (ATLs) and coaches need only basic facilitation skills. This chapter lays out the top techniques you need for great results.

9.1 What Is the Most Vital Ingredient of an Effective Meeting?

Stephen Covey has popularized the phrase "Begin with the end in mind" as one of the habits of effective people.[1] This principle underpins many Agile practices: understanding a story's value before scheduling its development; figuring out an iteration goal, not just a list of user stories; writing a piece of code only after writing a test to demonstrate the code's expected behavior. The same principle applies to any meeting: a clearly defined *purpose* is the most critical factor in its success.

> Key members of the project community filed into a defect triage meeting. In their hands they held spreadsheet printouts showing 160 defects. Knowing that the delivery team was not going to fix all 160 anytime soon, I suggested we just identify the top 20. The participants agreed, and I improvised a process for identifying and prioritizing the 20. When we were done, a half hour later, one attendee said, "This was the best meeting in a very long time!"

When you hear someone say, "This meeting was a waste of time," look first to its purpose: that is where everything begins. When attendees have a vague or incorrect grasp of the meeting's intent, they can't participate effectively. It feels long and goes off-topic — because they don't know what the topic is. If any element of it was worth their time, it probably happened accidentally.

The meeting's purpose answers the question "Why?" Why should we pause from value-adding work and get together? How will it make a difference? Why have this meeting instead of another activity? Just as every standard Agile meeting has a clear purpose, so should any additional meeting you hold. It may have other valuable benefits, such as sharing information, strengthening the team through collaboration, or even offering a chance to relax — but make sure you keep your eye on the main purpose.

When you invite people to attend and when you open the meeting, express the purpose and articulate how the process achieves it. For example, the first few times I lead a new team's daily standup, I start off like this:

"We're here to identify obstacles to progress and make necessary adjustments to our iteration plan. Would each one of you please share your update since our last standup, your ideas for the next 24 hours, and what's standing in your way?"

Despite common complaints about meetings, people seem to enjoy the opportunity for face time and conversation. This is valuable from a social aspect — just get them to accomplish the meeting's intent first. For instance, if your daily standups tend to devolve into design conversations, raise your hand and remind people to "take them offline" (discuss them at a later time).

The ritual and ceremony of a meeting can be a good starting point, but without introspection, they can also cause its purpose to be forgotten. At one company, team members lost patience for the retrospectives, so they shortened them to 30 minutes. They still held them, though: every two weeks they engaged in a perfunctory review of hastily written "opportunity" cards, without any real discussion, action items, or follow-up.

If you're having doubts about a particular meeting or are thinking of convening one, ask yourself: How does this meeting move us forward as a group? This simple question will help you discover the purpose.

> I observed a delivery team that held a sprint demo every two weeks — without their product owner or any stakeholder in attendance. They were visibly bored going through the meeting's motions, since they did not need the demo for their own sake. I suggested canceling that meeting until the product owner became more involved (which was the greater impediment).

Ultimately, a recurring meeting — even an obligatory one — will need to change if it no longer provides good value. For instance, if your team has been together for a while and is performing well, the retrospectives might not be yielding much anymore. Running them a little less frequently, or finding other forms for continuous improvement, might yield better results. A team that sits in tight quarters and communicates constantly may well find the daily standup too heavy for its needs and reduce its frequency or change its format accordingly.

> "If I could change corporate culture with only one sign, I'd post the following on every conference room door: 'If the meeting you are about to attend has no stated purpose, please return to something that does!'"
>
> — *David Spann, executive coach*

9.2 How Can We Focus on Our Work With So Many Meetings?

I hear this complaint *a lot*. Of all the objections to meetings, this one worries me the most, because knowledge workers do need periods of time to concentrate. It's one thing if meetings and nonproject obligations leave people only 60% of their time for work; it's another thing if that 60% is made up of little spurts of activity. Frequently switching contexts and going in and out of focus are sure ways to lower productivity and solution quality. Unfortunately, this concern eludes conveners; as meeting space is often at a premium, they use whatever available slots they find.

One solution is to group the distractions. Meetings are one type of distraction from value-adding, focused work. Another type of distraction is the lunch break. Can you hold the daily standup at 11:45, just before people break for lunch anyway? Can you run the iteration bookend activities — closing one iteration and planning the next — in a single afternoon, back to back?

Another solution is to allow nonbookend meetings only at certain hours, typically before 10 a.m. or after 4 p.m. By synchronizing team member distractions this way, you increase the overlap between their schedules, allowing them more time to work with each other.

You might be tempted to shorten a recurring meeting's duration in order to get back to work. Indeed, there is no magic in the heuristics "planning should take an hour for each week of iteration" and "limit retrospectives to one hour." But if you feel inclined to halve their length for reasons such as "We don't have the patience," "We just go through the motions," and "There are no surprises anyway," *pause*. Question your thoughts: Why don't you have the patience? (Is the meeting agenda not respected?) Why do you just go through the motions? (Do participants not understand the point of the meeting?) Why there are no surprises? (Do you allow time and a helpful process for generating insights?) All process meetings should have value. Make sure you don't lose it in the attempt to get out of them quickly.

Whenever you are on the receiving end of a meeting invitation, you are within your rights to ask the organizer about its purpose, process, and product. If the answers are less than satisfactory, consider offering your help. Or, if the organizer just intends to wing it, feel free to sit that one out. You have a right to have your time respected.

9.3 Who Should Attend Meetings?

While participation in numerous meetings may be the norm for managers and team leaders, it is rarely the case for team members. In traditionally run projects, most team members do not participate in cyclical planning, rarely demo their product, and do not conduct retrospectives every other week. Their daily standup is in the Starbucks line. The fact that most Agile meetings involve the whole team is a common cause for concern.

The concern runs deeper than labor costs. Participants lose patience for the meetings and can't wait to get back to "real" work. They have less time available for value-adding work and might need to make up for it. And they sense pressure — real or perceived — from management to optimize coding and testing time. A common unfortunate consequence is that teams choose longer iterations (such as three or four weeks) so as to reduce overhead.

Whole-team meetings are not inherently ineffective or inefficient; it's all a matter of how they are run. For instance, the value of standup meetings diminishes greatly when participants focus almost exclusively on the first question ("What have you done since the last standup?"). Make sure to facilitate whole-team meetings properly, keeping them on track toward their goals. Allow participants the time and space to generate important insights, which might yield time savings and course corrections. When participants get used to purposeful, on-point meetings, they won't consider them wasteful.

Nevertheless, even with proper facilitation, some team meetings may not be the best use of all participants' time. A few people will just sit there quietly, some of them listening, others engrossed in their laptop or smartphone. Should you still invite everybody?

Choosing meeting attendees requires a careful balance of competing needs. As the convener, balance *being inclusive* with a design for *maximal participant contribution and learning.* You can delegate the choice to attend to the invitees in a process known as "self-selection." In its basic form, invitees receive an early meeting description and can use that to opt in or out.

Further, you can suggest to your community the following rule: "If you are in a meeting and not contributing or learning, feel free to go do something else." If they agree to this rule, you might even post it prominently on meeting room doors.

Be aware — this rule requires a lot of courage. In some environments, attending certain meetings is a political matter. The rule might also have unintended consequences if most of the team sits out most meetings. If that happens, you probably have a buy-in problem (see 5.2).

9.4 What Do I Need to Prepare Before a Meeting?

Before you ever invite people to a meeting, be clear on three elements: *purpose*, *process* (agenda), and *product* (deliverables). In the case of the standard Agile meetings, such as iteration planning, review, and the daily standup, these elements are documented and well known. If you convene any other kind of meeting, such as for reviewing a design or selecting a tool, make sure attendees are aware of its purpose, understand how the meeting will proceed, and know its expected product or deliverable. Meetings go south quickly if even one of these elements isn't well prepared.

A powerful pattern for agenda design is as a *list of questions* that attendees answer in order to meet the purpose. For instance, the famous "Three Questions" of the daily standup result in identifying action items and artifact updates. Retrospectives include questions such as "What worked well?" and "What still puzzles us?" In design reviews, participants often rely on checklists. When you think of the agenda only as questions to answer, your focus on the purpose will be stronger and the meeting will be more productive.[2]

When you prepare the process of a meeting, also determine the space. If the team has a welcoming, comfortable open space, use it for iteration planning, because they associate the space with project action. Hold the review and retrospective in another room, to help the team take a step back from the cycle that just ended and to reduce the likelihood of their being distracted by their computers. For longer meetings, consider going offsite.

By occasionally varying the process of a recurring meeting, attendees will produce additional ideas and perspectives. This is particularly true of retrospectives: the popular "Worked Well/Needs Improvement" format gets old really quickly. Read up on available techniques,[3] and you can also design your own. A process that achieves superb results in Agile meetings is called ORID, or the Focused Conversation Method.[4]

Regardless of your meeting's type, consider including *silent work*.[5] Allow time for individuals to think and write down their contribution silently, followed by group time for collaborative processing of that input. You might know silent work from retrospectives that begin by having each participant write down their Worked Well and Needs Improvement items on sticky notes before posting them on a shared flipchart. This kind of work can be applied to many other group activities, such as writing stories or brainstorming a user interface.[6] It is effective for eliciting contributions from the quieter people and preventing the louder ones from dominating.

Observe trained facilitators, and you'll notice they make heavy use of the physical space. They organize the room for easy movement and group activities; they fill the walls with information captured on flipchart paper; they use many colors and sticky notes. They also *move around a lot*. Consequently, participants use more senses and move their bodies, becoming much more engaged and less likely to check out. They own their data and results — the facilitator merely makes the process happen.

The meeting will flow better if its process is visible and participants have precise, detailed instructions. They should always understand what they are doing now and what will come next. Bring flipchart sheets depicting the process steps and each step's instructions. Don't worry about being too specific or detailed; it's better for participants to become impatient about getting started than for them to whisper to each other, "What are we supposed to do now?" or "What did he mean?"

You already know to be prepared with data for the meeting, such as a groomed product backlog for iteration planning. Also be ready with the technology and supplies that enable the process. Participants quickly lose patience and interest if the data doesn't come up, pens don't write, or computers can't connect. Your time spent preparing is much less expensive than the entire team's time spent waiting.

Think very carefully: Is any participant likely to upset the meeting over the content, the process, or some external factor? If so, start preventing that dysfunction now. A preparatory conversation with the person might be in order. Formulate ground rules that will neutralize that person's negative influence. You might also design your process accordingly (for instance, include more silent work).

One reason people dislike meetings is the need to sit in one place for a long time, often without saying much. Arrange activities that have them moving about and doing something. (That is why release and iteration planning sessions are much more powerful with index cards or sticky notes, as opposed to looking at a software tool on the projector.) If you can't have people moving about, bring supplies that have them do *something*, such as pens and paper for doodling, or squeeze balls. Holding the occasional meeting standing up will also inject some originality and change, and — as with the daily standups — it's likely to make the meeting shorter.[7]

Facilitation takes substantial energy and focus. It's much harder if you're also contributing content as a team member. You might need some help, and often the best task to delegate is that of capturing input and decisions. Having a scribe will also allow you to move faster, because writing — especially in big letters on a flipchart — takes time.

If you're hosting a creative-type meeting like design, chartering, or visioning, make it interesting. Go beyond brainstorming and use games and simulations. They might take a bit longer than traditional meetings, but the creativity, stimulation, fun, and engagement will be well worth it. (Remember, work ought to be effective *and* fun; it doesn't have to be ultra-serious.)

Keep an arsenal of questions in your back pocket. As participants generate ideas, use your cheat sheet of content-independent questions to challenge their thoughts, prompt them for more ideas, and prioritize their contributions. Questions include, "How would that work?" "Why is that important?" "What else?" "Can anyone see additional benefits or disadvantages to that?" or "Now let's look at the challenges."

9.5 How Should I Start a Meeting?

Imagine it is 2:30 p.m. and you walk into another team's iteration planning meeting. Half the team is already sitting around the boardroom table. A few are checking email on their smartphones, and the others are chatting about their kids' schools. The Scrum-Master is sitting at the head of the table, looking harried. Another team member enters and sits down next to her buddy. A few minutes pass. The ScrumMaster is shuffling some papers, occasionally raising his head to see if people are settling down. Around 2:37, the room is finally quiet. Then he rises slowly and opens in a tired tone, "OK, team, you know the drill." As he continues talking, some people are staring out the window.

At 3:00 you walk into another planning meeting, where the team is sitting around a similar table. Their ScrumMaster, standing in front of the room and looking tall (which she isn't), says in a confident voice: "Good afternoon, team! Welcome to another edition of our iteration planning. I hope you've all had a great day; let's conclude it on a high note by producing a great plan for the next two weeks." The team members are all looking at her (some smiling, some not). There is no smartphone or tablet in sight.

Which meeting do you like better? Which kind would you prefer to lead?

Participants in a meeting of the first kind sometimes refer to it as "getting the life sucked out of them." In some companies, these meetings are the norm. Their iteration planning sessions are day-long affairs, which people do *not* look forward to. In fact, they tend to be one of the reasons people abandon Scrum or think it doesn't work.

The first minute determines the entire tone of the meeting. As the meeting's facilitator, that minute is entirely up to you — so make it an engaging, effective one. Here's how.

As people walk in — and before the meeting starts — welcome them. This simple acknowledgment establishes in their minds that you're facilitating and that the meeting is starting. I like to say "Hi," then smile or nod to every person who walks in, and I start the meeting with, "Hello, everyone."

Then, start on time. Untimely starts are a waste of time and goodwill, and they're disrespectful to the people who *do* show up on time. Have the courage to be punctual and announce your intent clearly in your meeting invitation. If meetings never start on time in your company because attendees rush in from other meetings, push your starting time back by 5 or 10 minutes — and *then* be punctual. No exceptions.

Follow with a strong opening. You don't need drama, gimmickry, or treats to make a meeting compelling. All you need is to bring people into the experience. A powerful, simple four-step format for that is called 4MAT:[8]

1. Explain *why* they should be there (the meeting's purpose).

2. Lay out *what* they will do (the meeting's product or deliverable).

3. Explain *how* that will happen (the meeting's process).

4. Address relevant *what-ifs*.

For example, you could open iteration planning this way: "We are here to plan our next iteration. We'll discover its goal or theme, its deliverables, and our activities. We intend to come out of this meeting with well-understood, prioritized stories as well as their tasks. We'll do this the usual way: our product owner will walk us through the stories she hopes to see delivered, and we'll clarify the details and acceptance criteria, determine our tasks, and identify a coherent set we can accomplish. I know some of you have to leave at 5:00, so if we happen to run out of time today, we'll reconvene tomorrow morning at 9:30. Are you all OK with this?"

Have presence: sit upright, or stand, in front of and slightly apart from the group. Speak at a teaching volume, which is louder than your conversational voice. Direct your attention to the entire room. Smile occasionally. Talk with your hands. Tune all these techniques to the particular attendees so you can establish and maintain rapport with them.

Establishing ground rules with the participants will increase the meeting's effectiveness. Popular rules, which teams usually reuse across most meetings, include:

+ Start and end on time

+ No side conversations

+ There are no stupid ideas

+ No blaming

✦ When you comment on an idea, start by saying what's good about it

✦ Electronics by exception (i.e., use a phone or computer only in exceptional cases)

You must guarantee safety — the safety to speak freely without fear of attack or other consequences. Personal safety can make or break retrospectives and other sensitive meetings, since the less safe people feel, the less they will share. Get early agreement on clear ground rules for personal safety and post them visibly in the meeting room. One of my mainstays is the powerful rule "No jokes about people, present or absent."

In the first retrospective I held with a new Agile team, they got visibly agitated when I suggested that we post our Worked Well/Needs Improvement stickies in the team space. After I verified my hunch that they weren't comfortable sharing this data with people outside the room, they agreed to make only the action items known. We proceeded usefully after that.

Anyone who speaks in the first couple of minutes is likely to be far more engaged than another person who merely sits passively. So get everyone to say something. You can go around the room and have everyone share a bit of news, their highlight of the week, or how they are feeling that day. Don't make this step optional if you want complete participation.

Make a quick decision if critical people are absent. Nothing will kill your strong opening and confident presence like protracted vacillation as to whether to continue with the meeting. Lead the team to a decision: should we continue toward our objective despite the absentees, or reschedule and disperse now?

9.6 What Should I Do During a Meeting?

This section summarizes your most important actions during a meeting. Based on my experience coaching many team leaders and managers to become better facilitators, *mere awareness* of these points will take you half the way to mastery.

Ensure the process. Respect all the time-boxes and breaks. Constantly monitor the ground rules and take immediate action when a rule is broken. Remember that the rules belong to the participants; you only help set and enforce the rules. If a rule turns out to be unworkable, help the group revise it.

Adapt the process as necessary. Expect the process you envisioned before the meeting to need real-time adaptation. That is within your control, and the group will likely not mind much. Just remember that the purpose and product belong to the group, not to you, so you can't change anything about them without the group's consent.

Be clear on consensus. The self-organizing, collaborative Agile team makes its best decisions using *consensus*. A consensual decision is one that the entire team can live with and support, even if it did not enjoy widespread support or enthusiasm. This kind of decision making, quite distinct from compromise or hierarchical decision making, strengthens the team. It is also a widely misinterpreted notion, so make sure your team understands its meaning and implications.

Before putting a proposal to a *consensus check* or *vote*, make sure it is clear. Don't rush into voting before giving folks a chance to consider both their positions and their colleagues' positions. The team also has to choose their *decision rule*, which is the required level of agreement. The simplest rules involve counting those in favor of a proposal: majority, a certain percentage, or unanimity. The team might use the same decision rule across all meeting types, or change the rule as they see fit.

In my experience, two other rules that lead to greater acceptance and support for proposals are "Thumbs" and "Fist of Five."[9] In Thumbs, every participant raises a thumb. Thumb up means "I support it." Thumb down means "I'm against it." Thumb sideways means "I'm not supporting it, but I'll go along with the team's decision." A single thumb down suffices for blocking the decision, in which case the discussion is renewed and the proposal potentially revised.

In Fist of Five, every participant raises a number of fingers. (If you want to inject some humor into the meeting and possibly defuse some tension, tell them, "You know which finger *not* to raise.")

+ 0 (fist) = blocking the proposal

+ 1 finger = serious concerns that have not been heard or addressed

+ 2 fingers = still have unaddressed concerns

+ 3 fingers = consent, with a major reservation: I can live with that and support it if that's what the group decides

+ 4 fingers = consent, with slight reservation

+ 5 fingers = full consent (unbridled support)

Fist of Five is similar to Thumbs but more informative; you can also use it to check for consensus before a more formal vote. In the first round of voting, if all participants raise three, four, or five fingers, the proposed decision is accepted. Otherwise, discuss concerns and proceed with round two, or revise the proposal and restart voting. In round two, if all participants raise two to five fingers, the proposed decision is accepted. Otherwise, more discussion takes place and, again, proposal revision would cause a restart. On the last round, only a fist can fail the proposal. Explain the Fist of Five process very clearly to the team and write the meaning of each number of fingers on a large flipchart before you begin.

I once did this exercise with a large group and didn't notice the single vote of two fingers on the first round. When I proceeded as if we'd gotten consensus, some people whispered that I was rigging the vote. Fortunately, someone pointed out the mistake quickly, and order was restored.

Once a decision is made — according to whichever decision rule you choose — capture it visibly so everyone is clear on what just happened.

Make sure you get to the important stuff. Having early clarity on the purpose, product, and agenda will help you keep the meeting on track, but it is not enough. The following techniques will help you avoid the occasional sidetracking or protraction:

+ Keep a visible "parking lot" flipchart. When someone brings up a good idea that doesn't align with the meeting's purpose and product, capture it in the parking lot. Review the parking lot at the end and make follow-up decisions accordingly.

+ Some activities have participants generate all their ideas before evaluating them. (Brainstorming and the popular Worked Well/Needs Improvement retrospective format are structured this way.) If you see that the available time will not suffice for evaluating all the generated ideas, have the participants narrow the list down using *multivoting*, also known as *dot voting*. All participants receive an identical number of votes, typically three to five, to allocate to any ideas as they see fit. When everyone is ready, they indicate their choices with one dot per vote (using stickers or markers). You can then focus on the ideas that received the most votes.[10]

✦ Have the group agree to a practical decision rule. Some groups want to have unanimity on most proposals. That takes time, and isn't always truly necessary.

Let them talk. As the ATL, you are expected to lead the standard Agile meetings. Yet the more you talk, the less your team talks. For instance, when a ScrumMaster asks each team member the three questions, they naturally direct their answers at the ScrumMaster, not their teammates. On the other hand, I've attended standups where the team knew the process and just ran with it. The ScrumMaster was taking notes and occasionally asked clarifying or prompting questions. In those meetings, the team was clearly more open and talkative. I've observed the same openness and richer discussion in iteration planning meetings where the ScrumMaster simply kept the meeting on track but didn't offer *any opinion* about a story, a task, or an estimate.

> It doesn't take much to get a team talking. In one standup I observed, the ScrumMaster started by asking the technical leader for updates. They proceeded to talk among themselves for a few minutes while 12 people watched them in silence. Once the ScrumMaster turned to the group and asked, "Does anyone have any issues to report?" the floodgates opened.

Maintain safety. Keep monitoring the room for personal safety. If safety rules are violated, halt the meeting. If you cannot reestablish safety and resume the meeting, you probably have a bigger impediment to remove once outside the meeting.

Have checkpoints. While you must constantly be aware of the meeting's progress vis-à-vis its purpose and agenda, don't expect your participants to be aware of it. When you've finished a step in the process, say so and review the results. Then give a preamble to the next step. This will keep everybody with the program and avoid detours.

Make information visible. The larger or longer a meeting, the harder it gets to keep track of the collected data and the produced insights. Capture the highlights of what's said on flipcharts and post them on the walls. (*Tip*: Alternate colors between lines for easier legibility.) Folks can refer to that information during the meeting, which makes it richer, as well as after the meeting, which makes it more valuable. A skilled facilitator is likely to capture a dozen flipchart sheets, or more, during a large meeting. Make sure to take down the speakers' exact words or ask them to "headline" their words if they speak at length. Do not interpret or paraphrase; it's their meeting and their meaning.

Encourage everyone to contribute clearly. Throughout the meeting, you will ask questions to propel the conversation and obtain input. When you pose your questions to the whole group, you will sometimes get an answer, and other times you will get silence. To engage more people, call on individuals by name and make eye contact (but avoid making them uneasy or self-conscious). You might say, "So, Patrick, what do you think about that?" or "Sarah, what's your opinion?" Once the interaction is flowing, get better input by asking clarifying questions and precision questions (see 8.5).

Stop dysfunctional behavior. Even with the best preventive measures, dysfunction such as verbal attacks or passive-aggressive acts might still occur. Both for the integrity of the meeting and for the patience and goodwill of unaffected participants, you must restore order as quickly as possible — don't just wait for the offenders to settle down.

Some dysfunctional behavior is a symptom that the offender needs to be heard. Use techniques from chapter 8, possibly in combination with the parking lot, to help him get his thoughts out. If a person acts cynically, ask him to suggest a better idea. (See sections 7.5 and 7.6 for more on such behavior.) And if the dysfunction violates the ground rules, say so. If the offenders push back on those ground rules, remind them that the participants made the rules in order to run an effective meeting. If appropriate, offer to revise them.

If the offender's behavior recurs from meeting to meeting, she's actually taking on a role, such as aggressor, recognition seeker, or dominator[11] — quite possibly without being aware of it. Coaching, feedback, and follow-up outside of the meeting should help.

Ultimately, the meeting belongs to the participants. If they can't or won't handle it, call it off.

Maximize your neutrality. As a facilitator, your only concern is for the participants to achieve the meeting's objective. Therefore, remain as neutral as possible. You are being neutral when you are *attached* to helping the group reach its objective without being *committed* to the specific objective. This is easier said than done, because your duty is to help your team deliver on bigger goals than this one meeting. Fortunately, they know that. Whenever you diverge from pure facilitation to a more participative role, just say so.

9.7 What Is Involved in Closing a Meeting?

Always leave time for reviewing the meeting's achievements. Whether you take 30 seconds or five minutes, a brief recap gives participants a sense of accomplishment. If they didn't reach closure, the review will foster appreciation of the challenge. You should review:

✦ Decisions made

✦ Action items (next steps) and who signed up for what

✦ Deferred items and, in particular, the fate of the parking lot items

✦ What the participants can expect as a follow-up or record of the meeting (for instance, images of the flipcharts uploaded to a shared team space)

On occasion, finish a meeting with a three- to five-minute retrospective *about the meeting*. Simply ask the participants, "What did you like about this meeting?" and "What would you do differently?" Then, capture their answers on a flipchart.[12] Use this simple, unfiltered feedback to improve your facilitation of subsequent meetings.

9.8 Facilitated Meeting Example

I once facilitated a whole-day meeting. Dan, head of product development in charge of hundreds of people, wanted to examine the progress of their Agile rollout. The deliverables were key insights and a backlog of rollout activities for the next six months. Seven of his senior staff attended.

By 5:00 p.m., we had achieved our goals. All day, the managers had been engaged, and they produced several high-quality insights and decisions. They rated the meeting as very successful. Our process was based on just a handful of techniques:

1. Dan and I welcomed the participants and described the purpose and rough agenda.

2. Participants suggested several ground rules and reached consensus on four of them. (Many groups have trouble respecting one of our rules: turn off *all* electronics. This group abided by it *all day*, checking their email only during breaks.)

3. The managers took turns describing their units' rollout experience. I captured their points and the ensuing discussions on a total of 12 flipchart sheets, which filled up two walls.

4. Based on this data, everyone wrote down their insights, one per sticky note, in silence. When done, they posted all the stickies on the whiteboard and proceeded to read them all in silence. Without talking, they moved the notes around to cluster related insights. Then, anyone who felt strongly about a particular group read it out loud. Our scribe (Dan's assistant) captured each group as a key insight, with details.

5. After lunch, our scribe distributed printouts of the ten key insights. Silently, each participant chose the four they considered most important, and I tallied their choices. Three of the ten insights were clear winners, receiving twice as many votes as the next seven.

6. I reviewed the description of each of the top three insights, and every participant wrote suggested actions for the next phase of the rollout (again in silence, one action per sticky). The stickies went on the board, and folks clustered them. Each cluster became an activity in the rollout backlog, and the ensuing discussion around it provided that activity's details.

On first glance, having silent periods in a meeting might seem strange. One benefit you can see in the previous description is that everybody got to share their smarts without having their ideas critiqued. Those who needed time to collect their thoughts had that time.[13] Furthermore, everyone stayed engaged and awake: you won't see anyone nodding off when you use these techniques.

9.9 What Should I Do Differently to Facilitate a Virtual Meeting?

If a meeting's participants are in two or more locations, challenges abound. Participants calling from their desks are more exposed to distractions than those in a meeting room. The narrower the communication bandwidth, the harder it is for them to focus and remain engaged. As the facilitator, you can no longer "read the room" for feedback on emotions and energy. While the preceding sections' guidance still applies, virtual meetings require special treatment in order to maximize engagement.

Design a virtual meeting for minimal attendance and duration. Invite only people who will participate during most of the meeting, and solicit required input from others ahead of it. Prepare and disseminate as much of the data ahead of time; for instance, shorten distributed iteration planning by having subsets of the team task out stories and recognize dependencies the previous day.

Well in advance, distribute any artifacts that you would otherwise hang in the meeting room or review at the beginning — such as purpose, agenda, and ground rules. This gives everyone a chance to respond and self-select (if appropriate). The information will be accessible to them throughout the meeting, and you'll spend less time on the introduction before engaging the attendees.

Make it clear (perhaps in the ground rules) that all participants are responsible for their full participation. The fact that others can't see them doesn't allow them to multitask any more than in an in-person meeting. Consider yourself their guardian: help them remain engaged by designing activities suitable for a distributed meeting. Enrich their experience by including visual elements: share a screen, show slides that anchor the discussion, or use webcams in all locations. Even though these elements add little *substance*, they draw people's attention and keep them focused on the meeting.

In a distributed meeting, a timely start means that on the scheduled hour, you start talking — not dialing. You need to start the conference line, Web share, and/or camera a few minutes earlier, and all participants need to be dialed in by the start time.

> As an external coach and consultant, I attend dozens of distributed team meetings every year. Local members tend to be gracious about the extra effort involved in looping in their colleagues in other sites. Frequently, however, some remote participant doesn't call in. After waiting a couple of minutes, a local manager emails, texts, or calls the person. I can just see the room's energy dissipate and the participants' mood turn sour as they think about the time they are wasting.

Before your strong opening, call roll by location. Have everyone say their names and perhaps a word or two to indicate their mood; leave out "What's new?" and chitchat. This way, everybody knows who is present, and it's their first opportunity to engage by saying something.

During the meeting, call on people by name and have them identify themselves when they speak. Ask people to describe their emotional response to what they hear, because others can't see them (use phrases like "How does that make you feel?" and "What does that do for you?" to prompt them). Use active listening (see 8.2), even more than usual, for the same reason. Use a shared screen or dedicated software as a virtual flipchart for capturing notes. Put the parking lot to good use in order to keep the meeting moving — and short.

Since distributed meetings can be significantly more challenging than in-person ones, don't skip the quick retrospective at the end. Call on each person by name and ask for one thing he or she liked and one thing he or she would do differently. ("Pass" is a valid answer.) Remember, whether a remote attendee liked your style or rolled her eyes, you wouldn't know it unless you asked.

Even after applying all this advice, you will still hear some grumbling about time spent in meetings. You might even have your own doubts. Just remember, meetings are meant to help a group move forward. They are an opportunity for communication, feedback, decisions, introspection, course correction, even team building.

Most of my clients had had little exposure to facilitation before their Agile transformation. You can set an example for others by honing your meeting skills and leading your meetings properly. Read more on the subject and take a facilitation course. Hire a professional facilitator to lead long, sensitive meetings, such as project retrospectives, and learn from watching him. Shadow other managers and coaches who are skilled in facilitation. And use your influence to create a culture that doesn't tolerate bad meetings.

Supplementary Resource
Go to **www.TheHumanSideOfAgile.com** and download
"Meeting Leader Cheat Sheet."

PART IV
Be the Agile Leader

Thus far we've examined how you are the oil in the community's engine. You perform varied duties to help the team deliver valued product. You connect people, support their Agility, and help them collaborate. Your next step is to *lead* them. As the Agile leader, you inspire and guide the team to great performance. You are the team's *champion*, the person who shields them and fights for them. Agile's premise of improvement and adaptation means change is a constant — and with change comes resistance. In Part IV, you will learn techniques for leading your team in adopting and integrating all changes, including the deepest one: their initial transition to Agile.

CHAPTER 10

Champion Your Team

Every one of the preceding chapters had the same premise: to succeed with Agile, you must take care of the human element. You do that by designing a work environment that allows the human element to flourish and then mostly staying out of the way.[1]

Nevertheless, you're still "in the middle." To the team, you are the servant leader who helps them deliver results. To senior management, you are the obvious point of contact for coordinating the team's work with upstream and downstream teams. In reality, however, many teams turn to their Agile team leader (ATL) for direction, and many senior managers hold ATLs solely accountable for teams' execution on plans. Become your team's champion and enable them to take responsibility for delivering value.

10.1 How Is a Leader Different From a Manager?

Chances are you have spent the last several years in corporate environments. There you encountered hierarchical structures, high-level and detailed planning, and complicated workflows. These mechanisms are designed to maximize profitability and product value while minimizing risk. In software development, these mechanisms are intended to maximize efficiency and resource allocation.

Even basic software is quite complex. Factor in continuous requests for changes, new features and configurations, and ongoing maintenance, and complexity grows at an alarming rate. The traditional response is to manage complexity through careful planning.

Managers spend considerable energy and time determining and sequencing activities, shifting resources, and controlling changes. The Agile response is to manage complexity through evolution.[2] Managers and teams use feedback to evolve their work products and processes gradually. Their guiding principle is to address current needs while considering readiness for potential risks and developments.

As you consider this different approach to complexity and risk, you might hope for a process, or a set of "best practices," to optimize the Agile response. The temptation is even greater for classically trained project managers and executives, who have spent most of their careers applying such tools. One client CEO challenged me once, "I've shipped eight successful software products in my career. What could you possibly say that justifies paying two programmers to write together the same code they could write alone?"

This is the attitude I observe in companies that have adopted Agile (for instance, Scrum) *in name only*. They plan biweekly iterations based on year-long plans to which they've already committed. They spend inordinate energy estimating tiny tasks. They perpetuate silos by assigning work to task experts. When I ask their ScrumMasters or project managers to describe the purpose of their role, they say it is "to enforce the Scrum process." They expect each team to produce an amount of work equal to a made-up number times the number of developers, and they hurry to take corrective action when reality turns out differently. In these environments, project managers carry out the executives' plans by maximizing production and predictability.

What would effective *leaders* do differently?

Effective leaders rely on their teams to make improvements and adjustments. They help by asking questions of the team and of all levels of the organization. Rather than "plan the work and work the plan," they lead planning and continually question the plan. They pay attention to what works and what doesn't, so they can improve one and eliminate the other. Effective leaders reframe failures as feedback and apply that feedback forthwith. Whereas managers direct their teams to implement agreed-upon ideas, leaders take in the ever-changing context to update visions, concepts, plans, and programs.

According to research,[3] the same six behavioral characteristics that make facilitators successful also make Agile leaders successful:

1. **Strategic.** Agile leaders take a broad, long-term view, one that doesn't fret over optimizing the short term. Strategic thinking contributes to clarity of vision, which is vital for ensuring that a team isn't just delivering *stuff* but fulfilling a valuable purpose.

2. **Tactical.** Agile leaders are also pragmatic, making sure the team continuously delivers value and responds to changing realities.

3. **Innovative.** Agile leaders balance long-term thinking (why/what) and short-term execution (what/how) with reflection on results, openness to new ideas, and experimentation (what if).

4. **Excited.** Although low-key leaders can inspire people, teams react differently to excitement, energy, and enthusiasm. Passionate leaders inspire their followers to invest their energy and overcome challenges.

5. **Consensual.** Agile teams operate best on a basis of respect and trust. Rather than erode these by *telling* teams how to proceed, leaders increase them by supporting consensual decision making.

6. **Empathetic.** Rather than view their team members as code-producing units, Agile leaders step into their shoes. They tailor their communication and expectations to each person's state.

The same research also identified four behavioral characteristics that cause Agile leaders to fail and their teams to hurt. Interestingly, these are behaviors expected of traditional project managers:[4]

1. **Authoritarian.** Exercised positional influence (authority) tends to stifle Agility. By requiring permission or approval, the authority retains the singular right to limit change, innovation, and improvement.

2. **Structuring.** People often respond favorably to structure, drawing comfort from the predictability it affords. However, the more structure there is, the harder it is to change and adapt. Managers who structure the team's experience and plans too much (optimizing for performance and risk) effectively stifle change.

3. **Conservative.** Software is complex enough, and planning is hard enough, that leaders are tempted to minimize changes if they are not obviously required. This contravenes the tenet of continuous improvement.

4. **Technical.** Some technical grounding is helpful, and leaders should understand the economics of their domain. Still, a technical expert-turned-manager can be detrimental to the team, since he or she would be tempted to fill in for the team, answer for them, or second-guess their answers.

> At an iteration planning meeting, the development manager sounded genuine when he encouraged team members to share their opinions and estimates. No matter what any person said, though, he either nodded vigorously or proceeded to "correct" it. Team members felt little ownership over their tasks.

10.2 What Does the Team Need From Me in Order to Succeed?

Your team needs a number of conditions met in order to succeed. And they will turn to you, their servant leader, to put them in place.

These conditions are similar to what teams have always needed from their managers, with a few adaptations for the Agile context.

The parameters of the work. For each project (or any undertaking), the team needs to know:

+ What exactly they are building (the *mission*)

+ Why they are building it (the *vision*)

+ The conditions of success, best framed as business effects outside the project's boundary (also known as objectives, goals, or management tests)

+ Their purview: what the organization considers them responsible for, beyond new product development, such as production support and legacy defect fixing

+ The tradeoff matrix of the constraints: which of the following constraints — functionality, quality, time, and resources — is fixed, which is desirable, and which two are adjustable

+ Who is part of their community

These are the salient components of the *Agile charter*, which the sponsor owns and to which everyone contributes their perspective. You need to ensure that the charter exists, stays current, and is the target by which the project is governed.

An appropriately structured team. Most teams do not have complete control over their composition. All members nevertheless expect their teams to be formed appropriately for the work at hand. You are in a good position to know which qualities, preferences, technical skills, and social skills your team requires and to strive to bring those in.

A knowledgeable, empowered, and available product owner (PO). The team must work with a person who can articulate and refine the vision, then stock the backlog reliably and sort it effectively. Without that person, the team would probably work out *some* solution, but not necessary a *valuable* one.

A suitable work environment. The team should operate in an environment appropriate to their work. This starts from basic work-space design elements, such as lighting, comfort, and personal space. It continues with reducing distractions from outside the team, such as noise and foot traffic. You can aim higher with an environment that supports productive teamwork and social growth. For instance, it's best if the team has some control over the environment's config-uration or can personalize it, even slightly. (Uniform "cubicle farms" don't generally inspire productivity and teamwork.)

> "My team was looking to map their workflow using a white-board and sticky notes. Unfortunately, we were situated in the middle of an open-plan office without access to walls, nor did we have the necessary space for a freestanding whiteboard. In the end, we bought a roll of whiteboard sheeting and applied it to a nearby structural pillar. Even though work items flowed from top to bottom, and space was tight, it served our purpose and is still in use years later."
>
> — *Neil Johnson, development manager*

The right tools for the job. It is not enough to provide desks, chairs, and computers. Software teams also need good productivity, communication, and collaboration tools — as well as some autonomy in choosing those tools. If they are new to Agile, they need proper grounding in the methodology before they start sprinting.

Access to pertinent information. To effectively negotiate, design, and produce deliverables, the team must understand the context. They need to know constraints and be able to determine implications. You can amplify their understanding by securing access to product roadmaps, plans, designs, market data, and — perhaps most usefully — users.

Clarity about desirable behavior. Success in an Agile context is not just a matter of meeting iteration commitments. It often involves building organizational capability, increasing innovation, retaining domain knowledge, and doing a host of other things. You need to ensure that those desired performance attributes are well defined at the organizational level and well understood at the individual level. (That is typically a responsibility of the organization's managers; see Appendix.) If the organization conducts performance evaluations, do your best to align those with Agile-friendly expectations (see 5.7).

Air cover. A team can self-organize and continuously adapt their process only in an environment that allows these dynamics. In environments that have little tolerance for such team-level autonomy, you act as the buffer. For instance, if your Agile team finds little use for detailed estimates but management still wants numbers, help your team spend minimal effort on estimation while providing useful information for forecasting.

Caring, encouragement, and recognition. If you provide for all these needs in a rigid, officious, cold manner, the team might do an excellent job — and head for the door. They will *want* to stick around, be with each other, and do a great job if you care about each member individually and encourage their growth.[5] You — or the product owner or managers — can recognize the team for a job well done. (The iteration review meeting is a powerful opportunity for that.) Recognition is important for motivation, which requires active nurturing; ignoring people's work has similar effects to negative feedback.[6]

> **Supplementary resource**: Download "Conditions for Team Success" from the book's companion website, **www.TheHumanSideOfAgile.com**.

10.3 Should I Expect Accountability From the Team?

In traditional, plan-driven development environments, accountability can be a powerful yet simple management tool. Assign a task to a member of your team and expect him to deliver within a prescribed range of time and quality. If he doesn't, he should be able to render a reasonable account of the work's progress and why it missed expectations. If the account isn't satisfactory or the person misses expectations regularly, there will be consequences. The deal goes both ways: you can expect people to be accountable for their commitments, and, from their end, many solid performers pride themselves on their accountability.

Some companies use the accountability mechanism with their individual contributors because they don't quite trust them. It's a sanctioned, to-be-expected mechanism for extracting work from people. It also complies handily with the mechanism that allows terminating employees legally "for cause." If your organization uses accountability this way, Agile methods may not be a good fit. According to the Agile Manifesto, we "Build projects around motivated individuals. Give them the environment and support they need, and trust them to get the job done."[7] In those conditions, you don't need the team member–manager accountability mechanism in order to get people to work; peer accountability suffices.

Even in organizations that adopt Agile wholeheartedly, some managers, project managers, and team leaders experience an internal conflict. On the one hand, the new framework promises that *teams* will drive themselves properly and productively. On the other hand, years of management experience (often combined with senior management that isn't interested in front-line methods) have accustomed them to demand accountability from *individual contributors*. Some may keep using this mechanism, rationalizing that their particular team doesn't fit the mold. That is an ill omen for the team's Agility.

At the individual level, honest accountability can catalyze performance and build relationships, whether the methodology is Agile or not. Willpower and intrinsic motivation don't always suffice for sustained performance, so one thing that helps is being a member of a community whose members are up front about intents and activities.[8] Each member, knowing that her colleagues hold her to account, will consider her actions and responses. When a team drives together toward shared goals, the members are naturally accountable to each other.

You must distinguish between individual and team commitments. Most commitments in Agile are team ones. For instance, an iteration planning results in a team commitment to a set of deliverables, unless you assign tasks to individuals. Do you wonder, "Should I hold the team accountable for their commitments?" And moreover, "Why should they render an account to me, and not to someone else?" The answers might surprise you.

As the ATL, you *should* hold the team accountable for their commitments. The obvious reason is that you represent the organization, which has certain expectations of performance from its *teams*. It's your place and role to communicate these expectations and ensure that they are met. You do that through observation, assessment, feedback, and corrective action (and not necessarily through formal evaluations). However, this accountability holds water only if the right conditions for team success are in place (see 10.2). For instance, if the team is required to cram more features into the product than they can build reliably, blaming them for low-quality code is unfair.

The less-obvious reason for holding the team accountable is that you can thereby help them perform. In fact, accountability is an element of coaching. The most visible example of it is in the planning game. By planning and estimating openly, the team puts forth their intents; members know that at the end of the cycle they might need to give an account of their actions. Just as at the individual level, this expectation helps them put serious thought into their work. And if they don't have a good explanation for significant slippage, they ought to learn from that experience. True mutual accountability between team members builds trust and strengthens relationships, which leads to better performance.

Note the distinction between accountability, which is *given*, and responsibility, which is *taken*.[9] The best situation is when the team —

both as individuals and as a whole — *takes responsibility* for their work; they eschew defense mechanisms (see 7.2) and take care of the situation. This plays powerfully into the individuals' and the group's self-esteem.

The team should be accountable to the closest person within the organization who designs their work environment and can establish consequences for the actions within it. That usually means you or direct managers. Your role turns on helping them deliver (say, by removing impediments), so you can expect them to answer to *you* for their part of the deal. As the team's process steward, hold them true to the methods they picked and decisions they made.

"At one company, accountability for results was generally absent. Both IT and our customers believed large budget overruns, late deliveries, poor quality, and cut scope were normal. I was assigned to be the project manager for a team that had just finished a lengthy project with weak results.

"To help them achieve better outcomes in the next project, I wanted to instill a sense of pride in the team so they would hold *themselves* accountable for their work. This was difficult, requiring many challenging discussions and a tremendous investment of time and energy. I wouldn't accept excuses for why an iteration review would take long or why it was difficult to accomplish a task. I kept exhorting them (and helping them) to find better ways. I never allowed the team to blame others.

"After a couple of months, the team had realized an incredible turnaround. I no longer had to hold them accountable; they were holding each other accountable. When issues arose, the team quickly moved to find solutions to allow them to succeed. For the first time in years, a team in this organization had a big success on their hands! By the end of the project the team barely required my leadership; I mostly provided information and removed difficult barriers."

— *Mike Edwards, Agile coach*

10.4 What Will Keep Team Members Motivated?

For more than a century, the business world has been conducting a huge, uncontrolled experiment in motivating people. In parallel, the world of academia has been scientifically researching the same subject. For the past few decades, these two worlds have been diverging, and nowhere is the gap more evident than in creative development work.

Most organizations rely largely on *extrinsic* motivators to drive worker action. These elements typically include wages, bonuses, benefits, vacation time, and stock options. Some of the more enlightened workplaces provide additional extrinsic motivators, such as praise, stimulating spaces, and opportunities to relax on the job.

According to modern research (and plenty of industry evidence[10]), these elements do not work as intended. Unless the work is highly repetitive and procedural — which is not the case with your Agile team — extrinsic motivators might even do harm. Your organization must pay its staff enough to be competitive and to enable them to focus on the work, not on the reward. Additional perks might be motivating in the short term, but they can also have a reversal effect. For instance, the expectation of a sizable bonus can cause such anxiety as to degrade performance.[11]

Organizations have long known that *intrinsic* motivation — the worker's inner drive — can be very powerful. So they naturally look for "motivated employees." According to current thinking, all human beings start life with intrinsic motivation — just look at children — yet outdated work structures erode it. Recent research suggests that knowledge-work organizations can tap into their staff's intrinsic motivation by fostering *autonomy*, *mastery*, and *purpose*.[12]

Think back to a (preferably recent) situation when working felt as good as playing. You were engaged, interested, driven, even if the task was unfamiliar and your results were less than perfect. Did you act willingly, with a feeling of choice in what to do and how to do it? That is autonomy. Did you turn out good results, and did you feel that your performance was bound to improve? That is mastery. Did you feel that your work contributed to something valuable, important, and greater than you could single-handedly achieve? That is purpose.

According to extensive Gallup research,[13] employee engagement is closely linked to business performance. Unless your workplace consistently provides autonomy, mastery, and purpose, don't expect long-term engagement from your employees. However, another Gallup finding might surprise you: for your workplace to promote intrinsic motivation, what senior management does matters far less than what direct managers and leaders do. In the Agile team context, that means *you*.

While you personally cannot create motivation in team members, as a servant leader you can promote an environment that satisfies their intrinsic drivers. You need to do so for *every* team member because of the "principle of the least invested coworker"[14]: the less-motivated have a greater drag effect on their team than any boost provided by the motivated ones. Fortunately, Agile makes your work easier.

Autonomy. As a self-organizing, empowered group, the Agile team makes and owns most decisions regarding their work. The team collaborates with the product owner to define deliverables and decides when and how to produce them. Members are expected and encouraged to voice their opinions, contribute where they can, and reach consensus about choices. They pick their tasks and enjoy considerable latitude with regard to implementation.

How to decrease autonomy. Create your entire project's backlog in detail and have the technical lead or architect estimate the work and task it out. Have a brief planning meeting at the start of each iteration in which the PO tells the team what to work on next and the tech lead distributes the tasks. Design most of the implementation ahead of time and have the team follow that design. Leave any remaining design or refactoring work to the most experienced people.

Mastery. The continuous improvement tenet of Agile has members refine their work products, process, and skills. They do all that in the context of value delivery — that is, on something that matters. Folks increase their mastery (and craftsmanship) not only through individual practice; they rely on frequent peer feedback and collaboration, such as through paired work and regular reflection. Despite the fact that ownership is now collective, all members know full well the value of their own contributions.

How to decrease mastery. Decree that each developer must accomplish a certain number of story points per iteration and increase that number every few weeks. Shorten the team retrospectives to 15 to 20 minutes, during which you tell them what needs improvement and how you'd improve it. Practice demo-driven development — produce enough *stuff* to *show*, without regard to the quality of its implementation. Give people performance feedback once a year and tie it to rewards (see 5.7).

Purpose. The Agile organization manages its project portfolio with eyes wide open, spending its resources on the undertakings that matter most. The sponsors, product owner, and you keep verifying that your specific project remains valuable, its vision remains compelling, and success criteria remain meaningful. You keep delivering value to your users and learning about their experience.

How to decrease purpose. Forget the project's vision and charter; just assemble a backlog and get started. Make up a deadline and create a sense of urgency around it. Tell the team that everything on the backlog is a must-have.

A custom-development firm started a lucrative project for a high-profile client. The vendor's team understood the project's value to their firm (*purpose*), chose cutting-edge tools and methods (*mastery*), and enjoyed considerable leeway (*autonomy*). A few months into the project, rumors started circulating that the client didn't really want the product for its users' benefit; they merely wanted a fancy addition to their marketing mix. As schedule pressure increased, a few team members started wondering aloud, "What's the point of doing it, anyway?" Even though the project still held the same promise for their employer (the vendor), the *perceived* loss of the other purpose — giving users a valuable tool — tanked the team's motivation.

Autonomy, mastery, and purpose belong under the umbrella of one universal motivator: *to feel important*. Everyone craves feeling needed, having a say, and being listened to. You can see these desires manifested in interactions, meetings, and daily work. Two Agile mechanisms that help people feel important are team-wide planning and reflection, and delivering working and accepted features every few weeks.

Keep paying attention to team members' motivation. Check in with them individually, and observe them at meetings. When senior management makes announcements, you may have to translate them into language that the team finds motivating. Be watchful for demotivators, and address them to the extent possible. Be aware that some demotivators pack a strong punch in an Agile setting; for instance:

✦ Keeping around members who don't fit (see 7.3)

✦ Developing features in a rudimentary, ugly, or hacky form in order to get early feedback — and leaving them that way

✦ Working in a legacy code environment, where *everything* takes longer and *everything* is harder

At the end of the day, people are more complex and dynamic than any model of intrinsic and extrinsic motivators. Perhaps you've worked with teams whose strong personal bonds trumped limited autonomy, mastery, and purpose. Or maybe you've had a colleague for whom high pay was an effective long-term motivator — not so he could drive a Mercedes, but because he used the money to give his children an easier life than he had growing up. I have known people who enjoyed a healthy balance of intrinsic and extrinsic motivation, and yet a personal tiff with a coworker sufficed to push them out. In the quest to keep your team members motivated, keep your eyes and ears open to all evidence.

Supplementary resource: Download "Ten Simple Motivation Catalysts" from the book's companion website, **www.TheHumanSideOfAgile.com**.

10.5 How Do I Get Stakeholders and Managers on My Side?

If your organization is new to Agile, team members will feel the transition's effect the most. The change also affects the rest of the project community, but to a lesser extent. This often-sizable group includes several layers of management above the teams, who need to adjust their expectations and behavior. It also includes professionals in other departments, downstream or upstream from the core team, whose work depends on effectively interfacing with the team.

As your team's champion, establish bonds with those people, effectively becoming the glue of the community. Doing so will secure the collaboration — or at least the cooperation[15] — needed for effective development and will prevent them from sabotaging the team's performance (intentionally or otherwise).

Start by providing basic education. Unlike your team, the stakeholders and managers need to understand only the principles and motivation of Agile as well as the few practices that apply to them. Never assume that they'll read the books, show up to your team's training, or try to understand the finer details. Senior managers are the least likely to have time for this education, yet having an audience with them even for one hour is often enough. When you meet them, don't describe process mechanics or show slides. Instead, ask about the business effects and results that matter to *them*, explain how Agile would help achieve them, and discuss their involvement.

Invite the entire community to the iteration demo. Nominally, it's an opportunity for feedback and course correction, but it's also an opportunity for community building and the demonstration of commitments kept. I also invite the same people to the daily standup; they are allowed to share updates and ask for clarifications, but they are not allowed to meddle. (I never, *ever*, allow anyone to use the words "chickens" and "pigs" in this context.[16]) Invite them to visit the team space, observe the valuable artifacts and information radiators[17] on the walls, and socialize with the team. Be around to answer the questions that might arise about Agile. If the team is new to Agile, not all members may be able to adequately explain some of the contentious points.

In my experience, most senior managers in a company transitioning to Agile underestimate the time it takes to reach good productivity (see 6.8). To make matters worse, they are told that teams produce *potentially shippable* increments every couple of weeks. This appeals nicely to managers who wanted Agile for its promise of "cheaper, better, faster." They apply subtle pressure on the teams to perform and get quite frustrated and anxious when things turn out differently (see 10.6). You must manage their expectations regarding the team's performance so they can keep things in perspective. Introduce them to the Satir change curve (see 11.1). Explain the continuous improvement mechanisms you have in place. Keep them focused on winning the war instead of each battle. A charter comes in handy here, as it deflects attention from small-scale deliverables.

Understand what other managers care about, then tailor your responses to their model of the world. Most senior managers care about the project's schedule (and making it shorter); customer experience (which goes directly to customer attraction and retention); and revenue and costs. You probably live in lower-level details, such as user stories and velocity, which are less useful to them. When they ask you for information, seek to understand their purpose.

For example, suppose they ask for daily detailed progress. Using techniques from chapter 8, you learn that they want visibility. Visibility affords them control, which will reduce their concerns about the project's schedule. Now you can speak their language. Show them how your methods respect and possibly compress the schedule, and back up your words with data.

One thing that worries people both downstream and upstream from the Agile team is, "How is this going to make my life harder?"

As you have conversations with the various stakeholders — in particular, managers of non-Agile projects — listen and take note of their particular fears. Common fears include:

+ *"The team's choice of Agile may prevent me from meeting my objectives."* The stakeholders still need to follow the company's processes and manage dependencies. Seek to understand their objectives, expectations, and obligations. Collaborate with them to produce backlog items that address their needs.

+ *"They are asking for more time than I can spare."* Handle this by playing down their involvement. Since you don't truly know how much they'll need to be involved, don't try to secure guarantees you may not need. Explain that the team is autonomous. Emphasize that the team will do whatever they can, without encumbering others or treading on their turf. And demonstrate a genuine intent to minimize the impact on the stakeholders' workload and schedule, adjusting their involvement as time goes on.

+ *"They'll probably want me to change my process."* That fear is actually true, to some extent, but again its details are not known *a priori*. Explain that you'll work out the details as you go along, because you frequently inspect and adapt.

+ *"I'm losing control!"* Having a measure of predictability along with a perception of control gives a good deal of comfort. Agile provides excellent control while giving the impression that it doesn't. Explain the control mechanisms that the person still has.

To this day, more people are misinformed and confused about Agile than those who know what it is. Even those who've read a book on Agile might be confused by your team's particular adaptation. Executives still tell me, "What's the big deal? It's only a process!" while failing to realize the magnitude and ramifications of Agility.

Any moment you're not out there setting records straight, they are forming their own impressions and telling themselves stories that may not be in your favor. Keep the lines of communication open. Sometimes it's the people you don't see every day whom you need to communicate with a lot.

Remember that all project community members have needs, wants, and obligations, which they meet within the organizational power structure. Become familiar with that structure so you can be pragmatic about possibilities and expectations. You might need to make concessions, such as translating release and iteration plans into standardized project reports. Sometimes you'll want to have a certain item higher up in the backlog so as to get an influential person on your side. Other times you'll encounter resistance, such as the HR manager saying, "We can't include auditions in the hiring process," or the Operations team lead saying, "We can't deploy more than once weekly." Look for common ground and ask, "Here's what I want to do. What *can* we do, given the constraints of your job?"

10.6 What Should I Do If the Team Has Had an Unpleasant Slip-Up?

All Agile and Lean methodologies include mechanisms for regulating the flow of work. Whether you use iterations or WIP (work in progress) limits, the idea is that the team doesn't pull more work than they're capable of completing. However, that doesn't guarantee smooth sailing. The complex nature of software development means that most teams will experience slip-ups. Common examples are:

+ **An embarrassing demo.** It took long to get started, features didn't work as intended, commonsense behavior didn't get coded, or valid questions were met with unsatisfactory answers.

+ **A cancelled demo.** The team couldn't get it ready in time, even with a slight continuance, so the decision was made to cancel it.

✦ **"Easy" work that just doesn't seem to end.** What seemed like a small story or refactoring has dragged on, and the team really can't say when it will be over. Worse, they may have compromised their ability to demonstrate or deploy unrelated features.

✦ **A majorly slipped iteration.** Almost no story was actually finished.

While such events need not turn into unpleasantness, they *are* impediments to the team's performance. You and your team have three duties:

1. Recognize their significance and impact.

2. Take corrective action.

3. Prevent their recurrence.

A slip-up is *a team problem.* It is not your problem — you are not singularly accountable for it, and it's not yours to resolve. Instead, lead the team in resolving it. The best avenue for that is the established mechanism for resolving team problems and learning from mishaps: the retrospective. Use the regularly scheduled iteration retrospective, or call an impromptu one. Consider conducting root-cause analysis in order to *not* settle for obvious first explanations. Two powerful, accessible tools for such analysis are the Five Why's[18] and the Fishbone (Ishikawa) diagram.[19]

10.6.1 What if Senior Management Reacted Unfavorably to the Slip-Up?

Sometimes a slip-up makes a nasty splash. The team is gathered — usually in the demo meeting — and receives a verbal lashing from an executive. Many teams that recently adopted Agile have had that experience: senior managers, with whom they had rarely interacted, now show up every two weeks and demand completed, perfect work. In some cases, those executives start micromanaging both the team and the ScrumMaster, thinking they can turn the situation around. This is like Agile martial law.

This turn of events is *most problematic* from the team's perspective. What's going on in their minds?

"*We look bad.*" Team members probably believe that they did their best and spent their time on useful activities. The fact that they encountered trouble must put them in a bad light.

"*This isn't fair.*" This thought is particularly prevalent — and disastrous — early in an Agile team's life cycle. They haven't quite normed yet (see 6.1) or transformed their mind-set (since that takes months), and now they are constantly under a magnifying glass to deliver finished work *every two weeks*, which isn't how they are used to working. They also feel that the hoopla is unjustified, considering that an iteration accounts for maybe 5% of the entire project.

"*This isn't entirely our fault.*" Is the slip-up due entirely to reasons under their control, or is some of it due to external dependencies like technical environments and vendor support? Make sure to separate the two, because the blaming executive may not be aware of the details.

"*Oh, no!*" A verbal lashing from an authority figure usually creates a feeling of impending doom. Although the team worked together throughout the preceding few days and weeks, the thought process they go through is this: "They won't allow this kind of performance to go on for much longer. But there's no way they'll say, 'The entire team doesn't deliver, so we'll just fire them all.' They say we rise together and fall together, but we're certainly not going to fall together. So I need to hunker down and do my best to show that I'm worth keeping, even if I can't trust my team members to pull through." This sort of survivalist thinking is the death knell of collaboration and mutual accountability.

[*Note*: You might also notice that the team is complacent about or uninterested in the slip-up or management's reaction. That spells a problem with motivation, buy-in (see 5.2), or commitment (see 5.3).]

Since you are their servant leader, take care of them, both individually and as a team. Let them vent and heal. Convene a retrospective and also hold one-on-one conversations to assess the mood and help people work through the emotions. Do those things once the dust has settled, but not too late — otherwise the negative emotions and attitudes start growing roots.

You also represent the business's interests, so you need to work closely with the senior managers. Make sure to demonstrate that you (as an extension of the team) are taking corrective action and preventing a recurrence of the slip-up. Build goodwill and understanding for the team's situation and learning curve. Also, as delicately and sensitively as you can, educate managers on the effects of their behavior. In essence, you need to shield the team without appearing to take sides.

10.7 How Do I Take a Stand for My Team?

Even a well-functioning team in a well-functioning organization sometimes needs protection. Organizational constraints and dicta may threaten a team's well-being. No matter how proactively you bring stakeholders and senior managers to your side, you will have to take a stand for the team occasionally. This can be scary and in some cases, career-limiting.

In the extreme case, the company no longer values the team's project sufficiently. Otherwise, the common threats to teams include moving members in or out, pressuring them to deliver, and micromanaging. Those threats touch the human side; they are not about the process. And unfortunately, they usually emanate from a senior manager who has good intentions but doesn't appreciate the consequences. Most senior managers are still not aware of:

+ The damage caused by shifting people around (see 4.5 and 6.1)

+ How long it takes to incorporate change (see 6.8), what to expect along the way, and how to mitigate the performance dip (see 11.1)

+ Local vs. global optimization of process and results[20]

+ The difficulty and unreliability of estimation and the side effects of treating estimation as a commitment or guarantee

+ What truly motivates people, and their own staff in particular (see 10.4)

+ The greater performance potential of a synergistic team versus a "team of one"

Assuming your management is on board with these points, how do you take a stand for your team?

First, seek to understand management's objectives and reasons by asking open-ended questions. Suppose they want to add contractors to your team. Do they want to help the team produce more or increase a certain expertise for better results in that area? What are they worried about? What tangible results do they expect to get? Or suppose an executive demands, "I want to know what each developer is working on!" What will that information help him do or avoid?

Analyze their actions' potential benefits and disadvantages. Remember that every action has both intended and unintended consequences; explore these together before starting something you can't undo. As the situation warrants, consider involving the team in producing creative alternatives. Even if they don't offer better ideas, merely consulting them will mitigate the impact of the threat (see 5.1).

> "We wanted to cover our code with good automated tests. On a few occasions, we said the tests would take some time, but we were slapped and told, 'Just deliver.'"
>
> ScrumMasters and team leaders in several companies have told me variations on this story. They and their teams wanted to write safe, clean, quality code; they spoke about being professional. Their managers were more concerned with the schedule. Taking a stand in this case meant demonstrating to the managers that quick, get-to-done iterations without supporting technical discipline are actually a bad investment.

If your team's autonomy is under threat and you cannot mitigate the risk on your own, escalate the problem. But what if the person at the escalation point is the one *causing* the problem? With any luck, you have a safe, trusting relationship that allows you to be candid about the situation. Otherwise, if you are employing an external coach or consultant, her neutrality might make her a suitable person to carry the message. Your last recourse is to find another influential person in the organization who has the boss's ear.

Remember that managers are people too. If you find yourself imagining that the manager has nefarious intents and is out to get you, *pause*. Few managers are the bullies, control freaks, or egomaniacs that some of their subordinates like to think they are. Have patience with them; assume best intent, and attribute to ignorance what you'd otherwise attribute to evil. They too are learning, so cut them some slack. If you push back, complain, or argue, you're far less likely to achieve the results you want than if you treat them empathetically (see chapter 8).

Every Agile team functions within a larger organizational framework. This framework sets the direction and provides operational support; sometimes it also hinders performance and interferes with teamwork. By championing your team, you will assist with the former and negate the latter. Provide, fight, and advocate for the team so they can take responsibility for their commitments.

Supplementary Resources
Go to **www.TheHumanSideOfAgile.com** and download "Conditions for Team Success" and "Ten Simple Motivation Catalysts."

CHAPTER 11

Lead People Through Change

Imagine for a moment that everything in your team's experience remained the same for years. The same people are consistently transforming requests for value into releasable product increments using the same process. The same managers and stakeholders are maintaining a constant business atmosphere. Team members have virtually fused into a single unit, moving along on an even keel.

Whether you're delighting in this prospect or groaning audibly at its blandness, notice that this team does not need a leader. All they could want is an administrator to assist daily execution. But introduce even a single variable into the equation — such as occasional business pressure, an improvement initiative, or a staff reassignment — and all of a sudden, they need to adapt their ways.

The reality of software development is that change is everywhere, all the time, and it involves multiple variables. Teams cannot deal with all changes effectively on their own or in isolation from the rest of their organization. They can use *your help leading them through change*.

Some teams' journey starts with what is arguably the greatest change: adopting the Agile mind-set. Even though Agile development has been around for more than a decade, many organizations and professionals still consider it a novelty, and few software development groups truly follow the Agile Manifesto.[1] Most practitioners, coaches, and managers cut their teeth on Agile development on the job, through trial and error. Be ready: for many years to come, you are likely to lead people and teams with wildly disparate understandings and perspectives of Agility.

Each team will require different support in adopting, adapting, or correcting methods for their context. You will encounter different degrees of openness and tolerance for change, different qualities and attitudes, different politics, and different project constraints. Learn what to expect and do in the Agile context in order to be a successful change agent.

11.1 What Happens to Performance During Change?

You know that learning new skills involves a "learning curve." You know that successful changes take time — did you know that there's also a *change curve*?

It doesn't matter what change you experience. Whether you learn (or relearn) a certain sport, become a parent, or adopt a technique from this book, your performance will follow the qualitative progression predicted by the change curve. If your team undergoes a change,

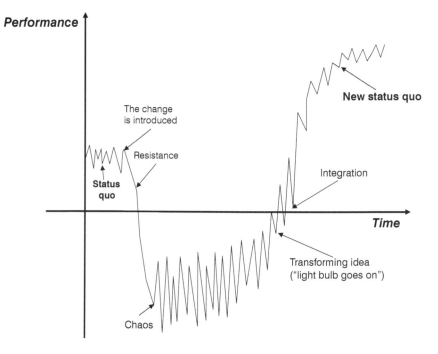

such as adopting Agile or revising a certain practice, the team will experience this shift in performance. Furthermore, each team member will move along his or her own curve.

Psychotherapist Virginia Satir first identified this curve in her work in family therapy. Others have helped determine the universality of the model.[2]

Before the introduction of the change (*foreign element*), your performance is stable; that is the old status quo, popularly known as the comfort zone. When the change happens, your performance will drop precipitously: you might lack pertinent skills, react inappropriately to stimuli, and *resist* the change. You will spend the next period of time — ranging from minutes to months, depending on the change — in *chaos*. You will still underperform, at times less so and at other times more. At some point, you will have the *transforming idea*: the light bulb will go on in your mind as you realize the meaning of the change and appropriate responses to it. In the next phase you will *integrate* the new skills, behaviors, expectations, and attitudes. You will eventually reach a *new status quo*, which is hopefully better than the old status quo.

If you review the curve of the Tuckman team evolution (forming, storming, norming, performing) model in 6.1, you'll notice that it has a similar shape. When a team is formed, it undergoes the change from not working together to working together. The departure or addition of a member triggers a similar change.

This model has several implications for you.

For starters, expect the bad times, and teach the team and your management to expect the bad times. Some changes — like transitioning the first several projects from a waterfall process to Agile — take months to sink in, and during that time the team flounders. Competent people who made the old process work now find themselves in unfamiliar territory. Treat them gently and help them be kind to themselves: the rocky period is not a reflection on their abilities but on their being human.

Don't give up! A person who is unfamiliar with this curve — especially a very logical person — might wrongly assume that simply by planning out a change and deciding to take it on, he will move directly from the old status quo to the new status quo. When he encounters the uncomfortable first state, chaos, he will not feel good or perform well. The natural reaction might be to reject the change as a failure or a bad idea. The proper response would be to have faith and tough it out — and that is not easy!

Don't fight the change curve. It depicts a universal human experience. Ignoring the curve makes as much sense as working while running a high fever. You can't manage away the performance drop. Although you and your team are unique, you are not exempt from the curve's effects. Performance will get worse before it gets better, and the latter will take time. Some changes are quick (such as introducing the daily standup meeting), while other changes take months (such as introducing test-driven development [TDD]). If your plans don't allow sufficient time, people will resort to familiar habits to make deadlines.

Even though the curve's shape is universal, you can affect the magnitude and duration of the dip. Typically, access to experts and servant leadership will do the trick. For instance, in an Agile transformation, your best recourse is to get an Agile expert to guide the change and prevent egregious mistakes. If several teams are transitioning at once, build alliances with other Agile team leaders (ATLs). In addition to a support network, you can collectively present needs to the management team and divide up some of the change work.

A team-level change causes members to go through two curves: their own and the collective one. As quicker-to-change members ingrain the new reality, slower-moving ones are apt to think, "I'm struggling while everyone else seems to be getting it just fine." (This will be painfully obvious when you introduce TDD, for instance.) Make sure individuals have frequent opportunities to check in on the larger group's progress, to understand that they are in it together, and to help each other. This is not an Olympic multilane sprint; it is more like a three-legged race.

11.2 What Are the Other Costs of Change?

Looking to improve a certain performance indicator, you contemplate a change. Expect an initial performance dip, as per the Satir change curve. That lost productivity is part of the cost of the investment you make in the change, which also includes:

+ *Time* used for planning, setting up, learning, implementing, and correcting

+ *Funds* spent on training and tools

+ *Equity* withdrawn from the "emotional bank accounts" of the people experiencing the consequences (see 3.3)

As you estimate the above, remember how bad people are at estimation. Most of us like to be optimistic and assume that most things would go well — after all, we are intelligent, motivated people. But as the chaos period in the change curve clearly demonstrates, change efforts are anything but smooth or predictable. So when you estimate the investment, leave a sizable buffer for surprises and risks.

If the investment required for the desired improvement worries you, ask yourself: What is the cost of keeping things the same? If a certain performance indicator is less than desirable (for instance, customer retention due to quality), what is the cost of keeping the indicator at its current level?

You can often choose among different investment avenues. Suppose you are introducing test-driven development. Expect to purchase books; expect the first dozens or even hundreds of tests to require substantial rework and refactoring; and expect the developers to feel confused, frustrated, or uncommitted on occasion. You can make an alternative investment in a live course and/or on-the-job coaching.[3] In exchange for the increased funding this requires, you'll decrease the time, effort, rework, and spent emotional equity.

The less you invest in a change, the more likely it is to fail or backfire. In other words, the less you invest, the more you hope to get lucky with it. A prominent example is when a company decides to adopt Agile and kicks off the implementation by sending a single person to a two-day Scrum course. Changes that receive inadequate investment can also backfire because of the perception they create. That's when you hear opinions like, "They don't take it seriously," "Management doesn't support us," "There will be consequences for failure," or "This too will blow over — let's just wait it out."

11.3 What Are the Preconditions for Successful Change?

For a change in methods or practices to succeed, the team must be willing, ready, and able to make it:

+ Willing: having the *motivation* to start the change and persist with it through the chaos period

+ Ready: having enough spare *bandwidth* to absorb the costs of the change curve

+ Able: being able to *focus* on the change enough to survive the chaos period, reach the transforming idea, and sustain the new status quo

11.3.1 Motivation

The most comfortable state for any person is the status quo. When your environment follows regular patterns, you can respond with your habitual patterns worry-free. If the environment starts behaving differently, you could be motivated to *reactively* change your responses. And if the environment remains stable, you could be motivated to *proactively* choose more effective responses or more efficient procedures.

Whether reactive or proactive, motivators for change fall into two categories:

+ "Away" (or "pain") motivators drive action to remove, fix, or avoid an undesirable thing. A familiar example is code reviews, which are meant to catch omissions and deviations early.

+ "Toward" (or "pleasure") motivators drive action to achieve or accomplish a desirable thing. Many Agile principles, such as satisfying the customer through early and frequent value delivery, provide toward motivation.

Away motivators are more likely to trigger action than toward motivators. Take, for example, having a fast, one-click build for your codebase. Agile teams believe it is a beneficial practice since it shortens feedback loops, automates a mind-numbing task, and reduces maintenance costs. Despite its value, few teams rush to implement it. The teams that are more inclined to put one in place are those who suffer the daily agony of an error-prone, hours-long build.

Nevertheless, away motivators lose their edge once the objective is met, which can trigger a bounce-back. Many weight-loss diets start with away motivation, such as "I can't fit into my old clothes anymore." Once the person can fit into the clothes, the drive is gone — unless it is supplanted by other motivators. Do not base all your change efforts on away motivation.

If the team's motivators are satisfied, they will consider the change. If the company's incentives are different or more abstract, they will gain little traction with the team. For example, in many mediocre transitions, managers have the motivation to develop products "cheaper, better, faster," but their teams don't. Developers, testers, and analysts see the same slipped schedules, complaining users, and highly defective products as their managers, yet their jobs and daily work stay largely unaffected by the customers' dissatisfaction. They do not feel the pain of the status quo as acutely.

Just as the whole team needs to understand the reason for the change, individuals need to have the motivation to take it on (see 10.4 for more on motivation). They also need clarity on the suggested new way — what it will look like, what will remain unchanged, and what the possible side effects are. Clarity helps get the motivation right and avoid the frustration of "that's not what I signed up for."

11.3.2 Bandwidth

A software vendor contracted me to coach one of its teams in advanced Agile engineering skills. The developers were quite open to working with me and loved to practice advanced testing and refactoring techniques. During this engagement, I also observed opportunities to improve their project management process. I helped the whole team try new methods of planning and reflection. However, there was little openness to deeper changes in team structure and dynamics or any other large change. When I came in — about three-quarters of the way through the project — they had already been pushing hard. Their client was moving the deadline up frequently and complicating their iteration commitments with urgent bug fixes. The team was working long hours and most weekends and holidays: they were tapped out.

Early Agile literature identified the need to practice *sustainable pace*: the team should be able to maintain its pace indefinitely. This practice guarantees a predictable, reliable rate of value delivery. It substantiates long-term planning. It also prevents the drawbacks of *un*sustainable pace, which include higher defect rates, burnout, sickness, and turnover.

The other disadvantage of unsustainable pace is that it drains people of hope and closes them to possibilities. Despite the fact that the developers were in favor of the techniques and changes I demonstrated, they applied only those that didn't appear to cost them time. In effect, they avoided anything that would give rise to a change curve with any significant chaos period. Test-driven development, for instance, wasn't widely accepted for this very reason. Unless you are already skilled in TDD, it requires considerable practice before you can realize its benefits.

If the team lacks bandwidth now, they might have some later. A natural point is the start of a new release or project. If your team sprints from iteration to iteration and can't spare any time for change, their pace might be sustainable — but a bad idea. A team that experiences a steady pressure of the here and now won't care to raise their heads and contemplate change. It is an indication that they don't incorporate *slack* into their plans, and they will pay for that, sooner or later.[4]

11.3.3 Focus

On one large-scale Agile transition, a certain team got off to an inauspicious start. During their kickoff, they estimated their ongoing obligations (including production support and migration to a new source code repository) at 85%. In other words, 15% of their time — six hours a week — was available for practicing Agile on new development. Worse yet, the asynchronous nature of some of the obligations meant they couldn't even block out those six hours in their calendars. That team never emerged from the change curve's chaos stage.

Any change that involves new skills or behaviors requires more than nominal bandwidth: it requires focus. People need dedicated, undistracted periods of time for practice. However, distractions and multiple obligations are a fact of life for software teams, especially in organizations suffering a staff shortage. Two effective techniques to increase focus are available to you.

The first is to *sacrifice* a team member. Dedicate one member to handle production support, deployment activities, and any other regular distractions. In rare cases (hopefully), she might need to pull others in to help. Rotate this duty every week or two to build skill and reduce frustration. If she happens to have some free time, she can be a "floating pair": available to pair up with other team members but not otherwise on the hook for iteration obligations.

The other technique is to *block time*. Dedicate certain hours of the week for a specific, mentally demanding activity. For instance, if the team should spend 10% of their time paying down technical debt, they can't do this in random spurts of 30 minutes. Instead, block off one afternoon every week. During those hours, they should do nothing but refactor legacy code.

11.4 How Can I Make Changes Stick?

A prerequisite for change is the decision to make the change, and a prerequisite for the decision is motivation. If motivation is not strong enough, the change may be short-lived, especially if it is a long-term proposition such as altering behavior, practices, or attitudes. How do you help people make *lasting* changes?[5] How can you help them take *responsibility* and *ownership* for change, including when they are not being watched?

These questions are particularly poignant for you in the context of Agile adoption: How can you help it become a true transformation? Many Agile implementations do in fact suffer from the bounce-back effect. The change is not deep enough or falls short of its promise, and after a few months, the process bounces back to the old status quo (or worse, a mishmash of "best practices" from the old and the new).

Following are several universal techniques for helping people make lasting changes:

State the outcome positively. It is not enough to say, "Team, we are putting a stop to 12-month release cycles because customers hate them." Instead, say what you *do* want to do. For instance, "We will move to three-month release cycles because that is how we will retain our customers." Describe the benefit you expect from changing successfully. Besides forcing you to consider your alternatives, positivity triggers more-helpful emotions in your audience (7.1).

Ensure safety during the change. All change involves some fear of the change process, of the outcome, and of the unknown. However, fear itself does not universally deter change and learning! Understand what sorts of fear your team feels, and determine suitable safety features. You can expect most team members to feel a very specific unvoiced fear: that of being attacked personally during the chaos period, when they still haven't integrated the paradigm. For that, you should establish a ground rule — applicable at all levels of management — that disrespect will not be tolerated.[6]

Provide replacements for any behaviors or beliefs you take away. Do you like sweets? I do. They are not healthy, but they have *some* positive value for me in their taste and occasional comfort. If you take away my sweets, I'll want something to satisfy the same needs or wants. The same goes for you, other individuals, and entire teams. If you take away sign-off on requirements because Agile processes don't need it, you must ask first: "How did sign-offs help us? What purpose did they fulfill? If we still have that need, can our new process address it, or do we need to adapt it somehow?" For instance, if the sign-off was a checks-and-balances mechanism to ensure that requirements satisfied the product's ultimate goals, your iteration review and backlog grooming discussions may suffice instead.

Change the environment. The physical environment is a powerful anchor for habitual behaviors, including those you are trying to change.

> One company's meetings never start on time. When people show up at a meeting's scheduled hour, they automatically pull out their smartphones. Merely entering the familiar, staid meeting room sends their subconscious minds this message: "Go on, check your email; nothing useful is going on here anyway." Even when all participants have arrived, the meeting is slow to start, as those people still take time to mentally check in.

If team members are stuck in their familiar single-person, high-partition cubicles, expect collaboration to be challenging. If senior managers frequently pass through the team's open area, expect a lot of heads-down, busy-looking typing instead of informal conversations. For new behaviors to succeed, try them in an environment that is less likely to trigger old behaviors.

Make it their idea. Help people feel that the suggested change is their idea. Even if you first brought it to their attention, let them develop and customize it. Once they feel *they* own the idea, not you, it doesn't suffer from the Not Invented Here effect.[7] Ownership increases motivation, and if the change works out nicely, its chances of survival become greater.

Offer frequent feedback, demand accountability, and help the team adjust. Any meaningful change means spending weeks or months on the least enjoyable parts of the change curve. Questions, concerns, and good reasons to quit come up from the very beginning. You can support the change by frequently offering constructive feedback, by holding people accountable to the change they wanted to make (but not to their performance in it!), and by helping them adjust. In other words, coach them. You will increase the chances of applying the change effectively and minimize the chances of a bounce-back.

11.5 Why Do Some Changes Stick Better Than Others?

Behavioral skills expert Robert Dilts has identified the Logical Levels of Change,[8] inspired by earlier work on a natural *hierarchy* in the processes of learning, change, and communication.

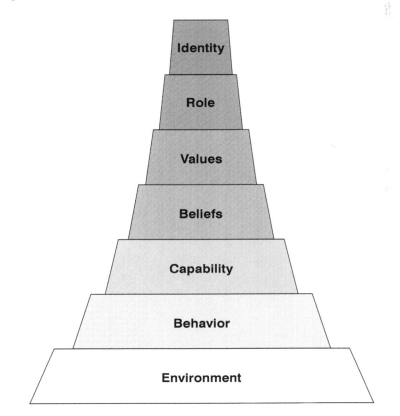

The lowest, most immediate, and most visible level is the *environment* in which you operate. For instance, you work in an open space and your desk is arranged a certain way. Above this level are your *behaviors*, such as the way you craft emails and speak with your team. Next up are your *capabilities*; for instance, perhaps you can facilitate an iteration review meeting with a difficult stakeholder. Above capabilities are *beliefs*: you may believe that a self-organizing team can shine. The highest levels are more closely related to your personality: your values (what's important to you), your role, and your identity. For instance, a harmonious working environment might be more important to you than timely delivery (*values*), you are a servant leader (*role*), and you know in your heart that this is the work you should be doing (*identity*).

Each level determines the possibilities in the levels beneath it. For instance, if you are a servant leader (*role*), you're likely to *believe* in an open-door policy but not likely to believe in having the final say over suggested process changes.

The logical levels are the backbone of personal and group change. Their implications for you are as follows.

It is easy to effect a change at a given level if it is congruent with the higher levels. For instance, if you consider collaboration important (*values*), and therefore believe you have something to learn from others (*beliefs*), you will be open to trying pair programming (*behavior*).

It is possible to effect a change at a given level if it doesn't agree with the levels above it. The change might be only short-term, or it might cause a reevaluation at the higher levels. For seven years, I worked as a developer in offices made up of individual or two-person rooms. Then I joined a company where the entire staff occupied a single open space. This new *environment* caused me to adjust my *behaviors* (what to do and not do in an open space) and to reevaluate, and ultimately discard, my *belief* that private offices are the best arrangement for productive software development teams. By contrast, if you'd like to form a team that would use Agile methods (*behavior*) in an open space (*environment*), but you don't build their *capabilities* — or you build them without helping the team espouse *beliefs* about their abilities and empowerment — then your effort is likely doomed.

If a change at a given level doesn't agree with the levels above it, it is best to focus on the requisite change at the highest affected level — and unfortunately, the higher that level is, the slower and harder the change. For example, suppose you want people to test-drive their code. Teaching them the TDD mechanics (*capabilities*) or encouraging them to use TDD (*behavior*) is rarely successful. For them to naturally *want* to test-drive their code, help them discover and form supporting *beliefs*. An example might be, "Code that was not test-driven is too buggy for my own good." You might need to go to higher levels. For instance, if they come to *value* craftsmanship, or *identify* themselves as software craftsmen, they'll likely believe that TDD is a necessary component. (Effective motivational speakers craft their talks this way, addressing the *beliefs* level and higher.)

It is a similar matter with the adoption of an entire Agile methodology. It's easy to make the superficial modification to roles, team structure, techniques, customer involvement, and planning cycles. However, those are merely *practices*: an imitation of others' successful techniques (*behavior* and *capability*). Even if they make for a great starting point, they might not suffice. Correct adoption requires a change from the *values* level down: buying into the Agile mind-set (*values* and *beliefs*), developing the *capabilities*, and getting considerable practice with *behavior* in a supportive *environment*.

When you contemplate a change that feels substantial, identify the logical level it resides in and see what lives at the higher levels, in order to determine your strategy.

When you are helping others align from a logical levels perspective, exercise caution about mind reading — guessing their thoughts based on your biases. As you come into contact with others, you will mostly observe *behaviors* and *environments*. To understand their higher logical levels, you must engage in deeper conversation — which they might not welcome. Get better traction with them using techniques from chapter 8.

As I was wrapping up a team's transition to Agile, one of their capable senior developers was promoted to technical lead. He and I started meeting weekly for coaching in his new role. We covered a lot of ground the first few weeks, but he was so busy putting out fires and helping developers get unstuck that he wasn't practicing the new skills and attitudes. Moreover, he started feeling unsuitable for this role!

In one session, I chose to focus on his negative emotions. He soon realized that he was subconsciously pushing away the behaviors and attitudes that would make him a technical lead. It turned out that he had the following logical levels:

Identity: I am a senior software developer. Therefore:

Value: Be a great programmer. Therefore:

Beliefs: (1) I should use my programming skills. (2) As a tech lead, I'm not using them anymore. (1) + (2) caused the angst, and subconsciously drove:

Behavior: Find all occasions, however small and tedious, to use my programming skills (and thus crowd out the angst-causing leadership activities).

With this realization, we started working on updating his self-identification from "senior developer who happened to be promoted" to "technical leader." He embraced the notion that as long as he helped his team deliver valuable code, his contribution was valuable, even if he wasn't programming. His behavior shifted dramatically within days, and the angst was gone.

11.6 How Can I Help People Shift Their Mind-Set?

Agile is a set of values, principles, and practices. As the previous section shows, these things reside on various logical levels, on some of which change is slow and arduous. You will therefore have more success helping people change practices than mind-set. When it comes to mind-set — values, principles, attitudes, beliefs — much of the change has to come from within a person. Still, you can help him considerably.

If you want someone to adopt a mind-set, walk the talk and lead by example. Suppose you are a senior manager and you'd like your teams and project managers to adopt Agile. If you expect them to form trusting, collaborative relationships among themselves, you're going to have to act this way with your direct staff as well. If instead you demand to be advised of every detail and to make every decision, they'll detect the incongruence, and their choice will be to please you, despite how un-Agile that is.

Don't knock what they are doing now. If you tell people that they are not doing something well, they will take your words as a claim about *them*. If you make them feel stupid or wrong, their coping mechanisms will kick in and resist the change. This is particularly hard if they studied and trained to act the way you are disparaging. Rather than negate what they do, use language of improvements, alternatives, or experiments.

Before you offer alternatives, help them explore what's not working. Suppose you've come to believe that test-driven development is the best invention since object-oriented design. Exhorting your developers or managers with "Let's try TDD, it's phenomenal!" won't get you far. Instead, find an opportunity to ask, "What's going on in our process that we could improve?" or "What actions do we take with regard to quality and defects that we wish we could take less often?" Help identify the pain, or the improvement opportunity, in order to make your offer of an alternative welcome. Be patient and never nag; intelligent people need to form their own ideas and convictions.

A powerful way to introduce change is with experiments. First, the time-bound nature of an experiment helps to temporarily disable those pesky logical levels. People may like the new behaviors and capabilities so much that the supporting beliefs and values will change. Second, the noncommittal nature of experiments can overcome skepticism and the fear of making irreversible mistakes. (See 13.4 for more.)

If you have the talent for telling stories, use it. Stories, just like open-ended questions and experiential learning, entice the listener to figure out the next step. The love of stories is hardwired into the human psyche — and people particularly like stories in which they can see themselves. Great stories inspire and provide guidance. They also give a glimpse of the outcome: when you take this leap, here's how this could end — it did in the story.

11.7 How Should I Coach People?

As a leader, one of your best tools is coaching. From being a virtually unknown concept outside of sports 20 years ago, the practice of coaching has grown by leaps and bounds. It is now a whole industry with its body of knowledge, certifications, and niches in almost all walks of life. Accordingly, it is vastly misunderstood. Some languages don't yet have the right equivalent for the English word "coaching."

As an Agile leader who draws and guides people toward a target, use coaching to foster intrinsic motivation and alignment. As an Agile leader who helps people and teams grow and change, use coaching as a facilitative tool.

A coaching axiom is that change and growth come from within the person (known as the coachee). Therefore cajoling, exhorting, pressuring, lecturing, obligating, tempting, and other forms of external compulsion are out. The coach acts as a true facilitator, helping the person see the desired outcome and effect the requisite changes. The coach supports the coachee's discovery and change process using facilitative techniques such as asking open questions, providing feedback, mirroring the coachee's internal state, and challenging thought patterns.

When it comes to changing the logical levels of values, beliefs, and attitudes, a fundamental coaching belief is that people have within them all the resources they need to make those changes. This belief stems from a deep-seated respect for people and their abilities. If you honestly believe that, your actions and words will manifest this respect even if you never verbalize it as such. Your coachees or followers will pick up on it and naturally try it on for size, thereby increasing their confidence and self-respect. If you do *not* truly believe that people have all the resources they need to change, that too will be evident in your actions and words. You will sometimes tell, rather than ask; you will appear as a "people fixer" or as someone who knows better; and your coachee will seek your approval.

One big caveat to the foregoing — and an occasional bone of contention among professional coaches — is what to do if the change requires new information, technical skill, or domain knowledge. This is a particularly thorny question in Agile transitions. Should the team's Agile coach (which might be you if there isn't a dedicated one) provide detailed how-to instruction, which can then be adapted through continuous improvement? Or should the coach expose the learners to the Agile principles (say, through simulations) and let them discover the implementation that works for them?

In situations where the coachee lacks the answers and resources to proceed, the coach would do better to act as advisor, mentor, or consultant. Still, the coachee can enjoy the learning process more, and the results can stick better, if she receives feedback, answers open questions, and owns insights. Once the coachee has developed sufficient skills or amassed sufficient knowledge to approach a problem competently, the coach can revert to the process-coaching model to help the coachee increase competence.

Being someone's servant leader does not give you automatic permission to coach him. Positional authority does not suffice either, because he may tune you out. You cannot coach the unwilling; either he requests coaching, or you offer it and he accepts. Furthermore, someone's permission to receive your coaching on a single occasion does not automatically extend to future opportunities.

In an Agile situation, you coach (willing) individual members as well as the whole team. Team coaching opportunities are usually formal. The iteration retrospective is all about change and adaptation, making it a prime opportunity to coach the team. Team planning meetings can offer opportunities for brief coaching.

Individual coaching can be formal or informal. The best formal approach is regularly scheduled one-on-one meetings. Their predictability is crucial for the same reason it is for team retrospectives: they become a habit, rather than an option. Coaches in every niche, including Agile, know that people show up to scheduled meetings, but if you tell them "Call me if you need my help," they will rarely do so. Having to make a conscious choice to do that usually falls victim to their daily realities, pressures, and internal conflicts.

Complement these formal one-on-one opportunities with the impromptu, informal style of "Coaching by Walking Around." Every day, drop in for brief individual visits (even virtual visits if your team is dispersed). Chat with folks. Keep your eyes and ears open to what they do and say — and especially to what they do *not* do or say. If you notice shortcomings in the team's behavior, choose whether to address them individually or in a formal team setting.

A person or group will receive your gift of coaching only if you have a trusting relationship. Once in a coaching situation — whether formal or informal, long or short — the coachee's receptivity increases the more curious, present, and empathetic you are.[9] The tools in chapter 8 will help you improve on those dimensions and thereby increase the efficacy and depth of your coaching.

Coaching starts with observations of the coachee's present state. With awareness comes the identification of desired changes and outcomes. The coachee can establish interim goals and plans for reaching those outcomes. (Make sure her individual plans and objectives do not run afoul of the overall team's direction.) Help her commit to following through on those plans, and then close the loop: hold her accountable to her commitment. Depending on the nature of the change, you might help her manage progress.

If you delight in working with people, you probably find coaching them to change and grow immensely satisfying. It also requires great skill and deftness, since it is a highly sensitive activity.[10] You will need considerable empathy, maturity, and confidence to coach properly rather than tell, teach, or consult. While you can study coaching formally and read about it extensively,[11] like many skills in this book, your best education will come from observing master practitioners and getting lots of practice.

In the 21st century, change is happening everywhere, all the time. Whether reactive or proactive, every conscious change is intended to have a valuable outcome. The challenge for every person, team, and organization is that the change experience is often uncomfortable. However, you can help make the change more desirable and its process more palatable: mark the destination, illuminate the way, and accompany the people. By ensuring the right preconditions, addressing the right logical levels, and coaching people, you can speed up the change and make it stick better. Even if your team never finds a change enticing, at least they won't fight it.

Supplementary Resource
Go to **www.TheHumanSideOfAgile.com** and download
"Change Leadership."

CHAPTER 12

Defuse Resistance

Even if everyone around you is perfectly motivated to reach the same goals, you will still encounter resistance on a daily basis. Resistance comes up in various situations, such as when you have a problem to discuss, a solution to consider, or merely an opinion to share. You're in for a greater challenge if you're trying to request a deliverable or effect change.

Polite professionals rarely resist openly. Instead, they speak in code. Common resistance codes include:

CODE PHRASE	MEANING
Yeah, but....	I wasn't paying attention to what you just said. Here is what *I* think.
I don't disagree with you, but....	Your idea might be OK, but *I* have a better one or a clearer perspective.
Our current solution already works well.	I don't want to consider your idea.
Have you checked with so-and-so?	I hope this idea blows over.
I don't need that.	You see value in that, but I don't.
Let's get some more people and have a meeting about it.	I don't want to think about it. Perhaps somebody else would.
I don't think this would work here.	*I* will have to live with the consequences, not you. I am not taking the risk.

Some resistance is a normal part of being independent, intelligent human beings. For many people, the very perception that they are being told what to do is bad enough. Any hint that someone else knows better is likely to trigger resistance.

In our industry, people are very busy dealing with complicated short-term and long-term commitments. Ask them for anything that might seem like extra work, and you're likely to encounter push-back. As many Agile coaches and leaders have discovered, teams sometimes even resist process changes that are supposed to reduce overall effort if the change itself is perceived as extra work.

As a leader, you may wish to encourage people to pick up additional skills and responsibilities. And while your fellow professionals naturally want to learn and grow, they don't want to do that all the time. In the daily balancing act between "important" and "urgent," between short-term obligations and long-term growth, an extra investment in learning and growth sometimes seems bigger than it is.

Resistance is a form of feedback, which you may interpret as negative or unhelpful. You might take it personally: others are resisting the message because it's coming from *you*. Yet their resistance can have two other objects: *your mode of delivery* and *the content* itself. Depending on your personality and your experience communicating with others, you might be inclined to lump all resistance into one of these categories. This limits your range of responses and can easily lead to impasses and hurt feelings.

The following sections provide advice for addressing all three resistance targets — you, your mode of delivery, and the content — so you can develop effective responses. Since professionals speak in code, it is sometimes hard to tell what they are resisting. Your clues include their choice of verbal and body language, your shared history, and your guesses about their perception of you.

12.1 How Can I Help Others Be Open to Ideas Coming From Me?

Someone might resist a perfectly useful or harmless message simply because it's coming from you. It's the hardest obstacle to overcome, because the deck appears to be stacked against you before you so much as utter a single word. You can turn that around by first *opening up to them.*

Start by accepting others for who they are. If they think you are trying to fix or improve them, they will resist you, because nobody likes to be considered broken or inadequate. They will only listen to you once they feel that you *truly* accept them, warts and all. They need to feel that you genuinely have their best interests in mind, whatever you stand to gain from the relationship. This may be challenging if your values don't match.

When your behavior and responses align with your values and identity, you are being *congruent.* Congruence, also referred to as authenticity, goes hand in hand with accepting people. Most adults pick up on incongruence quickly (albeit subconsciously) and reject it as manipulation. If you encounter frequent resistance to your overtures, watch yourself through other people's eyes: Are you sending mixed messages?

Ask respectfully for what you want, and be transparent about your motivation. Disclosure both requires trust and builds it. You don't have to bare your soul; just showing why you care about something makes you seem more human and like the other person. For instance, if you're asking the team to update the task board more diligently, it is perfectly fine to explain your request by saying, "When I see tasks remaining in the same place for a few days, I get nervous about meeting our commitments. I want to help, but I don't want to bother you or nag with pesky questions." In some situations, demonstrating vulnerability can strengthen your relationship.

Resistance may occur when you try to convince or influence others to take some course of action. If you take such actions yourself, you *lead* by example. If you open up to other people's influence (when appropriate), you *follow* by example. By doing both over time, you will build vital credibility and trust, which will increase others' openness to your ideas.

12.2 Which Modes of Delivery Don't Trigger Push-Back?

Chances are that your colleagues don't resist you all the time. They do take some of your guidance or address some of your requests, but sometimes they push back on perfectly sensible messages. In those cases, the way you delivered your message was probably unsuited to their mental state, or it turned them off.

One thing that can help any conversation along is rapport. It is a certain state of being when you're interacting with another person. The conversation flows; you feel good and energized about it. You may not be friends or have been acquainted for long, yet you feel some liking or affinity toward each other. When you are in rapport — whether you've established it consciously or not — both of you experience greater openness and reduced resistance. (Read more about rapport in 8.3.)

There are good times to ask for something, and there are bad times. Even in good times, if you just show up at somebody's door or cubicle and say, "Please start tracking actuals on tasks from now on" or "We should reexamine our use of the task board," chances are you'll encounter push-back or a deaf ear. Instead, take a little more time and engage in real conversation. Establish rapport and identify some common ground you have with the person in that context. For instance, "You know, Lisa, I'm having a hard time using our estimates." Or, "Have you noticed this iteration's task board? The tasks haven't moved in three days." Lead the conversation through one small agreement after another to a place that invites the other person to solve the problem or address the need with you.

> A newly Agile team was working on a large codebase with few automated tests. In support of their initiative to increase unit test coverage, they needed to create a new test directory. Lei, one of the members, emailed the Platform group, which maintained the build, asking them to add the directory. He sounded defeated when he told me he was flatly denied. I don't like to give up easily, so I convened a meeting. I spent the first few minutes establishing rapport with Dennis, the lead Platform developer, who had some deep-seated opinions against Agile. Once it was clear I wasn't pushing him into using Agile, I expressed the team's goal and why the current code structure was working against them. Lastly, I explained that a new directory appeared to be the smallest change that would allow them to proceed and added, "We're not wedded to that idea; let's look at more options." To that, Dennis responded, "It does sound fairly simple. I think we can fit it in over the next couple of weeks. Would that be OK?"
>
> On the way back to the team room, Lei whispered to me, "I never thought this could be done!"

If you want another person to do something, use the "Ask, don't tell" pattern.[1] Rather than *tell* her to do something, *ask* her to do it or to try it. Telling implies obligation, while asking implies choice — including the option of refusal. Requesting, instead of telling, also earns you points for goodwill and caring.

For greater ownership on the other person's part, use the "I have an idea" approach. Suppose you want to suggest a course of action. You might say something like, "We should do pair programming" or "You know, we should really split this story." The listener may perceive your opinion as firm, even *factual*, and possibly the only option available in this exchange. If instead you say, "I have an idea. How about we split this story?" you imply that there are options. It's not the one right way, and you're not vested in it. If you're having team buy-in problems, "I have an idea" is *very* powerful.

> "One of our online programs was running slowly due to its remote access to the master database. One day, I approached one of the analysts to brainstorm performance improvement ideas. After learning of the various improvements that had already been made, I asked whether the online program could have a local copy of the necessary data. Right away I got push-back: "We'll need more processing" and "This is not good design." I agreed with the processing consideration and with some of the analyst's other concerns, eventually asking, "How long would it take to prove whether having local data makes a significant difference?" Once the analyst realized that this test would be quick, she agreed to run it. The improvement turned out to be significant, and we later implemented this solution successfully."
>
> — *S. D. H., application support manager*

Does the team sometimes appear to reluctantly agree with you because you're in a position of authority? Before you offer an idea, you can evaluate their openness by asking permission to suggest: "Would it be OK if I suggested something here?" This puts the ball in their court and invites them to take an exploratory perspective and consider options. Asking *permission* to *suggest* disables the natural reaction of agreeing or disagreeing, where their minds race, "Quick, let me think: Am I for it or against it?"

Language plays a significant role in generating or reducing resistance. Do you think the other person will understand your words the way you meant them? Nope. (Using his preferred modality for the context greatly increases your chances — see 8.4.4.) He will interpret — mostly subconsciously — *every* word you use. And if some of these interpretations trigger an emotional reaction, the conversation is likely to derail quickly. For example, imagine hearing me say this to you:

"Can I tell you something?"

Did you hear "Can I tell you a story?" or "I have feedback you may not like"?

Many people get defensive upon hearing this sentence because they interpret it the second way. *Tell* is a loaded word, as are many words in common usage. If my real intent is expressed by the first sentence, a safer alternative is "Can I share something with you?" Another option is to preface your words: "I just heard a piece of news; can I tell you?"

When possible, frame your message positively. Although human beings have remarkable cognitive abilities, processing negation is not among them. (How quickly did your mind parse this last phrase, which included negation?) For you to process a statement such as "In a standup meeting, we don't just report status to the manager," you first need to interpret the words and create a mental picture of managers and standup meetings and reporting status — and then determine "that's not it." Anytime you want to encourage a change in behavior, saying "Don't do that behavior" requires the other person to first think about that behavior, which extends its roots. Use a positive suggestion instead. Rather than saying, "Don't write code without automated tests," try "What if your code always came with automated tests?" For practice, try avoiding "no" and "not."

12.3 How Should I Design the Content of My Message?

Suppose you have mastered the two preceding sections. You communicate carefully, and listeners are generally open to your influence — yet they may still reject a particular message's content. Influence your audience to give due consideration to your idea by *designing the content of your message.* That usually means saying more, and saying it differently, than you originally intended.

Before you get to your point, understand their perspective. If you believe you already know what they are thinking, this act of *mind reading* can be a valuable shortcut in the conversation — or a really bad idea. Instead, ask questions to elicit the other person's beliefs, assumptions, and perspective, using their own words.

For example, let's say the team has asked you for training in Agile engineering techniques, and you need the sponsor's approval. Rather than expecting her to disapprove, ask her questions like:

- ✦ "What do you think of getting additional training for the team?"

- ✦ "What sort of budget do we have for skill development?"

- ✦ "Now that we're using Agile, the team has identified some gaps in their technical approach. Would you help us get some external training, or offer an alternative?"

When you make a case for something, your choice of words and presentation is guided (often subconsciously) by your beliefs. For instance, if you ask a tester to write a test plan for each user story, your underlying beliefs might be that he would miss certain cases unless he predicts them all ahead of time, or that the benefits of a plan outweigh its labor costs. These statements are not facts. You *think* they are true, but you can't *prove* them. If your suggestion meets resistance, the tester might well be operating with a different set of beliefs, such as "I never really trust test plans." During your conversation or before it, you would do well to examine the beliefs that underlie your position and question their veracity.

Your listener will evaluate your content using the simple WIIFM criterion: "What's in it for me?" If you have a good handle on the benefits, express them. As described in 11.3.1, the benefits can be "away" or "toward"; expect to be more successful getting someone to consider ways to reduce pains and problems than ways to improve a positive experience.

Do you sometimes receive calls from telemarketers or service providers? Many start their pitch with, "I have a <survey/offer/special> for you, and *it will only take two minutes of your time*." They are *removing objections proactively* — in this case, your objection to having your time wasted. You can do the same. If your listener is not in a "buying mood," her stance — from the moment you start talking — is that of objection. She is likely to think: "How much is this going to cost me? What's the hassle factor? What do I stand to lose?" If you know how the person is likely to object to your offer, format your presentation — whether it's ten seconds or a whole minute — to put her mind at ease from the get-go.

When you initiate a conversation, you bring a certain set of ideas to the exchange. You have spent minutes, hours, or days forming those ideas, but the other person has not been privy to your thought process. Explaining why you're saying something lets them catch up to you *and* your message. Research has shown that people respond to requests more when they are accompanied with a "because,"[2] no matter how small the reason. Remember, though, that people have little patience for long-winded preambles and background stories before the main point. Moreover, since most people are emotional before they are rational, logical justification doesn't always get you far. Focus on the value in your idea: what it helps achieve or avoid.

Over several iterations, a team had shown inconsistent interest in pairing. They did not practice pairing uniformly and kept debating its costs and benefits. The ScrumMaster and I (their coach) wanted the team to give it an honest try, to make *some* decision. The team was receptive to me at this point; my challenge was to design the *content* and its *mode of delivery* for minimal resistance.

At the retrospective I said, "Let's try an experiment. Let's try full-on pairing for an iteration and see what we think of it. But we'll only try the experiment if all of you agree to it." (See 13.4 about the experimentation technique.) Then I explained the rationale of trying pairing in an all-or-nothing way. We were able to reach consensus, and the next iteration they paired full-time. Two weeks later, the team had amassed firsthand experiences for a meaningful examination during the subsequent retrospective.

Resistance to ideas and messages is a regular fixture of human interaction. Entire professions, such as advertising and politics, have to reckon with it daily. While there is no miracle antidote to resistance and no use attacking it head on, there are effective ways to reduce it: congruence and acceptance, careful wording, and respectful message design. Enough practice with this chapter's advice will help you build up a powerful ability to influence. Use it judiciously.

Supplementary Resource
Go to **www.TheHumanSideOfAgile.com** and download "Defuse Resistance."

PART V
Sustain Your Team for the Long Haul

The emergence of a new team — especially in a newly Agile environment, which yours is likely to be — is like the birth of a child. The first few months are an exciting time, full of hope and wonder. They are also challenging, with risks present on all fronts — people, product, process, and project. The first iterations can be exhilarating as a team discovers its autonomy, flexibility, and synergy. Retrospectives pack the hope of making things still better.

After a few tumultuous months, the team hopefully reaches the "performing" stage. They get comfortable turning out great product on a regular basis. As the initial thrill subsides, the team starts contemplating several more years of working together. In that time, they will have to keep improving their methods, if only to keep up. They will have to adapt to changes in both their composition and their organizational context. How can they maintain their greatness and even improve upon it? How should they break through plateaus? How do they keep from slipping back into the pre-Agile mind-set? Part V explores the human side of sustaining a team for the long haul: making continuous improvement a reality and staying the course.

CHAPTER 13

Make Continuous Improvement a Reality

Continuous improvement is among the most important principles of Agility. Successful Agile teams regularly consider improvements to their process and results. Both as communities and as individuals, they dedicate time for learning, reflection, and growth. That is how they provide better results for the same amount of investment, respond and adjust to changes in circumstance and needs, and stay competitive.

Performance will not improve unless some change takes place. Performance will naturally *fluctuate* — after all, you have people on the team, not coding units — but it will not trend upward without a change. In fact, it will trend *downward* if the overall process doesn't reduce technical debt. Many organizations have realized that their Agile teams' performance degrades over time, because they've racked up crippling technical debt and haven't adjusted their methodology to their system's growth.[1]

Wherever your organization and team are on the Agile transformation curve, you are probably constantly looking for improvements. *No matter how technical or impersonal an improvement might seem, it will rise or fall due to the human element.* Get used to exploring the human side of each suggested change so you can lead people through its application.

Take, for instance, two important performance-enhancing Agile/ Lean mechanisms: getting to done (i.e., proper story and iteration completion) and release readiness at the end of iterations. If you wish to implement them, several elements of human will and conduct must be in place:

+ Communication between the product owner and the delivery team needs to be clear, effective, and frequent in order to minimize rework and enable a viable decomposition of work items.

+ Communication among team members must be open and effective in order to shorten feedback loops.

+ Co-development, effort sharing, and fluid responsibilities are needed in order to minimize surprises and bottlenecks.

13.1 How Can the Team Embrace the Continuous Improvement Mind-Set?

Mind-set is one of the distinctions between good Agile teams and great ones. Good teams form their process from established "best practices"; great teams are constantly on the lookout for changes to make them more effective or efficient.

One way to inculcate the continuous improvement mind-set is to never take the status quo for granted. If your build takes ten minutes, would reducing it to five be useful? If your acceptance test suite takes 30 minutes, would halving that make a meaningful difference? If some team members say, "Nah, we don't see value in pairing," does that mean the pairing discussion is over and done with?

Beware the fine line between never taking the status quo for granted and never being satisfied. The former is a neutral, emotionally unattached perspective, and the latter is curmudgeonly and frustrating. Your team will pick up on your true feelings in the matter, since these will come across in your language. Adopt an attitude that is open and curious about potential improvements, while appreciating progress and contributions made to date.

Continuous improvement sounds like a Good Thing, and no one argues against it. But improvement spells change, which is uncomfortable and chaotic. In the short term it hurts results, and you have no guarantee of better results in the long term (see 11.1). Therefore, most people's natural instinct is to prefer the status quo to change. If you hope to ingrain the continuous improvement principle, you need to make it *a habit*.

To make something into a habit, *start small* and *make it easy*. Get people used to regularly making even small improvements. For instance, determine that every retrospective must include at least one action item that spells a useful change. If your team struggles with that, try counting change experiments: like any measurement, it will become a motivating target.

"The organization had very onerous and detailed process definitions. It was not allowed to do anything without prior approval and a waiting for a formal revision to the process. Changing a process meant going through three levels of bureaucracy, which took months to complete.

"Despite the team's skepticism, I insisted we would make improvements, and we would do so very visibly. I had the team start small and pick something minor that wouldn't trigger the bureaucrats' resistance. We made the change and publicized it to ensure it would eventually be 'made official.' We waited for the backlash, but none occurred. We built on this small win by introducing increasingly complex and visible changes. As the trust between management and the team grew, the skepticism and resistance to change diminished. Eventually we changed the bureaucracy from needing approval before making a change to one that captured and institutionalized new processes for future reference."

— *Mike Edwards, Agile coach*

Although the project community owns its process, most people don't notice process or care much about it. This inattention is exacerbated in a multiteam environment where folks have less influence over their process. Since you are their process steward, at least *you* will keep an eye on improvements. Observe performance, point out opportunities, and lead the charge if others won't. Celebrate successes, including small ones.

The continuous improvement mind-set cannot sustain itself without slack. People must have free mental cycles in which to think beyond the here and now (see 11.3.2). Without slack, they can neither contemplate change nor implement it.

13.2 How Do We Generate Ideas for Improvement?

Every improvement is an instance of change. Some improvements involve *doing less*, such as canceling a recurring, low-value meeting. These quick improvements are refreshing and easy to do. Other improvements involve *modifying* or *introducing* something in the process or teamwork. Such changes rarely occur spontaneously; they require investment (see 11.1 and 11.2), motivation, bandwidth, and focus (see 11.3). Where and how can you generate ideas for these improvements?

13.2.1 Team Forums

Even if you do nothing else, iteration retrospectives are your one institutionalized opportunity for triggering improvements. Frequent reflection promotes paying attention and helps prevent problems from taking root. Teams should also conduct release or project retrospectives, because they offer a deeper perspective.[2]

If your team has just picked up Agile, expect the push-back on retrospectives to start in a few weeks. Several hours in advance of a retrospective, a team member might tell you, "You know what, we're doing fine. I can't think of anything to improve." Or you might tell yourself, "Whatever improvement we could make doesn't justify stopping work for an hour." If you believe these thoughts, or if you keep hashing out the same things over and over in your retrospectives, then you're not using them correctly. The usual culprits are ineffectual facilitation and lax follow-up.

Allow time for deep discussion. Some Scrum teams regularly do 15-minute retrospectives. In my experience, you cannot get have a meaningful discussion about two weeks' worth of action and data in 15 minutes — unless you come in with preconceived solutions, which isn't the point.

Your team members probably have many more ideas than they ever voice. To get them all heard, facilitate your retrospectives properly. If someone tells you, "The process is simple and straightforward: we can just rotate leading the meeting," he is mistaking following an agenda for obtaining results. Retrospectives can get pretty dicey: people can become emotional, clam up, or act up. Some participants may dominate, while others might defer to seniority. You need skilled facilitation to run retrospectives that result in *actionable change*, and not everybody can do that. Most team members don't have the skills, the aptitude, or the willingness. Agile team leaders (ATLs) and Agile coaches are the natural facilitators of retrospectives. See more on facilitation in chapter 9.

As with any mechanism that's repeatedly used in a similar manner, retrospective fatigue can set in. One of the worst things about retrospectives is that week in, week out, they look the same. It's always "Worked Well/Needs Improvement," or "Keep/Change." Avoid boredom and disengagement by keeping your retrospectives fresh. For instance, after I showed one company how to replace its staid, separate-team retrospectives with a combined one based on Open Space Technology,[3] folks' engagement jumped sky high. For more ideas to vary your retrospectives, read *Agile Retrospectives*.[4]

Whatever the forum, folks must feel safe and motivated to put forth their ideas. Team members might not want to rock the boat, appear difficult, or be shot down. A trusting relationship with their team, or a "No ideas are stupid" team agreement, may not suffice.

Team members should have an avenue for ideas that cannot be traced back to them. Whenever I design a retrospective for a potentially loaded situation, I plan for maximum anonymity (read about tips for anonymity in section 3.4.1).

Make sure that your team knows that reflecting and improving are not limited to scheduled times in the week. Ideas often come up at standup meetings, if they are not rushed. (The team should agree to examine them after the standup.) Every few months, have a facilitated offsite meeting that combines work and fun. Whatever forum you use, capture those ideas before they disappear in the busyness of daily work.

13.2.2 Individual Members

Folks can also generate ideas on their own, outside of special-purpose meetings. Decades ago, companies had the suggestion box. Nowadays, some companies like to allot research time: team members spend some percentage of their time (each week or as banked time) on any creative endeavor that has the possibility of benefiting the company. (Famous examples of companies using this approach are Google, 3M, and Atlassian[5].)

Get people pairing; many times when I paired up with a developer or a tester, our minds wandered off our task and we came up with a bright idea. (In fact, daydreaming can spark some great creativity.[6]) Take members out to lunch or coffee — inevitably, they'll talk shop.

13.2.3 Process Analysis Tools

Look for published research and practitioners' reports that apply to your development efforts. On the process side, many theories and tools exist to analyze the process from various angles and identify intervention points.

For example, one of the seven principles of Lean thinking is to improve process performance by eliminating waste. One powerful yet simple way to identify opportunities is called Value Stream Mapping, which visualizes the activities and steps from idea to delivered product.[7] The waste is in activities that do not add customer or business value: typical candidates include meetings, estimation, defect fixing, rework, waiting, and relearning. Get ideas for improvements by considering how to eliminate or reduce such waste. Typical remedies include greater collaboration and fewer barriers, improved capabilities (skill set and expertise), effective automation, environment and tool enhancements, and less process.

13.2.4 Other Practitioners

When something is visibly wrong, it can be rather easy to produce ideas for fixing it. But when nothing is broken, people need an inspiration or a reference for the next step up. Often, inspiration comes from the outside — and there's a gold mine out there.

Around the world, thousands of teams have been experimenting with Agile implementations. Industry and academy researchers propose new techniques, theories, and interpretations. Interdisciplinary developments abound with ideas coming from such endeavors as the theater[8] and newspaper publication. That is why smart companies invest in sending their employees to conferences: they see clever solutions, consider new developments, and hear inspiring stories.

Other sources of inspiration, which consume less time and money, are local user group meetings. You could also contact Agile companies in your area and ask to drop in for a tour. Companies that do Agile well tend to be proud and open about it, so you're likely to get a yes.

Read professional literature. Books will educate you, inspire you, and open your mind. Many Agilists attribute their initial foray into Extreme Programming or Scrum to the early books on those methods. Books, however, are usually read once and then shelved.[*] For more regular exposure to inspiration and idea-providing resources, you can also subscribe to blogs, newsletters, and ezines, such as my free, biweekly ezine, the "3P Vantage Point" (**www.3PVantage.com/ezine.htm**).

---

[*] I would love to hear from you that this book is different. My contact information is at the end of the book.

Sign up for virtual events. Many experts lead free webinars and teleseminars on all matters Agile, and they can provide considerable inspiration and specific tips.*

13.2.5 Your Agile Coach

Many companies have turned to coaches to help them adopt Agile methods. Some of the large ones have espoused the recommendation, dating back to the early Agile days, to have an Agile coach on staff. On board as an Agile specialist, not as an individual contributor, an internal coach can be invaluable for helping teams establish, maintain, and improve their Agility.

If you're invested in achieving high performance, a skilled coach is also a must for a team that's doing well. Professional athletes, sports teams, and even chess players employ coaches all the way to the top. Coaching is not just skill building and knowledge transfer; an expert coach facilitates growth and change, gives feedback, prevents relapses, and provides guidance (for more on coaching, see 11.7).

The foregoing mechanisms have you tap into your team, experts, and other practitioners. Unfortunately, some of these avenues may be closed to you. Even if you have the time, energy, and open mind to access this veritable wellspring of ideas, your organization may not.

An organization's culture determines what it welcomes and what it resists. A company that prides itself on hiring bright, capable people is not likely to bring in a coach. Strong, entrepreneurial leadership is likely to put more stock in their industry peers' suggestions than in their teams' input. And some organizations will simply not pay for advice or conferences; their ideas for change come only from their own staff.

You can let this limitation deflate you, or you can get creative. If you cherish continuous improvement, keep at it.

---

* Every few months I lead the webinar "Top Ten Attitudes to Abolish when Adopting Agile," which explores holdover attitudes as a rich source of intervention points. Invitations to this free event go out in the 3P Vantage Point ezine (www.3PVantage.com/ezine.htm).

13.3 How Should We Approach a Substantial Improvement?

When you contemplate a complex improvement initiative, analyze its prerequisites, hurdles, and implications carefully. Ask yourself such questions as: Who needs to be involved, and when? Who is likely to resist the change, and how? What are possible side effects?

You may be able to carry out the change iteratively and incrementally — in other words, as an Agile undertaking. Break it down into smaller steps, each step having value and success criteria. Like user stories, some will be independent, whereas others will build on each other. Prioritize the steps, make them visible, and discuss them in retrospectives. Take one or two of those steps, collect feedback, and adjust accordingly. Be careful, though: experiencing multiple sequential change curves might be less palatable than proceeding more quickly through a larger change.

On one Agile transition engagement, the developers were very excited to pick up Agile methods and write automated tests for their code. However, they made no effort to embrace test-driven development (TDD). One time, I was paired up with a developer who agreed to test-drive the next feature. TDD involves quite frequent cycles of coding, compiling, and executing tests; she needed five minutes to compile just enough code to execute a single new test. No wonder the team preferred to code everything first, then write tests: a quick calculation showed that the TDD loop's mechanics alone would waste 15% of their time. That's equivalent to one of the team's seven developers being incapacitated! Before they could learn how to do TDD, this team needed to remove certain hurdles; most were technical, but one had to do with an internal standard.[9] Removing those hurdles was itself a valuable change. It required buy-in and some effort, and accomplishing it took two weeks.

Remember that every change involves a chaos period during which performance is much reduced (see 11.1). You may delay certain changes if you can't afford the drop. For that reason, I usually advise clients to undertake the mammoth change of Agile adoption during the first half of a project's life cycle. However, if the team is keen to get started, they could again carve out high-value, lower-impact practices such as the daily standup and sitting together.

13.4 Why Should We Approach Improvements as Experiments?

Some changes, especially those coming down from management, are enacted as rules. For instance, some companies put in place the rule "X new unit tests per programmer per iteration" before starting a more formal Agile transition. Another popular rule is "A story's not done until its owner has applied the code reviewer's comments." The team or management establishes these rules for a good reason, such as improving quality or reducing costs.

This approach usually has two shortcomings, however:

✦ The rules are predetermined to be the right measure. No attempt is made to assess their effect on performance. Sometimes they cause an unnoticed reversal elsewhere.

✦ The rules are an imitation of others' success. When you hear someone refer to a tactic or rule as a "best practice," you know that the context for its success has been lost. No practice is universally best; all practices have contexts in which they are costlier or less effective than others.

A better approach is to consider each improvement an experiment, with all the implications of the scientific method. Formulate a hypothesis; test it out, and collect data; then analyze your data and draw a conclusion. Since a work environment is a complex adaptive system, other techniques such as variable isolation and control groups might well be a stretch. In addition, objective measures are not always possible, but having a hypothesis to prove or disprove, and data to analyze, will get you far. Just make sure the experimentation period allows the team sufficient time in the integration phase of the change curve (see 11.1).

Several teams were theoretically interested in pairing but resistant to it in practice. They became considerably more receptive once I suggested experimenting with pairing. (I used the magic phrase, "Let's give it a try.") We usually limited the experiment to two or three iterations. I helped the teams establish clear rules (what to pair on, how often to switch, and the like), collect objective measurements such as defect data and completed story points, and solicit subjective measures such as satisfaction and knowledge acquisition. Time-boxing the experiment assured the participants of having a way out if they didn't like it.

Reframing a change as an experiment — and carrying it out as a bona fide experiment — is a great way to get buy-in. For stronger buy-in and participation in an experiment, it's better to have the team *agree* to run it. If the team can reach consensus on an experiment, they'll feel more curious about the hypothesis and more enthusiastic about participating than if they're told, "You are going to pair up for the next two iterations, and after we process the results, we'll tell you whether to keep pairing or not."

It's important to realize that you're not just reframing a change as an experiment. Agile teams and organizations are such complex systems that you don't truly know whether the change will result in net improvement. For instance, many people consider code reviews a "best practice" for enforcing standards and finding omissions. In some teams, code reviews do achieve those targets, but they also cause considerable context switching, delays in story completion, and costly overhead of managing review findings.

Beware the Law of Unintended Consequences. Whatever action you take, you might receive an unexpected benefit, cause an undesirable effect, or make the underlying problem worse. As you formulate your hypothesis and the experiment, consider what other consequences might occur. For instance, one Agility assessment I conducted revealed that senior developers used the code review mechanism to sneak in many changes and gold-plating tasks, thereby messing up estimates and bypassing the backlog prioritization mechanism. For a systematic exploration of possible unintended consequences, consider their five possible causes: ignorance, error, immediate interest, basic values, and self-defeating prophecy.[10]

Finally, each experiment has value on several dimensions. The obvious one is the added learning. Another one is team building: the team committed to a shared activity, performed it, and followed up on it. And there is the value of humility when an experiment's results are nothing like the hypothesis.

13.5 How Can We Know We're Doing It Right?

You have chosen to adopt an Agile methodology to reap certain benefits. Typical benefits include higher product quality, shorter time to market, and quicker response to market needs. The Agile approach presupposes that you would customize the methods to your business, staff, culture, and technology. As you invent techniques, change practices, and add or remove steps, you might be wondering, "Are we doing it right? Is that Agile?"

A quick way to assess your implementation is to check it against the Agile principles. Refer to the principles in the Agile Manifesto and the values in the Declaration of Interdependence[11] as checklists for your entire methodology as well as for each suggested change.

For example, suppose your team has been working in two-week iterations and they say, "This is too short for meaningful work. Let's extend to three weeks." I would ask whether the following four principles from the Manifesto would apply to your team as strongly as before:

✦ *"Welcome changing requirements, even late in development."* Iterations are intentionally short, so they can be undisturbed. Would the customer care to wait longer for features and changes? Can he still give the team frequent feedback to reduce the risk of discovering that a feature is unwanted?

✦ *"Deliver working software frequently, from a couple of weeks to a couple of months, with a preference to the shorter timescale."* Would an additional week significantly improve the team's ability to deliver working software, or is something else standing in their way of getting to done?

✦ *"Simplicity — the art of maximizing the amount of work not done — is essential."* The two-week time limit constrains the team to consider creative solutions and alternatives. Will they be as creative in a three-week cycle, or will they do more work than necessary?

✦ *"At regular intervals, the team reflects on how to become more effective, then tunes and adjusts its behavior accordingly."* Would having one-third fewer retrospectives work to the community's benefit?

Many Agile experts teach the practices with some variations. By examining your implementation from the principles and values angle, you'll avoid the "Which expert do we follow?" trap. You will shift from *doing* Agile to *being* Agile.

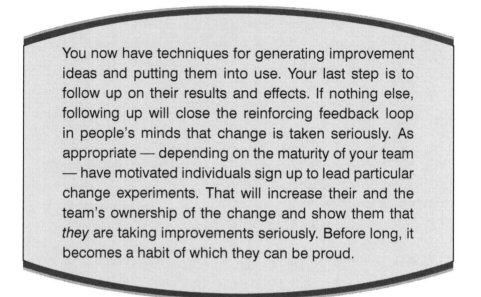

You now have techniques for generating improvement ideas and putting them into use. Your last step is to follow up on their results and effects. If nothing else, following up will close the reinforcing feedback loop in people's minds that change is taken seriously. As appropriate — depending on the maturity of your team — have motivated individuals sign up to lead particular change experiments. That will increase their and the team's ownership of the change and show them that *they* are taking improvements seriously. Before long, it becomes a habit of which they can be proud.

Supplementary Resource

Go to **www.TheHumanSideOfAgile.com** and download
"Mindful Continuous Improvement."

CHAPTER 14

Stay the Course

The needs and challenges of a young Agile team will keep you busy for months. Helping them reach the performing stage will be a most satisfying accomplishment. But you can't start coasting. Instead, help your team stay current, grow as individuals and as a team, and keep adapting.

14.1 How Long Should the Team Stay Together?

From the early days, Agile methods called for a Whole Team (the "community" in this book). They suggested co-locating team members and, moreover, having the two main roles — developer and customer — sit as close together as possible. More recently, Agile practitioners have embraced Lean thinking, which sees value in having the team *pull* the work, stay together over time, and be minimally spread across other communities.

These practices are not critical for Agility. A partly dispersed cross-functional team, time zones away from their product owner, with members entering and leaving, can still be Agile and deliver good value. However, these practices — which are all about *keeping together* — would radically improve productivity, quality, and adaptability. By self-identifying as the complete project community, they build shared ownership and reduce friction. Minimizing people's assignment to other teams (see 4.5) and emphasizing co-location (see 5.5) help them norm and perform by building trust, facilitating collaboration, and removing hurdles.

Successful, motivated teams love being together, which helps them become even more successful and motivated. Furthermore, highly productive teams are more valuable to the organization than their productive individuals utilized at 100%. Therefore, your best strategy for long-term performance is to *keep teams stable*. Rather than disband a team when their project is over, have standing Agile teams that pull work from a shared queue. They have the potential to create shared history, trust, collaboration, and long-term goodwill. Until they eventually adjourn, they can spend proportionately longer in the performing stage than teams that come and go.

Unless the team is naturally entrepreneurial and fast-moving, most members will appreciate having the same set of familiar faces around over time. They can develop effective habits, customized practices, and their own subculture. They can stop worrying about process and teamwork and focus on results. And the longer that team members stay together, the more their personal fate is tied with others' and the more responsibility they'll take. They will naturally take care of team needs, because the team's good is the individual's good.

Still, that does not mean teams should remain frozen. In software development, most individual contributors move up, sideways, or out every few years. Business considerations give rise to reorganizations and refocusing even in the most stable companies. If neither change affects your team significantly, the stability of even a high-performing team might lead to atrophy — akin to being asleep at the wheel on a long road trip. *Some* level and frequency of change may be necessary.

14.2 How Much Change Is Good Over Time?

When a software group follows a siloed methodology, each of its functional subgroups experiences *seasons*. Developers, for instance, have a relatively relaxed time early on in a project, which they pay for in a "death march" closer to the ship date. In a cross-functional Agile community, by contrast, everybody goes at a fairly even tilt, one iteration at a time. When people work in the same environment on the same products for years, they can get into a rut. Waterfall's seasons can break the rut; Agile's iterations can quickly turn into a hamster wheel.

Some people are attracted to sameness, stability, and slow evolution. As long as they are motivated to work on your team, they can contribute solidly for a hundred iterations. They are the people who appreciate a regular schedule and accept gradual, slow change, but won't generally initiate it. They have mastered useful tools and processes and don't care to switch to more modern ones.

Some folks are attracted to differences and thrive on variety. Give them different problems to solve and new product directions, and they will flourish. They are the people who embrace new methods and technologies (even practicing on their own time), who are keen on refactoring and renovating code, and who don't mind experimentation.[1]

In a work context, only a third of professionals are motivated by difference. The others will prefer slow evolution or stability.[2] You are likely to have both kinds on your team. This diversity is valuable, because they pay attention to different things. Their approaches to pattern recognition, problem solving, and innovation are different. (Notice how my choice of words in the last two sentences gives away my difference filter.)

Nevertheless, over time this diversity becomes problematic. The environment doesn't have to be as dynamic as a startup to cause nervousness among sameness people. Conversely, if the team's backlog contains little variety and the work is largely incremental, difference people will get restless.

"I just can't see this stuff in front of me anymore. I've done the same things so many times, they don't interest me anymore. I no longer have the ambition to approach them creatively. We had a person transfer from an office in another country, where she'd had a similar role to mine. She's seeing opportunities for change and she's injecting new ideas. I thrive on variety and newness, but, having seen the same things over and over, my mind has atrophied. I even feel physically tired, not just mentally so. Other long-time colleagues are also giving signals that they are growing impatient. When somebody makes a mistake, we don't just clean up and move on; instead it's 'Oh, come on!'"

— *A project coordinator*

Some difference people will channel their energy toward technological and process changes; others may wish to move to neighboring teams for the variety. The speaker in the story above had satisfied her difference preference through the varied needs of her role, but over time that variety became too repetitive. Without sufficient mental stimulation, difference people won't stay around long. This is particularly unfortunate, because they tend to pick up miscellaneous team tasks and dropped balls, if only for the novelty.

Difference people don't necessarily expect every experience to be dynamic. They can also enjoy variety outside of work situations — in their hobbies, their social life, their volunteer work. If their work environment is attractive enough, many will be patient with short-term sameness if it holds the promise of later exciting changes. Unfortunately, that promise is rarely yours to keep.

Bryan was a dynamic architect, working a flexible schedule at an established company. The company's codebase was a mess and its foray into Agile was lackluster, but he held onto the hope of a product rewrite and an Agile reboot. "When they extended the horizon of our ancient codebase by another three years," he told me, "I posted my résumé."

How much change is good over time will depend on your team's mix of personalities and preferences. It is a balancing act, and you may not make everybody happy. To increase your team members' engagement, look beyond motivation (see 10.4). What aspects of work attract them? Which activities excite them? What types of team success recharge their batteries? Do they find their team environment socially satisfying? How else can they build up their skills?

14.3 What Should We Do About Personnel Changes?

Software organizations are exposed to personnel turnover every bit as other industries are. Even if an employee wishes to stay with his organization, he may not want to stay with the same team for the whole time. Employees rely on many variables to determine their work path, and their particular team and methodology are but two of those variables. When a valued member moves to another role, another team, or another company, the remaining members have to restorm and renorm (see 6.1). As long as they see their colleague's move as voluntary — rather than as a managerial intervention — the regrouping should be rather smooth.

Most software teams develop products that have *longevity* — version 1.0 is typically the first of many versions. The product evolves over its life cycle; new parts emerge, some parts grow, others morph, a few vanish. As the product's capabilities grow, so does its complexity, if only because of configurability and backward compatibility. The product needs continuous maintenance simply to remain functional on new platforms. As the team that authored version 1.0 proceeds to work on later versions, they pay a sort of tax on their system's being in users' hands. They need more people in order to keep up.

When the team is still small, the typical recourse is to hire additional people into the team. If the existing team has been around for a while, they might not like the intervention — so *obtain their consent* first. In some teams, the hiring of new people causes unintentional unfairness, for two reasons. Since veterans know the existing parts (the "legacy") intimately, but newcomers know nothing about them, all the boring maintenance and defect-fixing work falls to the veterans. The other reason, which is easier to get around, is that newcomers receive new, powerful computers while the veterans are stuck with yesterday's models. Before you bring additional people in, discuss the situation with the team, identify the expectations of the new hires, and make sure everyone is clear on — and OK with — the likely effects of enlarging the team.

Hiring and reassignment into the team might cause it to grow too large. A team isn't "too large" by virtue of exceeding some magic number of members, such as ten. It is too large when fractures occur, usually along such fault lines as technology, product components, and social cliques. Now the team needs to make a choice: should they stay together and resolve their conflicts? Split into two smaller, still cross-functional teams? Or reorganize further into component teams? Your support and facilitation are critical here because the larger the team gets, the harder it is for individuals to look past self-interest and consider the group's good. If they do choose to split, help them determine the new teams' makeup, roles, and planning mechanisms.

14.4 What Are the Team's Options for Developing Skills and Knowledge?

People love learning. In knowledge work, learning is a prerequisite and a fact of life. It is critical for keeping your business running and employees employable. Your staff has to learn better methods and tools — and do so faster than the competition — in order to innovate and adapt. Learning starts with each individual member. The benefit of such learning to the organization is amplified, the more open, trusting, and collaborative the relationship between those members is.

According to management guru Peter Senge,[3] a learning organization exhibits five main characteristics: systems thinking, mental models, a shared vision, personal mastery, and team learning. As an Agile team leader (ATL), the two characteristics that are closest to you, and that you can influence the most, are personal mastery and team learning. The challenge I see everywhere is that organizations don't invest enough in these aspects of learning, which affects their adaptability to change, the quality of their products, and their competitiveness.

However, you can introduce several low-cost practices to amplify learning and personal mastery:

Study groups. A small group of people, usually from a similar discipline, study a certain topic over a period of time. They typically study a book or an online resource. Study groups work best when a leader keeps everybody accountable and on task, and when the group can apply the subject matter to work. For instance, when I was a developer in the early 2000s, one of my colleagues started a weekly design-patterns study group. Of the myriad known patterns, we focused our attention on a few we could immediately apply to our work.

Communities of practice. Even though Agile methods prefer vertical teams in order to deliver complete value, there's still room and demand for skill transfer across teams. Participants, usually from a similar discipline (such as UI designers) share information, experiences, stories, and practices. They might do so in scheduled, formal meetings or just get together weekly to have lunch and talk shop. Many communities of practice exist in online discussion boards and social media groups. These technologies help them scale, retain and search discussion history, and continue conversations asynchronously. Many corporations support internal communities of practice behind their firewalls, using social media–like technologies through which participants can also discuss specifics of their products.[4]

Facilitated discovery meetings. Schedule a few hours for the team to amplify its learning in specific areas. You can bring in a guest expert for a facilitated discussion. The team can analyze a specific topic together, such as in a "technical retrospective." They can also identify their own agenda in real time — for example, using Open Space Technology.[5]

I noticed a recurring theme in one team's retrospectives: members felt they didn't know enough. They wanted to learn more about the system, about its intended use, and about each other. Frequent collaboration and knowledge-transfer sessions didn't move them as far ahead as they wanted. At my suggestion, the project sponsor arranged a day off site for the 20-person project community. The first half, dubbed "Know-It-All," included a round of presentations on the most burning questions, plus an Open Space hour for the topics of greatest interest. For the second half, we went bowling, where inevitably some people talked shop. The team rated the event highly for both learning and engagement.

Conferences and local user group meetings. These are great opportunities for learning new ideas from other practitioners and experts. For deeper learning, present at them: there's no better way to learn a subject than having to teach it.

Team member pairing sessions with frequent pair switching. This tactic spreads knowledge of the system, tools, assumptions, constraints, and techniques like no other. It is great for communicating tacit knowledge. It is particularly *effective* because it is situated learning ("learn by doing"): the learner applies newfound knowledge immediately. The team doesn't have to formally buy into pairing to realize learning value from each pairing session.

Ambassadors. Team members act as ambassadors when they temporarily join another team for the express purpose of knowledge transfer and cross-pollination. The other team can be next door or across the ocean; the ambassador approach works extremely well for bringing dispersed teams closer. The ambassadors ought to go voluntarily so the change in team composition doesn't trigger a big productivity hit (see 6.1).

The following popular practices might *not* be as helpful as you think:

Knowledge transfer sessions. Such sessions usually involve someone spending a few days preparing a presentation and then delivering it to a number of people who listen politely before heading back to work. In my experience, the retention and application value from these sessions is extremely low, which frustrates everyone. This is particularly true of the popular format known as "lunch and learn" or "brown bag," during which listeners also eat. Many people prefer to spend their break time doing something else. Moreover, if you expect them to bring a packed lunch, some will inevitably think you and the company are being cheap.

Detailed documentation. While capturing knowledge in written form has its advantages, it also has significant downsides. It's time consuming, tacit knowledge gets easily lost, and the cost of maintaining the information can be rather high.

14.5 How Can People Grow Beyond Their Current Roles?

A person's professional growth typically involves positional advancement (on a technical or managerial track), skills development, and additional responsibilities. All still apply in an Agile environment.

Individual contributors generally advance from junior through intermediate to senior positions. The title confers recognition of a person's growth and professional acumen: she is expected to apply better expertise to problem solving, do higher-quality work, and have a greater positive effect on her team. Some individual contributors continue along the technical track. For instance, architects and other highly skilled developers can solve the hardest problems, kick-start new teams from a technological perspective, and facilitate effective design and programming practices. Veteran Agile testers do the same for a team's testing discipline. The critical point to remember is that while on a team, they are *team members*. They bring their added value but not their titles into the room. Their highest contribution can be in mentoring others rather than cutting code or testing.

On the management track, senior contributors become team leaders and then managers. In command-and-control environments, these transitions are problematic: all of a sudden, the person needs to adjust to leadership and then to being other people's boss. A manager's role requires different talents, preferences, and skills than an individual contributor's role. In an Agile framework, however, the manager–subordinate relationship is different because of team autonomy and empowerment. In fact, a person's experience in a people-first Agile environment should make his adjustment to leadership or management easier.

When it comes to additional responsibilities, individuals are welcome to want to do more and to be correspondingly empowered. Just beware of pigeonholing. With their new responsibilities, they might perceive themselves — or be perceived by others — as the sole specialists or experts, leaving no room for others.

One universal area of growth is craftsmanship, fueled by the desire to be ever better at one's craft. Human beings need *a great deal* of practice to develop true mastery — at least 10,000 hours, according to recent thinking.[6] Over the last few years, *software* craftsmanship has grown into a movement.[7, 8] An Agile team — especially one invested in technical discipline — is a welcoming environment for developing one's expertise. So you might not need to worry about promotions and seniority when, in fact, many of your team members will be perfectly content with the continued opportunity to hone their craft.

14.6 How Can the Team Insure Itself Against Human Failings?

When you need to estimate the effort and duration of a piece of work, you know that the actual numbers might fall on either side of your estimate. The universal cure for estimation overrun in plan-driven environments is to pad estimates, or add a "buffer." Agile teams have a different way to *protect their planning and forecasting* from various risks. They use the relative, rough estimate of story points, work with small items, and don't plan to 100% capacity. (In other words, they include some *slack* in the planning cycle.)

Smart Agile teams also invest time and effort to *safeguard their work products* from exorbitant costs of change and maintenance. This insurance policy takes the form of comprehensive automated developer testing (also known as unit testing or microtesting).[9] As appropriate technologically, they will take a risk-based approach, directing their coverage efforts to the areas of highest risk.

These two types of insurance address the process and the product. Ultimately, both are used by people. This book and many other resources help you address those people's motivation, build their soft skills, and foster teamwork. This is all fine…until things go wrong.

Being human, team members occasionally experience personal trouble. They are susceptible to mood changes. Their preferences and motivation change over time. Even your best people can suddenly lose focus. Thus, great Agile teams also need the third type of insurance: against human failings.

Basic "people insurance" takes the form of skill distribution. Team members coach each other, work in pairs, study, and practice. By spreading the skills, they increase redundancy, which is famously indicated by the "lottery number" (that is, the smallest number of people who, if they won the lottery and left your team, would cause the project to stall or die).[10]

You can have skilled individuals who deliver value, communicate well, and leverage their process effectively, yet if they can't pull together as a team when they need to, they won't succeed under adverse circumstances. Great teams don't just perform well; they are resilient and adaptable. The insurance policy for that is to *have each other's back*.

Like the estimation slack and the unit test suite, the main intent of having each other's back is not higher performance. It is to respond reliably when things don't turn out as hoped.

Having each other's back is a form of shared responsibility. When one person needs help, another will be there for her. More than being civil or professional, it is about the team, the team's work, and the actions of the team. You might offer help without someone asking for it. When someone gets in trouble, others in the team handle it. It is moral support for when the situation turns emotional. It is helping someone finish a task when you are available. It is helping others notice when they are speaking or writing without thinking, and providing feedback.

Shared responsibility doesn't always require you to do anything; sometimes, it means you avoid certain things. You won't use a team member's known weaknesses to your own advantage, you won't blame team members for mishaps, and you won't placate people when their actions are truly not helpful.

Like regular insurance, these forms of insurance require an investment of time and effort. You might make that investment simply to protect against risk. Yet there is also a hidden gain: *insurance liberates you.* Just as purchasing car insurance allows you to drive your car without fear of financial ruin in the case of an accident, team members who know that others have their backs will be more relaxed, innovative, and confident. Did you ever wake up one morning sneezing and coughing, only to think, "If I don't go to work today, things will fall apart"? Now imagine that the team had each other's back, *including yours*. Would you be making the same call?

Building shared responsibility at the team level is a gradual process.

First, the team truly needs to *be* a team. Everyone needs a common goal and interdependent commitments, so that everyone has the same long-term view and the feeling of being together in the same boat. Individual ownership, obligations, and objectives take away from being a team.

Second, members need to have a strong affiliation to their team. When their primary allegiance is to their team, they are more likely to have the trust necessary to have each other's back. They know they'll keep working together, without the organization pulling them apart. See chapter 5 for advice regarding both steps.

The third step is to build rapport (see 8.3). Rapport underscores mutual respect and approachability. Encourage your team members to build individual human connections with their colleagues. Provide opportunities for them to find common ground, both professional and personal. This step will be much easier with continuous face time than if they are dispersed, but you can use high-bandwidth technology to help in the latter case.

Team members who can give and receive congruent feedback can share responsibility and have each other's back. Congruent feedback means they don't blame each other for problems. They don't placate, which implicitly permits bad behavior to continue. They don't ignore colleagues or work around them. They actively build healthy relationships with others, including those they don't always like.

Even if your team never needs to make a claim on their insurance, sharing responsibility will increase their sense of collective accomplishment, improve their teamwork, and result in greater satisfaction from their work.[11]

14.7 How Do We Avoid Reverting to Old Behaviors?

The software industry is littered with Agile implementations whose success and performance did not last. In some cases, new senior management came in and undid Agile, whether intentionally or through a reorganization. In most other cases, however, Agility eroded gradually. Your ongoing leadership and influence are vital — and limited. Since every team is part of a bigger whole, management has to actively back Agility in order to stop and reverse erosion.

Someone must protect the chosen methodology. The single Agile team has a process steward, typically called ScrumMaster, ATL, Agile project manager, or coach. A large program or a division should also have someone look after the integrity and development of its methodology. Some companies dub this role their "Agile evangelist," "head coach," or "practice lead." The project management office (PMO), if it focuses on budget, schedule, and scope, is probably not the place for that.

Your project community applies the Agile methodology in the context of a larger organization, which has additional procedures and expectations. Some can be innocuous nuisances, like filling time sheets. Others can be downright detrimental to the Agile philosophy. The usual suspects include annual performance appraisals (see 5.7), stack-rating people, and publicly singling out individuals for outstanding behavior. You might have your own habits and holdover beliefs from a waterfall environment, which are less effective in Agile — such as hiring into the team without their involvement and consent. Keep reevaluating your actions to make sure you don't ruin the team's accomplishments unintentionally.

Teams' good results today are no guarantee of good results tomorrow — because their members are human. Some team trouble is immediately apparent, while other trouble is a slow-progress malady. Keep your eyes and ears open to symptoms of apathy and unhappiness, and address them forthwith: just like personal health, sickness sets in some time before its symptoms are visible.[12]

Left unchecked, every system grows more complex over time. As it needs to address new demands, rules, and risks, its users add mechanisms, which increase complexity. (Just consider the extra costs and processes of doing business since the Sarbanes–Oxley Act.) The same is true of your Agile implementation. The antidote is to continuously refactor it: simplify, remove duplication and variations, and minimize steps in your process. For instance, teams have simplified their process by eliminating task estimation. They kept using points at the story level, and split every task that seemed large or unmanageable. A process owner or evangelist can lead or take responsibility for this activity.

Many companies have turned to Agile *processes* in the hope that they would fix certain problems. But they only *do* Agile — imitating others' successful practices — without truly *being* Agile. It's akin to going on a "process diet": without a congruent change in habits and attitudes, its effects won't last. Agility is more than just sprints, customer involvement, and cross-functional teams; it's a philosophy — a complete set of attitudes, beliefs, and values. It must be supported at those logical levels (see 11.5) in order to be sustainable. That's why culture matters so much. If you don't do it like you mean it, it won't last.

Finally, get a second opinion. Human beings manage the constant deluge of sensory input by tuning out the familiar; they notice change only when it is above a certain threshold. The same is true of groups of people. The erosion in your team's Agility might be too gradual for you to notice. Consider having an Agility assessment done, either by an outside expert or by another Agile leader in your company.[13] At the least, an objective report of findings ought to inspire ideas for remedial actions.

Are you the kind of manager or leader who thrives on building great teams from scratch? Or do you derive greater satisfaction from helping strong teams *stay* strong? Even if you consider one challenge more appealing than the other, you'd do well to get comfortable with both. As Agile development is still new — and operating in a business context that hasn't quite embraced its premises yet — most Agile teams are young. Few managers and team leaders have extensive experience in sustaining teams for the long haul. So if that's the challenge you're drawn to, there's much to learn and practice. Perhaps you'll write your own book someday.

Supplementary Resource
Go to **www.TheHumanSideOfAgile.com** and download
"Keep up the Good Work: Ten-Point Team Checkup."

WHAT DO I DO NEXT?

At the time of writing (2012), tens of thousands of professionals are active as ScrumMasters, Agile project managers, and functional leads. Relatively few people self-identify as Agile team leaders (ATLs). The role, as defined in this book, demands a great deal from its practitioners. Then again, aiming high is a natural part of Agile thinking, and the other Agile roles are also quite demanding.

If you're mostly helping your team on the process front (as some ScrumMasters do), or on the project front (as some Agile project managers do), increase your effectiveness by becoming an ATL. You don't have to change your title, wait to be promoted, or ask to be formally designated as such. Effective Agile teams endorse shared leadership, personal responsibility, and self-organization, so just *act* as an ATL.

You may want to browse the table of contents again and notice elements in your current practice upon which you can improve. As situations arise, notice which questions you ask yourself, then look them up in order to prepare yourself quickly.

Choose one specific topic to study more deeply. (Why not more? So you can "get to done"!) Use the chapters' notes to find additional background information and related resources. Some of these resources are books; some are workshops. If you'd like to learn more from me, simply go to **www.3PVantage.com/ezine.htm** for my free ezine containing articles, interviews, and access to online events. Check the back of the book for my other products and services and more opportunities to interact with me.

Books are by nature general. This book addresses 80-odd questions that professionals like you have posed to me (or publicly) over the years. You will naturally have questions and issues that the book doesn't address, or you might feel that your team's challenges call for dedicated guidance. If you want to get an opinion, ask a question, or see how I can help your team, feel free to write to me at **gbroza@3PVantage.com**.

APPENDIX

What Do Functional and Line Managers Do in Agile?

In Agile, cross-functional teams self-organize to deliver working software. A typical team has enough needs to justify appointing a dedicated Agile team leader. That person guides and supports the team with no assumption of positional authority or a reporting relationship. But should the team also have a manager? Or should the programmers (from this team and maybe others) report to a development manager, the testers to a test manager, and so on for every other function? And what value does a manager — functional or otherwise — add in an Agile setting?

Team-level Agile methods make no reference to managers. Early Agile proponents even claimed that managers are overhead, hold-overs from the old command-and-control regime who get in the team's way. However, managers become highly valuable once an Agile organization looks beyond the single team, the tactical level, and short-term goals. Various needs and questions appear that belong in two categories:

+ **Strategy and roadmap.** "Where do we go, beyond any single project?" and "How, and when, will we get there?" The questions raised are about portfolio management, staff deployment, and business development.

+ **Capability development.** The questions raised are about horizontal (cross-team) aspects such as overall staffing and retention, technical specialization, skill enhancement, career development, standardization, and tooling.

No longer encumbered by the details of daily execution and work assignment, managers support the organization's long-term needs. In the following depiction of the dimensions of managerial needs, managers take care of the left-hand side, while project managers take care of the right-hand side:

MANAGEMENT	PROJECT MANAGEMENT / TEAM LEADERSHIP
Strategic	Tactical
Employees' long-term growth and path	Team members' engagement with their project and their team
Capability	Execution
Organizational Agility	Team Agility
Horizontal (systemic)	Vertical
Roadmap and project portfolio	Single project

Managers focus their attention on people — both individual contributors and leaders. They lead the hiring decisions and process. They provide feedback and coaching to facilitate employees' growth and performance. They cultivate relationships with staff that increase motivation and retention. Keeping their eyes on the organization's long-term needs, they invest in appropriate staff development and capability building. They shepherd organizational learning — for instance, by supporting communities of practice.

Managers evangelize Agile and help it take root and grow within the organization. They leverage their influence and relationships to remove organizational obstacles to Agility, such as individual objectives and performance appraisals.

Working horizontally across projects and programs, managers can notice and tackle systemic problems. They grease the wheels by eliminating organizational waste, such as cumbersome processes or bureaucracy, and by easing bottlenecks, such as specialists in high demand. They help identify technical dependencies, point out opportunities for reuse, and coordinate local effective practices across similar functions.

Managers are in the best spot for managing the project portfolio[1] — a critical activity for sustained value delivery at the organizational level. Even if portfolio rebalancing occurs only quarterly, managers need to prepare and analyze the requisite data more frequently. Their freedom from tactical, daily project management makes that possible. They are able to manage staff allocation to organizational initiatives and remove structural obstacles to optimal portfolio execution.

Some development environments rely on both functional managers and project managers. Other environments combine the project manager and the functional (line) manager role into one Agile manager or leader role. As long as the managers are competent leaders and strategic thinkers, they do *not* need to specialize in a function such as development or quality assurance (QA). Moreover, if teams remain largely stable (as advised in section 14.1), managers can perform many of their duties effectively without requiring a reporting relationship. The essence of Agile management is leadership: putting people first in support of the organization's success.

ACKNOWLEDGMENTS

Since childhood, I have believed I had a book in me. However, the required effort always appeared daunting and the bar of excellence too high. And what would I even write about? Three years ago, Henrik Kniberg delivered the first blow to my wall of limiting beliefs by telling me the hilarious story about how his popular *Scrum and XP from the Trenches* came to be. All of a sudden, I opened up to the possibility that writing a book did not have to be a huge project, and a year later I started writing. By the time I realized that the book had indeed turned out to be a huge project, I was hooked. I held myself accountable for completing it by talking about it to anyone who would listen.

Two friends deserve special recognition for this particular book's existence. Johanna Rothman and David Spann gave me the support I needed to start writing and persevere to the end. Their support was critical since, like many projects, the book took far longer and evolved much further than I expected (or, more accurately, wished). They helped me overcome the aspiring author's mental obstacle, "There's nothing I could write that hasn't been written already." They reminded me that every person has a unique background, voice, and truth. My particular combination owes its development to two other special people: my parents, Ruti and Zvika, with whom I have spent countless hours talking about managing and being managed.

Eight years ago, I stopped climbing the ladder in software development organizations. I was going to be a full-time, external XP coach, a role that barely existed at the time. Joshua Kerievsky bet on me by hiring me to train and coach Industrial Logic (and Cutter

Consortium) clients. Over more than four years, I learned a lot from Josh and from the other great thinkers and practitioners he hired.

When I realized that I knew how to develop content but not how to write a book that matters, I turned to Mission Marketing Mentors. John Eggen, Lorna McLeod, and Kim Olver taught me all I needed and supported me throughout this endeavor.

I am fortunate to know many kind and knowledgeable people, a number of whom stepped up to review early revisions, excerpts, and entire chapters. My gratitude goes to Christopher Avery, Sharone Bar-David, Brent Barton, Stevie Borne, Suzanne Danis-Harkness, Rachel Davies, Bob Fischer, Michael James, Rob MacGregor, Gino Marckx, Darryl Minard, Enrico Palummieri, Luiz Parzianello, Keith Ray, Dave Rooney, Johanna Rothman, Steven Smith, Dan Snyder, and Ted Young. The preface became what it is now thanks to help from these kind souls, as well as from Christoffer Baar, Ivan Basch, Mike Edwards, Chris Ellefson, Jack Jones, Chris Leslie, Philip Lo, and Ron Skruzny.

After applying all their feedback, another group of experts and practitioners provided excellent feedback on the entire manuscript: François Bachmann, Ian Brockbank, Sekhar Burra, Steve Gray-kowski, Joy Kelsey, Rajesh Makhija, Gary Marcos, Yavor Nikolov, Vanessa Roberts, and Laura Woten. When I arrived at critical junctures, Johanna Rothman, Patrick Wilson-Welsh, and Brent Barton helped me make the necessary decisions. Four outstanding executives and delivery leads — Eugene Kiel, Chris Beale, Anas Fattahi, and Melody Zukowski — showed me how competent Agile team leadership contributes to a healthy environment and demonstrable results at their company, Cengage Learning.

My thanks go to all the practitioners who contributed stories to the book, some of whom did not wish to fully identify themselves.

When I interviewed potential editors, I experienced a common hiring dilemma: Which of two leading candidates to choose? Having made the conscious decision early in the project to favor quality over time and investment, the dilemma didn't last long: I chose both. Karen Pasley and Mark Woodworth brought complementary experiences and perspectives to improve my writing and catch my gaffes.

Writing a book is much like writing software code. True to form, hundreds of sticky notes were sacrificed in the making of this book, and countless hours went to refactoring its content and architecture. My family was incredibly patient with me throughout the writing journey, which involved several long periods of being physically present but mentally absent. Particular thanks go to my wife and soul mate, Ronit. Despite her completely different professional background, many years of hearing me go on about Agile — and years of coordinating projects and people — have enabled her to give meaningful feedback at every step of the book's evolution. I could rely only so much on coaches, editors, colleagues, and reviewers; with Ronit by my side, I never had to write alone.

Gil Broza
Toronto, Canada
June 2012

NOTES

Preface

1 Human beings have subconscious, contextual working preferences: Information/Systems, Things, and People. Some folks naturally gravitate to working with information or systems: they might enjoy spending a whole day examining fields in a spreadsheet, or putting systems and processes in place. Others gravitate to working with things: writing code, or building stuff with their hands. The third group gets excited by working with other people; coaches are like that. Data provided by jobEQ.com for a more granular categorization, based on a European stratified sample of 1,003 respondents taken in 2011, shows that the People preference is not prevalent. This means that the natural tendency of most people at work is to deal with artifacts and activities rather than to talk, collaborate, or cocreate.

Chapter 1

1 I learned this term from Joshua Kerievsky, who applied it in the Industrial XP methodology. I believe the term originated with David Schmaltz.

2 *Principles behind the Agile Manifesto*, 2001, agilemanifesto.org/principles.html.

Chapter 2

1 Johanna Rothman presents a very pragmatic take on project management in *Manage It!: Your Guide to Modern, Pragmatic Project Management* (Raleigh, NC: The Pragmatic Bookshelf, 2007).

2 An antipattern is a specific repeated practice that may appear to be valuable but ultimately results in negative consequences.

3 Johanna Rothman makes this point with respect to strategic vs. tactical work in *Hiring the Best Knowledge Workers, Techies, and Nerds: The Secrets and Science of Hiring Technical People* (New York: Dorset House, 2004).

4 For Jerry Weinberg's approach to giving and receiving feedback, consult Charles N. Seashore, Edith Whitfield Seashore, and Gerald M. Weinberg, *What Did You Say?: The Art of Giving and Receiving Feedback* (Columbia, MD: Bingham House Books, 1997).

5   An often-quoted management truism is that "You get what you measure." If a certain aspect of work is measured (because it appears to be valued), the performers of the work may (perhaps subconsciously) alter their behavior to satisfy the measurement. For instance, if you insist that iterations yield a higher number of "done" points without introducing supporting process change, the team may relax the definition of "done" in order to satisfy that metric. Read more about "You get what you measure" in the context of Agile in Deborah Hartmann and Robin Dymond, *Appropriate Agile Measurement: Using Metrics and Diagnostics to Deliver Business Value*, at www.innovel.net/wp-content/uploads/2007/07/appropriateagilemeasurementagilemetrics.pdf.

Chapter 3

1   Marcus Buckingham and Curt Coffman, *First, Break All the Rules: What the World's Greatest Managers Do Differently* (New York: Simon and Schuster, 1999).

2   Jerry Weinberg has been leading the world-renowned "Problem Solving Leadership" (PSL) workshop for many years with various other hosts. www.estherderby.com/workshops/problem-solving-leadership-psl.

3   Stephen R. Covey, *The 7 Habits of Highly Effective People: Powerful Lessons in Personal Change* (New York: Free Press, 2004).

4   Johanna Rothman and Esther Derby, *Behind Closed Doors: Secrets of Great Management* (Raleigh, NC: The Pragmatic Bookshelf, 2005).

5   Johanna Rothman, *Hiring the Best Knowledge Workers, Techies, and Nerds: The Secrets and Science of Hiring Technical People* (New York: Dorset House, 2004).

6   This is an abbreviation of Norm Kerth's Prime Directive for retrospectives. *Project Retrospectives: A Handbook for Team Reviews* (New York: Dorset House Publishers, 2001). In retrospectives I often shorten it even more to "Assume Best Intent."

7   Buckingham and Coffman, in *First, Break All the Rules*, claim that great managers do play favorites, because they invest more in their performers than in those not likely to reach the top. If you agree with this perspective, be careful not to create a perception of unfairness.

8   Byron Katie and Stephen Mitchell, *Loving What Is: Four Questions That Can Change Your Life* (Three Rivers Press, 2003).

9   This practice is documented in Esther Derby and Diana Larsen, *Agile Retrospectives: Making Good Teams Great* (Raleigh, NC: The Pragmatic Bookshelf, 2006), 119–120.

10   I have introduced this practice to many teams. Initially, some folks feel embarrassed to participate; I mitigate this by going first. Two other common reactions are "We did this in kindergarten!" and "This is too touchy-feely." Once a few people have offered appreciations, those concerns evaporate.

11 These questions are an application of the ORID process, mentioned in chapter 9.

Chapter 4

1 Groupthink occurs when a group strives for a unanimous decision or interpretation that wouldn't ruffle anyone's feathers.

2 Johanna Rothman, *Hiring the Best Knowledge Workers, Techies, and Nerds: The Secrets and Science of Hiring Technical People* (New York: Dorset House, 2004).

3 Marcus Buckingham and Curt Coffman, *First, Break All the Rules: What the World's Greatest Managers Do Differently* (New York: Simon and Schuster, 1999). Also find examples of such questions in Rothman, *Hiring the Best Knowledge Workers, Techies, and Nerds* (2004).

4 Thomas J. Allen, *Managing the Flow of Technology* (Cambridge: MIT Press, 1977). The "Allen Curve" shows that the probability of communicating technical information at least once a week drops below 8% when a ten-meter distance separates people, and levels off below 5% at 30 meters and higher.

5 Walter Leite, Marilla Svinicki, and Yuying Shi, "Attempted Validation of the Scores of the VARK: Learning Styles Inventory With Multitrait–Multimethod Confirmatory Factor Analysis Models," *Educational and Psychological Measurement* (2009): 2.

Chapter 5

1 I learned this powerful question from Christopher Avery.

2 A famous early example from the software industry is the Black Team, a testing team at IBM. The story is recounted in Tom DeMarco and Timothy Lister, *Peopleware: Productive Projects and Teams*, 2nd ed. (New York: Dorset House, 1999).

3 Jeff Weiss and Jonathan Hughes, "Want Collaboration? Accept — and Actively Manage — Conflict," *Harvard Business Review* (March 2005) (HBR Reprint R0503F, p. 1).

4 Read more stories and examples of this approach in Diana Larsen and Ainsley Nies, *Liftoff: Launching Agile Teams and Projects* (Hillsboro, OR: Onyx Neon Press, 2012).

5 The "Begin with the end in mind" principle, which you might recognize from Stephen Covey's *7 Habits of Highly Effective People*, underpins many Agile practices.

6 Robert Cialdini, *Influence: The Psychology of Persuasion* (New York: Harper Collins, 2007), 96.

7 Ibid., 98.

8 Gil Broza and Yehoram Shenhar, "From Struggle to Success: How a Third Chance, an Eleventh Hour Rewrite, and Strict Adherence to XP and Evolutionary Design Turned Our Flailing Project into a Marketable Product," *Agile Development Magazine* (spring 2007).

9 The output of team retrospectives — public feedback and action items — can be made available to managers, who might review it in a second-tier retrospective.

10 Samuel Culbert with Lawrence Rout, *Get Rid of the Performance Review!: How Companies Can Stop Intimidating, Start Managing — and Focus on What Really Matters* (New York: Business Plus, 2010).

11 Esther Derby, *The Payoff in Merit Pay (Not)*, www.estherderby.com/2009/01/the-pay-off-in-merit-pay-not.html.

Chapter 6

1 The original paper is Bruce Tuckman, "Developmental Sequence in Small Groups," *Psychological Bulletin* 63 (1965): 384–99. For a recent review of the concept, see Mark K. Smith, "Bruce W. Tuckman — Forming, Storming, Norming and Performing in Groups," *Encyclopaedia of Informal Education* (2005), www.infed.org/thinkers/tuckman.htm. In 1977, Tuckman added a fifth stage, "Adjourning," to describe the dissolution of the team (Bruce Tuckman and Mary Ann Jensen, "Stages of Small Group Development Revisited," *Group and Organizational Studies* 2 (1977), 419–27). While this important stage is potentially stressful for some members, it is outside the scope of this book.

2 Based on Jon R. Katzenbach and Douglas K. Smith, *The Wisdom of Teams: Creating the High-Performance Organization* (Harvard Business Review Press, 1992).

3 Self-organization is defined as the emergence of order in a complex adaptive system. Glenda Eoyang's CDE model (Container — Difference — Exchange) integrates diverse theoretical and practical approaches to self-organizing human systems. Read about it in Glenda Eoyang, "Conditions for Self-Organizing in Human Systems" (PhD diss., Union Institute and University, 2001), hsdinstitute.academia.edu/GlendaEoyang/Papers/518048/Conditions_for_self-organizing_in_human_systems.

4 A famous example of the potentially negative consequence of taking decisional cues from other people is the Kitty Genovese story, recounted in Robert Cialdini, *Influence: The Psychology of Persuasion* (New York: HarperCollins, 2007), 129–32.

5 Simulations, in particular, are helpful in all stages of a team's life cycle. To be advised of my upcoming workshops and simulations, sign up at www.TheHumanSideOfAgile.com.

6   These behavioral patterns (from a total of eight) appear in the Success Insights Wheel of Target Training International. Their underpinning is in the DISC model, which dates back to William Marston, *The Emotions of Normal People* (London: K. Paul, Trench, Trubner & Co., 1928).

7   M. D. Seery, E. A. Holman, and R. C. Silver, "Whatever Does Not Kill Us: Cumulative Lifetime Adversity, Vulnerability, and Resilience," *Journal of Personal Social Psychology* 99, no. 6 (December 2010): 1025–41. This multi-year, longitudinal study of a national sample found that people with a history of some lifetime adversity reported better mental health and well-being outcomes than not only people with a high history of adversity but also than those with no history of adversity.

8   Kent Beck with Cynthia Andres, *Extreme Programming Explained: Embrace Change*, 2nd ed. (Boston: Addison-Wesley Professional, 2004).

9   Arlo Belshee, "Promiscuous Pairing and Beginner's Mind: Embrace Inexperience" (proceedings of the Agile Development Conference, July 24–29, 2005, Washington, DC: IEEE Computer Society), 125–131. dx.doi.org/10.1109/ADC.2005.37.

10 For my take on the inherent misunderstanding in the question "What's the best tool for Agile testing?" read my article by the same name at 3pvantage.com/articles/the-best-tool-for-agile-testing.htm.

Chapter 7

1   Charles N. Seashore, Edith Whitfield Seashore, and Gerald M. Weinberg, *What Did You Say?: The Art of Giving and Receiving Feedback* (Columbia, MD: Bingham House Books, 1997).

2   Wikipedia contains a comprehensive entry on "Emotional Contagion": en.wikipedia.org/wiki/Emotional_contagion.

3   This exposition of responsibility and its absence is largely informed by the teachings of Christopher Avery (www.christopheravery.com), Esther Derby (www.estherderby.com), and Johanna Rothman (www.jrothman.com).

4   Learn more about the Responsibility Process in Christopher Avery, *Teamwork Is an Individual Skill: Getting Your Work Done When Sharing Responsibility* (San Francisco: Berrett-Koehler Publishers, 2001), or consult his website, www.christopheravery.com.

5   Otto Kroeger with Kanet M. Thuesen and Hile Rutledge: *Type Talk at Work: How the 16 Personality Types Determine Your Success on the Job* (New York: Dell Publishing, 2002).

Chapter 8

1   Dale Emery's *Untangling Communication* dissects communication problems using Virginia Satir's "The Ingredients of an Interaction." dhemery.com/articles/untangling_communication/.

2   Jamie Smart, in *How to Get Rapid Rapport*, discusses rapport and offers exercises: www.purenlp.com/articlecontributions/jamiesmart.htm. Jonathan Altfeld, in *Rapport — Mirroring*, discusses it further: www.mynlpresources.com/articles/20071220/print.

3   These terms, and the joke they hail from, are a veritable part of Scrum lore. While the point comes across, the reference to barnyard animals has caused some backlash. The terms, and the joke, were stricken from the 2011 Scrum Guide (www.scrum.org/storage/scrumguides/Scrum Guide - 2011.pdf).

4   Another strong indicator of modality is called eye accessing: which way the person's eyes look when he's accessing internal information. Read about it at www.renewal.ca/nlp13.htm.

5   Read about modality and representational systems at www.saladltd.co.uk/salad pages/Nlp tips/nlp_tip_6.htm.

6   Barbara Fredrickson, *Positivity: Groundbreaking Research Reveals How to Embrace the Hidden Strength of Positive Emotions, Overcome Negativity, and Thrive* (Crown Archetype, 2009).

7   Asking you to pause your reading and look around you is meant to *break your state*, specifically by distracting you. The two dialogues are supposed to trigger different states, which can work well only if the states are separated by a break.

8   These filters were first described in Richard Bandler and John Grinder, *The Structure of Magic: A Book About Language and Therapy*, vol. 1 (Palo Alto: Science & Behavior Books, 1975).

9   These patterns and their associated precision questions (challenges) are known as the Neuro-Linguistic Programming (NLP) Meta Model. Read about it at www.nlpls.com/articles/NLPmetaModel.php.

10 Luiz Claudio Parzianello and I first adapted the NLP Meta Model to Agile development this way for a joint workshop at the Agile 2011 conference in Salt Lake City. We combined and renamed some patterns, because we found their names in the Meta Model opaque.

11 These questions correspond directly to the Logical Levels. Explained in 11.5 in the context of change, logical levels apply also to growth, thinking, and self-expression.

12 Otto Kroeger with Kanet M. Thuesen and Hile Rutledge, *Type Talk at Work:*

How the 16 Personality Types Determine Your Success on the Job (New York: Dell Publishing, 2002).

13 DISC is an acronym for four aspects of behavior: Dominance, Influence, Steadiness, and Compliance (see note 6 in chapter 6). Several companies provide DISC assessment tools.

Chapter 9

1 Stephen R. Covey, *The 7 Habits of Highly Effective People: Powerful Lessons in Personal Change* (New York: Free Press, 2004).

2 For question-centric agendas to common Agile meetings, see Section IV in Jean Tabaka, *Collaboration Explained: Facilitation Skills for Software Project Leaders* (Boston: Addison-Wesley Professional, 2006).

3 Tabaka, *Collaboration Explained*; Michael Wilkinson; *The Secrets of Facilitation: The S.M.A.R.T. Guide to Getting Results with Groups* (San Francisco: Jossey-Bass, 2004); Esther Derby and Diana Larsen, *Agile Retrospectives: Making Good Teams Great* (Raleigh, NC: The Pragmatic Bookshelf, 2006).

4 R. Brian Stanfield, *The Art of Focused Conversation: 100 Ways to Access Group Wisdom in the Workplace* (Canadian Institute of Cultural Affairs, 1997) (a condensed version is available at topfacilitation.net/Docs/AFC.cfm).

5 I learned this term from Lyssa Adkins. You can read examples of it in her book, *Coaching Agile Teams: A Companion for ScrumMasters, Agile Coaches, and Project Managers in Transition* (Boston: Addison-Wesley Professional), pp. 153 and 249, and at www.coachingagileteams.com/2010/11/29/uncategorized/using-silent-work-techniques-to-get-to-astonishing-results/.

6 In another example, Derby and Larsen, in *Agile Retrospectives*, describe "Triple Nickels," a silent-work activity for generating ideas.

7 "Sit-down meetings were 34% longer than stand-up meetings, but they produced no better decisions than stand-up meetings. Significant differences were also obtained for satisfaction with the meeting and task information use during the meeting but not for synergy or commitment to the group's decision." From Allen Bluedorn, Daniel Turban, and Mary Sue Love, "The Effects of Stand-up and Sit-down Meeting Formats on Meeting Outcomes," *Journal of Applied Psychology* 84(2) (April 1999): 277–85.

8 4MAT is a way to organize teaching material that follows the four common learning styles. www.aboutlearning.com/what-is-4mat.

9 See Wilkinson, *The Secrets of Facilitation*, and Tabaka, *Collaboration Explained*, for decision rules and various interpretations of Fist of Five.

10 Derby and Larsen, *Agile Retrospectives*, 92–93.

11 Kenneth Benne and Paul Sheats described 26 such group rules back in the 1940s. For a recent summary, see www.mindtools.com/pages/article/newTMM_85.htm.

12 This activity is known as "+/Delta" (Derby and Larsen, *Agile Retrospectives*, 116–17).

13 Extraverts need to talk in order to think, and introverts need to think in order to talk. Since most teams will have both extraverts and introverts, choose activities that suit both.

Chapter 10

1 For a hilarious take on management, read Neil Johnson's "How to Do Nothing," at fragile.org.uk/2010/02/how-to-do-nothing/.

2 I heard this concise comparison between the traditional and the Agile approaches to complexity from Mary Poppendieck.

3 David Spann, "Being a Collaborative Leader (and Getting Things Done)," Cutter Executive Report (Agile Product & Project Management), vol. 12, no. 4, 2011.

4 The Project Management Institute, *The Project Management Body of Knowledge* (*PMBOK*), www.pmi.org/PMBOK-Guide-and-Standards.aspx.

5 Marcus Buckingham and Curt Coffman, *First, Break All the Rules: What the World's Greatest Managers Do Differently* (New York: Simon and Schuster, 1999).

6 Dan Ariely, *The Upside of Irrationality: The Unexpected Benefits of Defying Logic at Work and at Home* (New York: HarperCollins, 2010).

7 *Principles behind the Agile Manifesto*, 2001, agilemanifesto.org/principles.html.

8 This is related to the deliberate practice concept. See Geoff Colvin, *Talent Is Overrated: What Really Separates World-Class Performers from Everybody Else* (New York: Portfolio Trade, 2010).

9 I first learned from Christopher Avery the power of distinguishing the two concepts — both in my mind and in conversation.

10 Daniel Pink, *Drive: The Surprising Truth About What Motivates Us* (New York: Riverhead Trade, 2011).

11 Ariely, *The Upside of Irrationality*.

12 Pink, *Drive*.

13 Buckingham and Coffman, *First, Break All the Rules*.

14 See Christopher Avery, "How Consensus Decision-Making Creates Shared Direction in a Team" at www.christopheravery.com/blog/how-consensus-

decision-making-creates-shared-direction-in-a-team/ (blog post retrieved on May 23, 2012).

15 Cooperation and collaboration are another pair of terms that are often used interchangeably. They have different meanings, however. In collaboration, people have a single shared goal; in cooperation, they have individual as well as common goals. Collaboration is rooted in cocreation; cooperation is rooted in mutual assistance.

16 These are the terms used in some Scrum implementations to distinguish the team from the rest of the community (see section 8.4.1).

17 Alistair Cockburn coined the term "information radiators" in 2000 to denote "a publicly posted display that shows people walking by what is going on. Information radiators are best when they are big, very easy to see (e.g., not online, generally), and change often enough to be worth revisiting." Read more at alistair.cockburn.us/Information+radiator.

18 Esther Derby and Diana Larsen, *Agile Retrospectives: Making Good Teams Great* (Raleigh, NC: The Pragmatic Bookshelf, 2006), 85–86.

19 Ibid., 87–89.

20 One of the seven principles of Lean Development is "Optimize the Whole." See Mary and Tom Poppendieck, *Implementing Lean Software Development: From Concept to Cash* (Boston: Addison-Wesley Professional, 2006).

Chapter 11

1 The Agile Manifesto at agilemanifesto.org/.

2 Virginia Satir et al., *The Satir Model: Family Therapy and Beyond* (Palo Alto: Science and Behavior Books, 1991); Gerald M. Weinberg, *Quality Software Management: Anticipating Change*, vol. 4 (New York: Dorset House, 1997). Steven Smith's article "The Satir Change Model" at stevenmsmith.com/ar-satir-change-model/ summarizes the model well.

3 If you'd like to learn Agile engineering from me (in a public course or privately), browse available offerings at www.3PVantage.com or write to me at gbroza@3PVantage.com.

4 Tom DeMarco, *Slack: Getting Past Burnout, Busywork, and the Myth of Total Efficiency* (New York: Broadway, 2002).

5 One popular model for leading change is Dr. John Kotter's 8-Step Process for Leading Change. A good starting point for it is www.kotterinternational.com/kotterprinciples/changesteps.

6   DeMarco, *Slack*.

7   Dan Ariely, *The Upside of Irrationality: The Unexpected Benefits of Defying Logic at Work and at Home* (New York: HarperCollins, 2010).

8   Robert Dilts, *Changing Belief Systems with NLP* (Capitola, CA: Meta Publications, 1990). Like so many other mental models, Dilts's Logical Levels model has received its share of controversy. As statistician George Box famously said, "All models are wrong, but some are useful." I've found Dilts's model useful in helping people embrace Agile thinking and behaviors.

9   David Spann and I led a workshop called "The Curious, Present and Empathetic Agile Coach" at the Agile 2010 conference in Orlando, Florida. Write to me at gbroza@3PVantage.com if you'd like David and/or me to lead it at your company.

10 Esther Derby, "Are You Ready to Coach?" at www.estherderby.com/2011/02/are-you-ready-to-coach.html.

11 Rachel Davies and Liz Sedley, *Agile Coaching* (Raleigh, NC: Pragmatic Bookshelf, 2009); Lyssa Adkins, *Coaching Agile Teams: A Companion for ScrumMasters, Agile Coaches, and Project Managers in Transition* (Boston: Addison-Wesley Professional, 2010).

Chapter 12

1   If you have a programming background, you might know that Object-Oriented Programming favors the opposite pattern: "Tell, don't ask."

2   Robert Cialdini, *Influence: The Psychology of Persuasion* (New York: HarperCollins, 2007), 4–5.

Chapter 13

1   Chris Sterling, *Managing Software Debt: Building for Inevitable Change* (Boston: Addison-Wesley Professional, 2010).

2   Be aware that release or project retrospectives require deeper facilitation skill. Consider engaging an external expert to do the first few ones so your coaches and ATLs can learn by example. If you'd like me to lead such a retrospective for your company, or to provide a referral, contact me at gbroza@3pvantage.com.

3   Harrison Owen, *Open Space Technology: A User's Guide*, 3rd ed. (San Francisco: Berrett-Koehler Publishers, 2008).

4   Esther Derby and Diana Larsen, *Agile Retrospectives: Making Good Teams Great* (Raleigh, NC: The Pragmatic Bookshelf, 2006).

5   Read about Atlassian's version, called "FedEx Days," in Daniel Pink, *Drive: The Surprising Truth About What Motivates Us* (New York: Riverhead Trade, 2011).

6   Marty Baker, "The Connection between Daydreaming and Creativity," creativity central.squarespace.com/creativity-central/2011/6/13/the-connection-between-daydreaming-and-creativity.html.

7   MIT, "Product Development Value Stream Mapping (PDVSM)" manual at lean. mit.edu/products/product-development-value-stream-mapping-pdvsm-manual.

8   Robert Austin and Lee Devin, *Artful Making: What Managers Need to Know About How Artists Work* (Upper Saddle River, NJ: Financial Times Prentice Hall, 2003).

9   Specifically, the team needed to do three things: (1) set up their IDEs to compile the code (they were using only shell scripts to build code), (2) untangle some dependencies so they could compile just a few modules instead of everything, and (3) get the rule revoked that forced each test class to subclass the company's test base class. The latter caused a major slowdown, since it required a server to be up before a test could be run — even if the test had no need of the server.

10   Robert Merton, "The Unanticipated Consequences of Purposive Social Action," *American Sociological Review* 1 Issue 6 (December 1936): 894–904.

11   *The Declaration of Interdependence*, pmdoi.org.

Chapter 14

1   The sameness/difference distinction is a metaprogram identified in Neuro-Linguistic Programming (NLP). See Shelle Rose Charvet, *Words That Change Minds: Mastering the Language of Influence*, 2nd ed. (Dubuque, IA: Kendall/Hunt, 1997).

2   Proprietary data provided by jobEQ.com based on a European stratified sample of 1,003 respondents, 2011.

3   Peter Senge, *The Fifth Discipline: The Art and Practice of The Learning Organization*, rev. ed. (New York: Crown Business, 2006).

4   Read more on communities of practice at www.cutter.com/bia/fulltext/webinar/2011/communities-of-practice.html.

5   Harrison Owen, *Open Space Technology: A User's Guide*, 3rd ed. (San Francisco: Berrett-Koehler Publishers, 2008).

6   Malcolm Gladwell, *Outliers: The Story of Success* (New York: Little, Brown and Company, 2008).

7   *Manifesto for Software Craftsmanship*, manifesto.softwarecraftsmanship.org/. In addition to the manifesto, this website has a deep Further Reading section.

8   Gil Broza, "Today's Business World Needs Contextual Craftsmanship," in the "Software Programming as Craft: The Impact of Agile Development" issue of the *Cutter IT Journal*, 2010.

9 Gil Broza, "Could You Use Software Development Insurance?" at 3pvantage. com/articles/could-you-use-software-development-insurance.htm.

10 You might know this concept in its more morbid form, "bus number" or "truck number," which involves being run over instead of winning the lottery.

11 Much of this section's material first appeared in Johanna Rothman and Gil Broza, "I've Got Your Back," TechWell, January 2011, at manage.techwell.com/articles/ weekly/i-ve-got-your-back.

12 Carlos Buxton, "Go Ahead, Rock the Boat: Spot 3 Warning Signs of Apathy," www.bigvisible.com/2011/10/how-to-spot-and-combat-three-warning-signs-of-employee-apathy/.

13 If you'd like my help to analyze your company's Agility, write to me at gbroza@3PVantage.com.

Appendix

1 Johanna Rothman, *Manage Your Project Portfolio: Increase Your Capacity and Finish More Projects* (Raleigh, NC: The Pragmatic Bookshelf, 2009).

INDEX

An *n* following a page reference indicates information found in the notes.

MEET GIL BROZA

Agile Specialist and Mentor
Owner, 3P Vantage, Inc.
Email contact: **gbroza@3PVantage.com**

In writing *The Human Side of Agile*, Gil Broza has tapped into fundamental concerns — and challenges — of Agile practitioners. For not only does the "human" in the book's title refer to the people that make up any Agile team, it also pertains to those who lead them, to those who run the company, and to the people who purchase and use the end product. Gil encourages Agile team members to take up the mantle of team leader and to steer all involved toward the excellence promised by properly executed Agile.

Gil's experience and observations confirm that many who adopt Agile pay too much attention to the mechanics of the process, and are disenchanted with the results. Some are in denial and some are searching for a magic bullet. They're mired on a mediocre performance plateau, stalled in a mishmash of "best practices," and looking for answers. In the last 10 years alone, he has mentored more than 1,500 professionals who then delighted their customers, shipped working software on time, and rediscovered passion for their work. Gil has also:

✦ Served as a development manager, team leader, and programmer for 12 years, successfully applying Agile methods since 2001

✦ Coached more than 40 private- and public-sector clients, large and small, including independent software vendors, custom development firms, and organizations that build software for internal use

- ✦ Written several practical papers for conferences and trade magazines, including the prestigious *Cutter IT Journal* (Gil also co-produced the Coaching "stage" at the *Agile 2009* and *2010* conferences)

Throughout his career, Gil has focused on human characteristics that prevent positive outcomes in software development teams. These include limiting habits, fear of change, outdated beliefs, and blind spots. In helping teams overcome these factors, he supports them in reaching ever-higher levels of performance, confidence, and accomplishment.

Gil offers much-needed services (beyond basic education) to help ScrumMasters and other Agile team leaders grow in their roles. In addition, he provides workshops, consulting, facilitation services, and enablement programs to fix lackluster Agile attempts and support ongoing Agile improvement efforts. He is in high demand by individuals and companies looking to fully realize Agile's potential.

 Want a taste of what makes Gil different? Scan the QR Code, or visit **www.OnTheWayToAgile.com** to receive Gil's popular (and free!) "Something Happened on the Way to Agile" mini-program. Consisting of 20 daily training segments, it will help you break the cycle of Agile mediocrity and move toward the promised benefits of Agile.